John Alberger

Monks, Popes, and their Political Intrigues

John Alberger

Monks, Popes, and their Political Intrigues

ISBN/EAN: 9783743306912

Manufactured in Europe, USA, Canada, Australia, Japa

Cover: Foto ©ninafisch / pixelio.de

Manufactured and distributed by brebook publishing software (www.brebook.com)

John Alberger

Monks, Popes, and their Political Intrigues

MONKS, POPES,

AND

THEIR POLITICAL INTRIGUES,

BY

JOHN ALBERGER.

"*Like lambs have we crept into power; like wolves have we used it; like dogs have we been driven out; like eagles shall we renew our youth.*"—ST. FRANCIS BORGIA.

"*Eternal vigilance is the price of liberty.*"—WASHINGTON.

IN ONE VOLUME.

BALTIMORE:

1871.

PREFACE.

The object of the present work is to show the political nature of the Catholic church, and its treasonable designs with regard to the American republic.

In the course of the following pages the author has endeavored to show that the Catholic Church is intrinsically a gigantic conspiracy against the liberties of the world; ingenious in its construction, opulent in its resources, extensive in its ramifications, and formidable in its character. In proof of this assertion he submits to the consideration of the reader a mass of irrefragable authority, and indisputable historical incidents. The authorities on which he chiefly relies are papal bulls, briefs, and encyclical letters; the canons of Catholic councils; Catholic periodicals under the supervision of priests, such as the *Civita Cattolica*, *Bronson's Review*, the *Boston Pilot*, the *Tablet*, the *Rambler*, the *Shepherd of the Valley*, the *Paris Univers;* also the works of Dens, the author of the Catholic system of Divinity; of Llorente, the secretary of the Spanish Inquisition; of Bellarmine, the celebrated Catholic controversialist; of Ferraris, the author of the Catholic Ecclesiastical

Dictionary; of Fra Paola, the Catholic ecclesiastical historian; of St. Thomas Aquinas, entitled by the church "*the Angelic Doctor,*" "*the Angel of the School,*" "*the Fifth Doctor;*" of St. Bernard, called "*the Honeyed Teacher,*" and his works "*Streams from Paradise;*" of Labbeus, of St. Liquori, of Moscovius, and of a host of other oracles of Catholicism.

By means of these authorities the veil of piety which conceals and decorates the papal church is partly drawn aside, and her monarchial character, political organization, despotic nature, ambitious designs and treasonable principles, are distinctly presented to view.

The author pretends to no originality. The diction and logic are, of course his own, but the facts and principles upon which he bases his charges are the avowals of the church, the records of history, and the official affirmations of civilized nations.

The Infidels, as faithful sentinels on the watch tower of liberty, have often uttered the cry of warning; the Protestant pulpit has at intervals startled from its drowsy slumbers, and echoed the same alarm; but neither the one nor the other has been able to arouse the people from their profound slumber. Gavazzi has lectured, Hogan, Colton, Hopkins have written, but so profound and death-like is the torpidity which holds the senses of Americans in indifference, that the warnings of writers and speakers have died away with the

PREFACE.

tones in which they were uttered. But Americans must awake—they will awake—if not soon enough to avert the impending doom overhanging their country and their posterity, yet soon enough! alas, too soon! to weep in despair over their present apathy and indifference, amid the ruins of their republic.

JOHN ALBERGER.

BALTIMORE, MD., July 4th, 1871.

CONTENTS.

CHAPTER I.
Catholicism a Political Organization. . . 6

CHAPTER II.
Political Machinery of the Papal Power, . . 15

CHAPTER III.
Monastic Vow of Perpetual Solitude, . . 22

CHAPTER IV.
Monastic Vow of Perpetual Silence, . . 32

CHAPTER V.
Vow of Silent Contemplation. Part First, . 40
" " " " Second, . 46
" " " " Third, . 35

CHAPTER VI.
Monastic Vow of Poverty, . . . 85

CHAPTER VII.
Monastic Vow of Celibacy, . . . 106

CHAPTER VIII.
Monastic Vow of Unconditional Obedience, . 129

CHAPTER IX.
Pagan Origin of the Monastic Orders, . . 136

CONTENTS.

CHAPTER X.

Popes — their Pretensions, Elections, Character and Administrations, ... 153

CHAPTER XI.

The Papal Monarchy—Crown, Banner, Cabinet, Court, Decrees, Jurisdiction, Coinage, Army and Navy, Revenues, Oaths and Spies, . . 181

The Papal Monarchy. Section Two. The Pope's Direct Authority; his Opposition to Marriage; to Slavery; his Claim to Temporal Power on the Forged Decretal Letter of Constantine; on the Fictitious Gift of Pepin; on the Pretended Donation of Charlemagne; on the Disputed Bequest of Matilda, Duchess of Tuscany; the Title of Pope a Usurpation; the Papal Artful Policy; the State of Italy under the Papal Government, ... 207

CHAPTER XII.

Papal Political Intrigues in England—Papal Machinery; Intrigues under the Reigns of Henry II.; of King John; of Henry VII.; of Charles I.; of Charles II.; of James II.; of William and Mary, ... 226

CHAPTER XIII.

Papal Political Intrigues in France—During the Reigns of Clovis; of Childeric III.; of Pepin; of Charlemagne; of Hugh Capet; of Philip IV.; of Louis XII.; of Francis I.; of Francis II.; of Charles IX.; of Henry IV.; of Louis XIII.; of Louis XIV., ... 256

CONTENTS.

CHAPTER XIV.

Papal Political Intrigues in Germany—Under the Reigns of Otho I.; of Henry IV.; of Henry V.; of Frederic I.; of Frederic II.; of Conrad IV.; of Albert I.; of Henry VII.; of Louis of Bavaria; of Charles IV.; of Sigismund; of Charles V.; of Ferdinand II.; Papal Intrigues in Austria; in Prussia; and in the Netherlands, ... 289

CHAPTER XV.

Papal Political Intrigues in Portugal and Spain— Under the Reigns of Alphonso I.; Sancho II.; Dionysus; John II.; Emanuel; John III.; Sebastian; Philip II.; Joseph I.; Maria Francesca Isabella; John VI.; Pedro VI.; and Dona Maria, - . . . 323

In Spain—Under the Reigns of Recared I.; Charles V.; Philip II.: Philip III.; Charles II.; Charles III.; Charles IV.; and Ferdinand VII, ... 336

CHAPTER XVI.

Papal Intrigues Respecting the United States; Catholic Persecution; Protestant Persecution; Catholics in the Revolutionary War; in the late Rebellion; Catholic Enmity to Civil and Religious Liberty; an Alliance formed for the Subversion of the American Republic; the Duke of Richmond's Letter; Catholic Immigration; Progress of Catholicism; the Republic in Imminent Danger; Union the Only Means of Salvation; Conclusion, . . . 348

CHAPTER I.

Catholicism a Political Organization.

GUIZOT, speaking of the Christian Church, says: "I say the Christian Church, and not Christianity, between which a broad distinction is to be made." (Gen. Hist. Civilization, Lecture 11, p. 48.) The Catholic Church has little except the name of Christianity, while it is secretly a political organization to establish "the supremacy of the Pope over all persons and things," which, according to Bellarmine's view, "is the main substance of Christianity."

If we have recourse to the lexicon to ascertain the signification of the term religion, we may arrive at a definite conclusion respecting its classical use: but if we are guided in our inquiry by the popular acceptation, we will discover that its definitions are as numerous as the inhabitants of the globe, and as various as their features. We have Natural religion, Pagan religion, Hindoo religion, Jewish religion, Christian religion, and Mahometan religion. Among Christian sects some believe religion to consist in individual feeling, some in baptism, some in reverence for the clergy, some in problematical creeds and dogmas, some in observances of church ordinations, some in rhapsodies, and some in a species of sentimentalism.

The Boston Pilot says: "There can be no religion without an Inquisition;" but Thomas Paine, with nobler philosophy, thinks "religious duties consist in doing justice, loving mercy, and endeavoring to make our fellow creatures happy." The diversity and discordance which have arisen respecting the import of this term, originate from its compound nature adapting it to designate one idea, or a variety of ideas. But while we rarely encounter two persons exactly concurring in an opinion of what is religion, we find all readily admitting that it essentially consists in just principles and correct conduct. Principles are the fountains of thought and feeling; to be just, they must be formed in accordance with truth and reason. Conduct to be correct must be in harmony with the rights of others, and the principles and designs of the human organism. According to this definition, religion may exist with or without ceremonial observances. All forms are merely external appendages, unessential to the nature of religion, and as distinct from it as the casket is from the gem, or the body from the vital principle. If this definition should be construed into a definition of mere morality, it cannot invalidate any objection founded on it to Catholicism, as every such objection will then become demonstrative proof that the Catholic Church is not only destitute of religion, but even of morality.

The signification of a corporate organization is well understood, but how shall we ascertain its principles and designs? Not from the tenor of its professions; but from the nature of its constitution, the tendency of its measures, the sanctions which it has given, the recognitions which it has made in its official capacity; and above all, from the avowals it has uttered, under such a prosperous condition of affairs as made disguise unnecessary. In courting popular favor, an organization concocted to subvert the rights and interests of the people, would, from motives of policy, be prompted to conceal its nature and design; but when wealth and power had sufficiently fortified its security to enable it to scorn and defy public opinion, it would then as naturally unfold its latent principles, as a summer's sun would hatch an innocently loooking cluster of eggs into a nest of poisonous asps.

If among the members of an organization, which professes to be of an exclusively religious character, men should be found who are unquestionably religious or moral, this fact would no more prove it to be a religious or moral institution, than would the membership of the same persons to a railroad or municipal corporation prove such a corporation to be a religious and not a secular organization. But if at periods in its history, its most irreproachable and credible members should denounce it as a political power, and labor to transform it into a purely religious institution, and for such a "damnable heresy" were burnt alive, and their ashes thrown into a river to prevent the people from worshipping them, what would be the legitimate inference from such facts? Would it not be that it claimed to be a political organization? that it was high treason in its estimation to question its right to this character? and that to utter such a question in its domains was to provoke its heaviest penalty? Did not all these facts occur in Rome respecting Arnold of Brecia? And in Catholic history have not similar facts, from his time down to the Reformation, been incarnadined in human blood, too deeply for audacity to deny or time to obliterate?

But what is a religious organization? If religion is moral goodness, a religious organization must be an embodiment of its principles, a practical exemplification of its maxims, and a scheme in measures and policy adapted to extend the observance of its obligations. Such an organization must be consistent with itself, and in harmony with the natural principles of man. In integrity it must be invulnerable; in adherence to right inflexible; in hostility to wrong, uncompromising. It must be the champion of the rights of human nature; the friend of freedom, equality and liberality; the enemy of bigotry, intolerance, and despotism. Its claims must be commended by truth; its measures sanctioned by reason and conscience; its triumphs won by argument and persuasion. Its hands must be unstained with blood. It must never perpetrate a fraud, nor descend to intrigue, nor dissemble, nor cherish malice, nor slander an opponent, nor traffic for self-aggrandizement, nor prostitute its principles to political objects, nor accommodate itself to the vices of any age or country. Amid general corruption it must always be pure, amid bigotry it must always be tolerant, amid oppression it must always advocate the cause of justice, and amid ignorance the cause of education.

Such are some of the essential characteristics of a religious or moral organization. Any departure from them in an institution, proves its secularism. No church in which they form not a distinguishing feature, has any claims to be a religious or moral corporation.

Now when we see an institution, professing to be of an exclusively religious character, organizing its departments upon a financial basis; enjoining on its members the vow of unconditional obedience, in order to subject them to its despotic domination; the vow of absolute poverty, in order to enable them more successfully to administer to the increase of its wealth; the vow of celibacy, in order to prevent them from having legitimate heirs, to divert the ecclesiastical possessions from the church; when we see it establishing schools to select and mould to its designs the most promising among youth, instituting universities to enrich itself by the sale of their honors, absolving sins for money, selling indulgences for the commission of premeditated crime, erecting missionary stations among Pagans for the purpose of traffic and emolument, manufacturing evidence, committing forgeries, and corrupting and interpolating the text of ancient authors, denouncing reason, crushing liberty, circumscribing knowledge, anathematizing those who disbelieve in its arbitrary dogmas, torturing those who question its supreme authority, burning those who oppose its pretensions; having a national cabinet, ministerial offices, accredited ambassadors, maintaining a standing army, a naval force, religious military orders to extend and enlarge its domains, carrying a national banner, wearing a political crown, declaring war, concluding national covenants, coining money, and exercising all the rights of an acknowledged independent monarchy, it is more than credulity can admit, to concede that such an organization is not a corrupt, cruel, despotic, and political institution. That such is the constitution of the Catholic Church is a fact, attested by the existing Papal Government, and by the spirit and acts of its past history; and that it is now what in the past it has been, is established by the unanimous testimony of its acknowledged expounders.

Simplicity has been amused by modern Catholic apologists, who assert that the Papal monarch has resigned his former pretensions to universal temporal sovereignty, and that he now merley maintains his right to supreme spiritual authority. But this subterfuge can mislead only a superficial, ignorant mind. As spiritual sovereignty is absolute dominion over reason and conscience, it unavoidably involves temporal sovereignty; nay, temporal sovereignty of the most despotic and unlimited authority. Reason and conscience lay at the foundation of all political power; and if Catholicism is adapted to govern them, it transcends in despotism the most ingeniously contrived monarchy that tyranny has ever elaborated, or by which the faculties of man have ever been enthralled. Spain, Russia, or any other government is less tyrannical in its constitution than is the Catholic Church. He who would establish the contrary opinion, must first obliterate the Papal bulls, the decrees of the Councils, and the authorities of the Catholic Church; he must go to Rome and convert the present Pope and his college of Cardinals; nay, he must attend the coming Œcumenical Council and induce it to annul the canons of all the previous Councils, and to declare that all the preceding Popes were "damnable heretics," and have them accordingly excommunicated. These preliminary steps must be taken before he can avoid absurdity or the imputation of wilful prevarication.

But the Papal See has never resigned its preposterous claim to universal temporal sovereignty. The bulls and canons asserting this pretension have never been annulled. They still form the canon law of the Church. No official declaration has announced an abrogation of them. The Pope's reiterated and blasphemous claim to infallibility precludes the possibility of such a sensible act. Infallibility is inconsistent with change of principle or error of conduct, and when the Church of Rome arrogates such a divine attribute, she avers that her past history indicates her present character and future intentions. In this opinion all her authorities concur. Bishop Kendrick says: "All doctrine of definitions already made by general Councils and former Pontiffs *are marks which no man can remove.*" (Primacy, p. 356). Brownson says: "What the Church has done, what she has expressly or tacitly approved in the past, is exactly what she will do, expressly or tacitly approve, in the future, if the same circumstances occur." (Review, Jan. 1854). Again: "The Catholic dogma, in regard to every subject whatever, has always been the same from the beginning, remains always unchangeably the same, and will always continue in every part of the world immutable." (Review, Jan., 1850). Again: "Catholicity, as long as it continues Catholicity, cannot be carried to excess. It will be all or nothing." (Review, Jan., 1854). The editors of the *Civilita Cattolica,* the Pope's organ at Rome, say: "From the darkness of the catacombs she (the Catholic Church) dictated laws to the subjects of Emperors, abrogating decrees, whether plebeian, senatorial or imperial, when in conflict with Catholic ordinances. To-day, as in all time, the Church commands the spiritual part of man; and, in ruling over the spirit, she rules the body, rules over riches, over science, over affections, over interests, over associations — rules, in fine, over monarchs and their ministers."

The Dublin Tablet, Feb. 24, 1865, the accredited organ

of Romanism in the British realm, says: "The Pope is at this moment interfering in Piedmont, defending one class of citizens against the government; and in the House of Representatives (of the United States), a Christian (Mr. Chandler, in his speech, Jan., 1865), denies the right! Governments may and do prohibit good works, and the Pope interferes. They also commit evil, and the Pope interferes; and good Christians (Catholics) *prefer the Pope's authority to that of the State.* The godless (non-Catholic) colleges of Ireland, the troubles of Piedmont, all bear witness against the unchristian opinion." The Paris *Univers* says: "A heretic examined and convicted by the Church, used to be delivered over to the secular authority to be punished with death. Nothing has appeared to us more necessary. More than 100,000 persons perished in consequence of the heresy of Wickliffe, and a still greater number for that of John Huss; and it would be impossible to count the bloodshed caused by Luther, *and it is not yet over.*" De Pratt, formerly an Abbe of the Pope, says: "The Pope is chief of 150,000,000 of followers. Catholicism cannot have less than 500,000 ministers. The Pope commands more subjects than any sovereign—more than many sovereigns together. These have subjects only on their own territory, *the Pope commands subjects on the territory of all sovereigns*" (Flag of the Union.) But the testimony is voluminous, and I forbear further quotations on this point.

To understand, then, the past history of the Catholic Church, is of paramount importance to every freeman. What is it? It is the development of her nature. It is the unfolding of her treason to the world. It is uncovering the cruelty and despotism concealed under her religious profession. It is the revelation of her animosity to the rights of men, to the progress of society, and to the exercise of reason and conscience. It shows her to be a secret political organization, skilfully constructed for the acquisition of supreme political power, and hypocritically disguised under the semblance of religion. If in her infancy she did not always avow her ambitious designs, she always secretly cherished them; and, if in her adversity she has moderated her tone, she has not her natural thirst for secular power. As she grew in strength, she grew in arrogance and despotism; and when, by a system of artful intrigues and bold usurpations, she had created a colossal power that overawed the united monarchies of Christendom, she unsheathed the double sword, the symbol of ecclesiastical and political power, and asserted her right, as Vicar of Christ, to rule with or in preference to Princes, invaded the rights and liberties of independent nations, crowned and uncrowned monarchs, destroyed freedom everywhere, anathematized, shackled, tortured and burnt all who opposed her monarchical pretensions. Her triumphal processions have been the most magnificent when her hands were the bloodiest, and her *Te Deum* was chaunted with the most fervor when the smoke of her stakes ascended in the thickest volumes, and the gore shed by the double sword streamed in the broadest and deepest currents.

When Time, the avenger, hurled her from her despotic throne, she supplicated, because she could not command, and moderated her pretensions, because she dare not assert them. But if she presumes not now to tear the crown from the head of the mighty, who would annihilate her for her audacious attempt; if she does not now absolve subjects from allegiance to their governments, whose artillery, to avenge the insult would be marshalled against her; if she does not now attempt to burn at the stake those who reject her absurdities, and who would burn her for an attempt—the reason of the extraordinary change in her infallible holiness is palpable. It is not because she has discarded the doctrines consecrated by so many bulls, battles and treaties, but because she cannot carry them out without peril to her existence. But let Brownson, whom Pope Pius IX., in a letter dated April 29, 1854, blessed with an apostolic benediction for services rendered, solve this point. He says: "*The Church, who possesses an admirable gift of discretion*, has prudently judged that she would not declare all things explicitly from the beginning, but at a given time, and in suitable circumstances, would bring into light something which was hitherto in concealment, and *covered with a certain obscurity*. (Review, January, 1854).

CHAPTER II.

The Political Machinery of the Papal Power.

THAT the Holy Catholic Church is artfully constituted to subjugate all secular and ecclesiastical power under its authority, and that its object is not to advance the interests of moral goodness, but to acquire temporal dominion, must be admitted by every one that fully comprehends the principles upon which its religious Orders are organized. These Orders were founded by Catholic saints and Bishops. They have been confirmed by Popes and Councils. And though they have been suppressed, on account of their corrupt tendency and political intrigues, in kingdom after kingdom, yet in pontifical bulls they have been defended as being the most useful and pious class of the Catholic community. They may therefore be regarded as having been authoratively acknowledged to be constituted in harmony with the principles and designs of the Catholic Church. In fact they form the body of its organization, as the Pope does its head, and the Councils do its members.

In investigating the intrinsic nature of these orders, we are naturally led back to that period of their history which allowed them an unembarrassed development. As they are sanctioned by a church which claims the attribute of infallibility, whatever changes the advance of civilization has effected in them, must be regarded as a mere prudent accommodation to existing circumstances, to be tolerated no longer than they are imperative. If in 1900 the Catholic Church gain the supremacy in the United States which she hopes to gain, she will restore the despotism and superstition which characterized her domination during the dark ages. Pope Gregory XVI. in his Encyclical Epistle of 1832, says: "Ever bearing in mind, the universal church suffers from every novelty, as well as the admonition of Pope St. Agatho, that from what has been regularly defined nothing can be taken away—no innovation introduced there, no addition made, but that it must be preserved untouched as to words and meaning."

The religious Orders consist of anchorites, monks, nuns and knights. The anchorites in general lived separately, but sometimes in communities. The nuns lived in perpetual solitude, as also did the monks, with the exception of such as devoted themselves to the administration of the public affairs of the church. The knights were soldiers of the cross, instituted to defend and propagate the Romish faith by the force of arms. The orders differed from one another chiefly in the style of their dress, in degrees of rigidness of discipline, and in the assumption of additional vows. They all assumed the vow of absolute poverty, of perpetual celibacy, and of unconditional obedience to the rules of their Order, and to the commands of their superior. Each member was subject to the absolute authority of his superior, who resided in the monastery; each superior to the absolute authority of his general, who resided at Rome, and each general to the absolute authority of the Pope, who was the head and the chief engineer of the whole machine. By means of this machinery the monarchical power of the Pope has been, and is still, although the machinery in some places is somewhat damaged, exerted in every kingdom, in every republic, in every city, and over every Catholic mind in Christendom.

When a novice assumed the monastic vows, he became the absolute property, or chattel, of the institution which he entered, as irreversibly as if he had signed, sealed, and delivered a deed conveying to it his soul and body. By this act of piety he yielded up his personal freedom, and became ironed with the shackles of an eternal slavery. A culprit might hope for liberty when his time would expire, but the recluse could only expect disenthralment by death. If disappointed in finding the holiness which he fancied to hallow the place, or if, relieved of the misanthropic gloom, the isolating superstition, or the delusive representations which had induced him to enter the monastic walls, he should escape, he was pursued, and if captured remanded back by the civil authorities to the cold solitude of his prison house. Not only have these cruel deeds been perpetrated in the dark ages, but in this age of civilization—not only in despotic Europe, but in free America. True, the civil authority in Protestant countries has not interfered, but Catholic ingenuity has discovered means equally efficacious. How many escaped nuns have unaccountably disappeared from society? What infamous means have Catholic priests adopted to fill their nunneries? A young girl in Baltimore, who had just passed her sixteenth year, was carried to a nunnery, and although her mother and relatives invoked the interposition of the civil authorities, yet they were unable to reclaim her, because she had arrived at age. Who that has any conception of the numerous applications of distracted mothers at the police station-houses of some of our large cities, for their children, who have mysteriously disappeared; or that has read the account recently published in the New York papers, (of the recovery of the body of a young female who had been drowned, when in one day eight mothers called at the dead-house to see if the corpse was not that of a daughter whom each had missed), can avoid believing that if the nunneries were open to public inspection, some of these mysteries might be resolved?

After the ceremonies were concluded which sepulchred the novice forever in his monastic cloister, his thoughts, feelings, and desires were henceforth to be regulated, not by the operations of the brain, but by the rules of his Order. The most secret recesses of his mind were to be opened to the inspection of his confessor. For the intrusion of a natural thought he was liable to the infliction of the severest penalty; and the voice of the superior was the only reason, the only conscience, the only instinct he was at liberty to obey. Subjected to a systematic course of rigid discipline adapted to paralyze reason, suppress conscience and stifle instinct, he became a passionless, soulless, mechanical automaton, as well formed to bless, pray and preach, as to curse, forge and murder, and equally ready to do either at the mandate of his superior.

When the superstition of the masses, the ignorance of princes, the ambition of politicians, and the intrigues of the priesthood had favored or cultivated the growth of Catholicism until it was matured into a colossal monarchy, it was discovered that while its centre was in Rome, its branches extended to every section of Christendom. Its monasteries conveniently and strategetically located in different parts of the world, its confessors penetrating the secret designs and wishes of statesmen and princes, its spiritual advisers scrutinizing the conduct of opulent and distinguished personagas, its spies, under the license of Papal indulgences, professing all opinions, and entering all associations and societies, and its agents in constant communication with their superiors, their superiors with their generals, and their generals with the Pope, and all acting in concert in every part of Christendom toward the accomplishment of one grand design; the See of Rome became the receptacle of accurate accounts of the condition, events and characters of the various sections of the globe, and was capable of improving every occurrence to its best advantage, and of commanding in its support the power of every locality. As nothing was too great to transcend its aspirations, so nothing was too minute to escape its scrutiny. Monarchs, legislators, judges, jurists, statesmen, generals, bankers, merchants, actors, schools, colleges, men, women, children—all were objects which its spiritual machinery sought to control. Invisible, but omniscient, the Pope was seen nowhere, while his power was felt everywhere. He touched the secret springs of his machinery and the world was roused to arms or silenced to submission; kings were astounded with applauding subjects, or sat powerless on their thrones; armies rushed to battle or grounded their arms; statesmen were blasted, none could tell for what crime; miscreants were ennobled, none could tell for what virtue; men's business or domestic affairs were disarranged, none could tell for what cause. So sudden, secret and terrible were the revolutions wrought in the fate of individuals and nations, that they seemed like the vengeful interposition of Providence, and the mystery which concealed the hidden cause led the ignorant and stupefied world to interpret them, under the instruction of a crafty priesthood, as the manifestations of divine wrath.

When we calmly consider the disposition of the Catholic organization, it seems that all the inventions of ancient tyranny were condensed in it with improved malignancy. The ambition of Cæsar, which hurried him on to the destruction of the liberties of his country, while he imagined the cold hand of his departed mother clasped his heart; the jealousy of Commodus, who never spared what he could suspect; the cruelty of Mithridates, who fed on poison to escape the secret revenge of his injured subjects; the inhumanity of Caligula, who wished the world had but one neck, that he might cut off its disobedient head at one blow, are, indeed, terrible examples of despotism, but they were limited to one nation, and left reason and conscience unshackled. But in the Papal organization we find a scrutiny which penetrated all secrets, a despotism that ironed reason and conscience, an ambition that grasped heaven and earth, a malignity that blasted for time and eternity—a policy in which all the elements of bigotry, terror, malice, duplicity and obduracy were incorporated in their most frightful proportion. Before this conception we might well shudder, for its irons are secretly manacling our own limbs. Its triumphs, written in the blood of the millions it has butchered, commemorated by the monuments of ecclesiastical rubbish which it has erected, seen in the gloom of superstition it has cast upon the world, utter a solemn admonition to the freemen of

America. Think not that the present attainment in civilization is proof against this boundless Upas—this all-blasting tree, whose sap is poison and whose fruit is death. Think of Egyptian, Asiatic, Grecian civilization, and tremble lest their fate become your own. Let not confidence beget an apathy that may close the eye of vigilance, or enervate the powers of resistance. Listen to Pope Pius IX. when he declares that "the Catholic religion, with its rights, ought to be exclusively dominant, in such sort that every other worship shall be banished and interdicted." Listen to Father Hecker, who says: "The Catholic Church now numbers one-third of the American population, and if its membership increase for the next thirty years, as it has for the thirty years past, in 1900 Rome will have a majority, and be bound to take the country and keep it." Read the statistics and learn the fearful probability of the fulfillment of Hecker's prophesy. Then dream no more that your liberties are safe.

CHAPTER III.

The Monastic Vow of Perpetual Solitude.

THE religious Orders were the fundamental principle of the growth of the Papal monarchy. These orders assumed certain vows, the nature and tendency of which we will proceed to investigate in the spirit of candid inquiry. The first vow to which we will invite attention, is the vow of perpetual solitude and seclusion. Although at the first introduction of these monastic orders into the church, this vow, and those which we shall hereafter examine, were not formally assumed, yet they were invariably observed; and in the year 529, under the auspices of St. Benedict, the express assumption of them became an indispensable condition of membership. Until the tenth century, the hermits and the Benedictine monks and nuns were the only Catholic Orders that existed; the former generally, and the latter entirely, lived in solitary seclusion.

The devout misanthropy of the hermits induced them to select for their habitations the most gloomy, cheerless, and inhospitable regions they could hunt up. Piously scorning the salubrious and magnificent localities, so prodigally furnished by nature, they constructed their huts at the bottom of dismal pits, among the cliffs of rugged rocks, in barren deserts, and in solitary wildernesses. Some lived under trees, others under shelving rocks, some on the top of poles, and others in the deserted caverns of wild beasts. Some buried themselves in the gloomy depth of trackless forests, isolated from human contiguity, and assimilated in aspect and habits to the brute creation. Their bodies divested of decent apparel, and covered with a profusion of hair, and their aspect horrid and revolting beyond description, the hermits sought to acquire the reputation of saints by attaining the nearest possible approximation to wild beasts. Another class of these eccentric devotees constructed a number of contiguous dungeons, and formed themselves into a sort of monastic community. In these vaults they imprisoned themselves for life, the door being locked, and sometimes walled up, a small window only was allowed, through which to receive aliment and give pious advice. In these dungeons they manacled their limbs with ponderous chains, encircled their necks with massive collars, and clothed their legs with heavy greaves. In the depth of winter they would immerse themselves in icy water, and sing psalms. To make themselves revolting; to imitate the habits of wild animals, until they became more horrible, because more unnatural; to subject themselves to voluntary torture, severe and bloody flagellations, were deemed the highest acts of piety. Whatever conspired to comfort they considered profane; whatever was pleasurable they avoided as sinful; and whatever was absurd, filthy, and disgusting, they imagined allied them to gods and angels. St. Anthony, who was so holy that he never washed himself, nor wore any apparel except a shirt, was canonized by the Catholic Church for his extraordinary attainment in sanctification. The approbation which the church so readily conferred on oddity and singularity might at the first appear surprising, but when we recollect the immense pecuniary and political advantage she derived from them, we will no longer doubt her motive, nor avaricious sagacity. A singular custom suggested by this ludicrous institution may be worthy of a passing notice. The abbots of the monasteries, in order to dispose of a brother abbot, whose celebrity surpassed their own, or whose circumventive genius they feared, or who had excited their suspicion, jealousy or revenge, would congregate together, and declare that the fated brother had arrived at a degree of sanctification that better qualified him for the hermit's cell than for an abbotship of a monastery, and that to protect him from the contamination of the world, and to enable him to perfect his holiness, it was necessary to wall him up in eternal seclusion. In accordance with this pious regard for their brother's sanctity, they adopted summary measures for its forcible execution.

Silence, gloom and solitude, according most congenially with the designs of the monastic institutions, they were generally located in sterile wastes, dense and trackless forests, and other localities adapted to excite the sensation of loneliness, dreariness and desolation; but when secular considerations suggested they occupied picturesque and luxuriant localities, commanding the sublimest prospects of Nature. These edifices, which often rivalled gorgeous palaces, were nothing but religious penitentiaries, in which the inmates endured all the privations, and were shackled with all the irons with which criminals are punished in ordinary penal institutions; and though they were ostensibly constructed for religious purposes, they were really designed for the infliction of punishment, in accordance with the ecclesiastical code. With regard to this code Guizot says: "The Catholic Church did not draw up a code like ours, which took account only of those crimes that are at the same time offensive to morals and dangerous to Society, and punishing them only because they bore this two-fold character; but prepared a catalogue of all those actions, criminal more particularly in a moral point of view, and punished all under the name of sins. (Gen. Hist. Civil., Lec. x., p. 118). In what light these religious penitentiaries have been regarded by their inmates their eternal seclusion has prevented them from publicly divulging, but the few who have broken their enthralment, and the "heretics" who have been confined in them, have described them as the most intolerable of dungeons. In fact the modern penitentiary system has originated from them. Guizot thinks this is one of the great blessings which Catholicism has bestowed on society—(see Gen. Hist. Civil., Lect. vi., p. 135).

The vow of perpetual seclusion comprises a renunciation of the pleasures and business of life, an abnegation of the claims of consanguinity, friendship and society; and an abjuration of all filial, parental and natural affection. This vow is in contravention of the obligations imposed on man by Nature, to improve society by contributing to the advancement of its financial, social, political and scientific welfare. It precludes the exercise, and consequent development, of the varied powers of the human organism. It surrenders the personal refinement and moral strength which may be acquired by social intercourse, and conflict with opposing habits and principles. It ignores the imperative duty of understanding and judiciously relieving human want and misery, and of aiding the execution of efficient schemes of public utility and philanthropy. It is not only in violation of the obligations of humanity, and the noblest principles of human enjoyment, but it debars the recluse from correcting any error into which he may have been betrayed by false representations, or an overheated fancy; or, of modifying his condition according to the change which experience and reflection may have effected in his opinion and feelings. Yet, although such are the absurd nature and injurious consequences of the vow of perpetual seclusion, it is proposed by the church of Rome, as the surest means of obtaining the sanctification of the soul and the crown of eternal happiness.

If to bury our talents, to wall ourselves up in a dungeon; to sit for years upon a pole; to scorn the society of human beings; to reject the comforts of civilized life; to retrograde into barbarism; to assume the habits, and acquire the aspect of wild animals; to imprison ourselves where we can never respond to the demands of consanguinity, society, friendship and patriotism: where we can never contribute to the knowledge, wealth or prosperity of the country of our nativity—if this is religion, then Catholicism has the honor of confirming the most revolting condensation of these monstrosities that has ever disgusted the spirit of civilization. But if religion really consists in fair dealing, in noble deeds, in moral integrity amid moral turpitude, in individual purity amid general corruption, in unwavering virtue among the strongest incentives to guilt, then the organization that sanctions vows subversive of these attainments cannot be admitted, consistently with the most indulgent liberality, to be of a religious character.

Thus far in our judgment, we have presumed that the novices, in assuming their vow, were actuated by the laudable desire of obtaining the highest degree of moral purity. This worthy ambition was doubtless the governing motive of a proportion of them. Either from the instigations of moral insanity, or from the vagaries of a distempered fancy, or from the misrepresentation of artful and designing priests, or from the despondency which misfortune is apt to engender in weak, or too sensitive minds, or from a misconception of the natural tendency of solitude, men and women have at times been led to assume the vows, and submit to the penance prescribed by the religious orders. But there were other motives equally, and perhaps more generally, active. Ludicrous as were their holy isolation and penance, still the sanctity which the monks imitated, and the tortures which they self-imposed, were rewarded by a credulous and superstitious world with profound homage and admiration. By undergoing sufferings which appeared intolerable to human fortitude, they acquired the reputation of being sustained by divine agency; and, as their popularity increased in proportion to their wretchedness, they labored to extend their fame by adding to their misery. Their sufferings and fortitude alike incomprehensible to human reason, an awe-struck fancy betrayed the public into the delusion that what it beheld was the results of superhuman sanctity; of a sublime elevation above ordinary humanity; and of the interposition of divine power. These misconceptions, artfully cultivated by the priesthood, extended the fame of the self-tormentors beyond the celebrity of heroes, poets and philosophers. Kings and queens visited them with superstitious reverence; statesmen consulted them on abstruse questions of governmental policy; peace and war were made at their mandates; and pilgrims from remote regions bowed at their feet and begged their blessing. Thus favored by the profound homage of all classes of Christendom, they were enabled with more facility than any other profession to become opulent bishops, royal cardinals, or monarchical popes. Such being their eligibility to the honors and emoluments of the spiritual dignities of the church, vanity was quick to perceive that the anchorite's hut and the monk's cloister were the surest paths to universal adulation; religion, that they were the most respectable methods of becoming honored in life, and worshipped after death; avarice, that they were the most available means of obtaining lucrative positions; and ambition, that thay were the shortest roads to dignity and power. With these attractive facts glaring on the eye of sacred aspirants, it requires but little knowledge of human nature to conceive with what avidity the ambitious would crowd into the most repulsive cloisters; with what eagerness they would adopt the revolting habits and ludicrous privations of the recluse; and with what ingenuity they would indurate and torture the body, in order to win the applause of the world, and the privilege of selecting its most advangeous positions. Accordingly, monastery after monastery arose with sudden and astonishing rapidity, and their cells became supplied—not with aspirants after holiness and heaven—but with aspirants after secular and ecclesiastical dignities, and the indolence, luxury, and licentiousness which they afforded.

The pious flattery that was lavished on voluntary suffering, and the distinguished rewards which recompensed it, strongly tempted the feeble conscience of monks and hermits, to task their ingenuity in inventing contrivances for magnifying the apparent and diminishing the real sufferings of their self-imposed torture. By the aid of an improved invention an artful hypocrite could procure a greater reputation for sanctity than a contrite penitent, and become more eligible to the worldly honors and emoluments of the church. St. Simeon Stylites, who sat upon a pole for thirty years, convinced Christendom, by his wonderful absurdity, that he was miraculously supported; while living he enjoyed its profoundest respect, and when dead was canonized by the Catholic Church. But an observer by describing the numerous gesticulations of this sainted mountebank, diclosed the secret of his artifice. By means of a system of gymnastics, he kept up a vigorous circulation of blood through his frame, and thus acqired a health and longevity which would have been incompatible with a state of inactivity. But it appears that he was tormented with an ulcer on the thigh, inflicted by the devil, who had tempted him to imitate Elijah in flying to heaven, but who maliciously smote him upon his raising his foot to make the ascension. His mystical gesticulations not healing, but probably inflaming the wound, may have shortened the natural term of his miserable existence. As he had gradually arisen from a pole of seven feet high to one of fifty feet high, if had not been for his vanity and his evil company he might have gained a still higher position; but whether by this means he would ever have reached heaven may be questioned by astronomy and heresy: but there is no doubt he acquired by his folly and artifice the beatification of the Catholic Church.

The apathy with which the self-tormenters endured their excruciating penance and the severe rigors of the seasons, was chiefly the effect of artificial callousness, induced by an ingenious discipline, calculated to destroy the susceptibility of the nervous system to the influence of external agents. A similar course of training has always been practiced by the religious orders of the Hindoos and the Mohametans, who, like those of the Catholic Church, endure self-imposed torture which seems to surpass human fortitude, and acquire by this species of ambition unbounded popularity. Even the uncleanness of the holy brotherhood was an artifice. It formed a protecting incrustation on the surface of the skin, which, by covering the the papillæ, the sentient, organs, or destroying their capacity for sensation, enable the hermits to endure without apparent emotion the cold winters and bleak winds of inhospitable forests. This secret is known and practised by some African tribes, upon whom washing is consequently inflicted as a penalty for crimes. To the eye of superstition, clouded with ignorance, and fascinated by the *ignes fatui* of sacred fiction, the calmness of the monks and hermits under torments and exposures which seemed insufferable to humanity, appeared a palpable demonstration of miraculous interposition, and consecrated them in its estimation. Their acts, however, were as much tricks as are the mysterious capers of a conjurer. As the more artful and callous could endure the severity of penitential acts with greater indifference than the candid and sensitive they acquired a higher reputation for holiness, advanced to the enjoyment of more distinguished honors, and finally became canonized as paragons of virtue and objects of adoration.

Such are the nature and consequences of the vow of perpetual seclusion. Such is a portion of the "doctrinal definition already made by the general councils and former pontiffs," which, according to Bishop Kendrick, "are landmarks which no man can remove." (Primacy, p. 356). Such are some of the Catholic dogmas, which, "in regard to every subject whatever," according to Brownson "have been always the same from the beginning, remain always unchangeably the same, and will always continue in every part of the world immutable." (Review, January, 1850). Such is in part "what the church has done, what she has tacitly or expressly approved in the past," and according to the same authority "is exactly what she will tacitly or expressly approve in the future, if the same circumstances occur." (Review, January, 1854). "The same circumstances" is the universal church, which Jesuit Hecker, in his recent speech in Chicago, thinks the United States needs, and which the people (Catholics) will at no distant day proclaim.

CHAPTER IV.

The Monastic Vow of Perpetual Silence.

A vow of perpetual silence was assumed by several religious orders; but it was observed with different degrees of austerity. Some monks passed their whole lives in profound silence; others spoke on certain days of the week; and others at particular hours of specified days. The modern penitentiary regulations respecting the conversation of prisoners seem to have been derived from the singular customs of the dumb brotherhood.

The members of the mute orders, perpetually concealing their features with their cowls, and their thoughts by their silence, appear to have concluded that secrecy was the substance of religion. He who could conceal the best, and preserve silence the longest, obtained among the devout the useful credit of possessing the most grace. The effusion of the Holy Ghost, which, by a prodigal distribution of tongues, and their clashing jargon, had set the primitive ecclesiastical council in an uproar, and which, by its powerfully stimulating qualities had turned so many cities upside down, had a very different effect on the silent orders of the Catholic Church. While to the former it communicated intuitive knowledge of all languages, to the latter it interdicted as profane the use of any. To pass an entire life without uttering a word, was considered by the dumb friars, as an unquestionable evidence of their having received the unutterable fulness of the

Holy Ghost. Whether the primitive church and the Catholic orders were blest with the influence of the same Holy Ghost, or whether the divine spirit politely accommodates the nature of his unction to the demands of particular ecclesiastical exigencies, seems to require some proof, before it can be rationally admitted that profound silence and distracting discord are effects of the same cause.

But the question of truth and error is of a less intricate nature. Truth is candid, open and fearless; error is hidden, intolerant and cowardly. The one challenges investigation; the other denounces it; the one opens its breast to the scrutinizing gaze of the world; the other conceals its features from the most intimate associate. If such is the fearlessness of truth, and such the cowardice of error, the secrecy of the silent orders commends them less to the confidence which candor inspires, than to the suspicion which secrecy begets.

Secrecy is most generally adopted to cover objectionable designs; and, the profounder the former is, the more objectionable are the latter. I speak not of the secret signs by which benevolent societies recognize their members, but of those associations which, while they are professedly designed for religious purposes, conceal their principles and projects from public view. Although in some other respects secrecy may sometimes be suggested by discretion, yet it is often suggested by guilt. All that offend against the natural sentiments of propriety, shrink from the public gaze. Robbery, murder, and every other infraction of civil ordinations seek to shroud their intentions and machinations in the greatest secrecy. The traitor and the highwayman,' afar from the searching scrutiny of the inquisitive, retire to solitary forests, inaccessible retreats, and dismal caverns, to hold their conclaves and plot schemes of blood and depredation. Evasion, prevarication and disguise are the inseparable concomitants of guilt. So secret is crime that its perpetration can generally only be established by circumstantial evidence. Secrecy is, therefore, naturally calculated to excite suspicion; it seldom means good; it generally means evil; sometimes robbery, frequently murder, often treason, always some plot so antagonistical to reason and the welfare of society that its projectors are conscious that publicity would endanger, and perhaps defeat its execution.

The shocking crimes which the pious monasteries concealed have frequently been divulged by those who have escaped from their cloisters, but what unutterable deeds the taciturnity of the mute monks sanctioned may not be so clearly proved as naturally imagined. That it was exceedingly profitable will appear evident upon a moment's reflection. These dumb friars were confessors, and as they never uttered a word, they acquired the confidence of the most desperate criminals. The Jesuits, who could not disclose the startling secrets of their order without alarming the fears of temporal princes, confessed to none but to the silent monks. All the devout who contemplated the commission of the crimes of murder, sedition, or treason, preferred to unbosom their designs to the taciturn fraternity, and receive through their agency the absolution and indulgence of the Holy Roman Catholic Church. But the connivance of the church at criminal deeds could be commanded only by the power of gold; and the amount requisite for expiation was always in proportion to the atrociousness of the crime. Now, as the commission of the highest misdemeanors most imminently endangered the life and liberty of the perpetrators; it is as easy to see the munificent pecuniary advantages which perpetual silence obtained for the monks, as it is to see that the most flagitious criminals would prefer disclosing their intentions to the most silent lips.

It may here be remarked, by way of explanation, that confessors are not bound, as is generally supposed, to inviolate secrecy. The secrets of the confessional may be communicated from one priest to another; and, when a confessor desires to make public use of any information which has been confessed to him, he adopts the artifice of requesting the informer to communicate the matter to him out of the confessional.

The dumb friars, not less artful than secret, elaborated a system of sacred gesticulations, by which they managed to express their wants and desires with as much force as they could have done with their tongues. Although grimace and gesticulation were more clumsy and less varied in their signs than is vocal articulation, yet by this means the dumb monks contrived, as occasion suggested, to describe, command, supplicate, scorn, imprecate, curse or bless. This odd device was well adapted to the non-committal policy of the religious orders, as it enabled them to affirm, deny, impugn, slander; to threaten any dignity, anathematize any power, and commit any crime of which language is capable, without incurring responsibility, violating any legal enactment, rendering themselves amenable to any tribunal, or answerable for the breach of any code of honor.

The adoption of this ingenious device to avoid compliance with unnatural obligations, affords an instance of the singular duplicity into which the subtilty of pious craft may betray human nature. The misfortune of being born a mute is justly classed among the most deplorable calamities that can afflict a human being. The natural privations of such a person elicit in his favor the condoling sympathies of all considerate persons. Yet in order to accomplish secret purposes of ambition or cupidity, the dumb monks resigned the most important advantages with which Nature had enriched them, and gratuitously assumed all the disadvantages that the greatest calamity could have imposed. If there was nothing reprehensible in the taciturn fraternity but this curious departure from the natural use of the human faculties, it alone would be sufficient to subject them to the suspicion of the candid, and the aversion of the prudent.

The tongue, it must be confessed, is sometimes an unruly member, but it is also the noblest blessing of the human organism. It is among the most prominent characteristics that distinguish the human from the brute creation. It is mostly by the means of the judicious employment of speech that the ignorant are instructed, the afflicted consoled, and the cause of truth and freedom defended. It is by it that error is detected, vice intimidated, and superstition and despotism are exposed. The interchange of opinion, the animating power of debate, the searching inquisition of truth, the spontaneous sallies of wit, the exhilarating effusions of humor, the burst of eloquence, the lore of philosophy, art, science, all the natural overflowing of the soul, find

in the varied and expressive functions of speech their
most available avenues for the outlet of their respective
treasures. Speech is a reflective blessing; it blesses
him who exercises it, and him upon whom it is exercised. None can use with propriety their vocal
powers without improving them; none can instruct
without being instructed; none can advocate truth
without being enlightened by its beams. It is a means
which all possess of imparting consolation; which en-
riches the more prodigally it is dispensed; which the
poorest may bestow on the richest; which is always the
cheapest, often the most valuable, and sometimes the
only one that can avail. When speech is free and untrammeled by the fetters of intolerance, it is the most
efficacious mode of improving the moral and intellectual
tone of society. It is more powerful than legal enactments, and has been more successful than dungeons,
racks, and all the prescriptions of tyranny combined.
Laws may interdict and gibbets terrify, but neither can
convince the understanding, nor purify the sources of
action. But freedom of speech enters the soul, con-
verses with the intellect, sifts opinions, and moulds the
nature of man into order and justice. She enters the
halls of legislation and erects right into law. She
enters the court and gives equity to judicial proceedings. She enters a community and breaks the irons of
slavery, bestows equality on all, and enthrones in power
public opinion. She enters a nation of slaves and
makes them a nation of sovereigns. She is the great
redeemer of the moral world. Her touch has healed
its disorders; her voice has calmed its storms; her
spirit has reanimated its dead. Such being her mission,

none but impostors need fear her scrutiny; none but bigots need dread her vengeance; none but tyrants need tremble at her approach.

Yet, notwithstanding the immense advantages the power of speech confers on its possessors, the silent monks have resigned all right to its use and sought an equality with dumb brutes. Whatever motives of religion may have mingled with the consummation of this atrocious folly, it atones not for the good it has prohibited the monks from doing, nor the luxurious pleasure it has obliged them to forego. If it is consistent with the secret designs of any religious order to iron the faculties of speech in eternal silence, it is not consistent with the designs of Nature, the dictate of reason, nor the progress of man. If it is consistent with the obligations of any religious organization to prohibit the exercise of those powers by which error is checked, truth promoted, virtue fortified, and the world enlightened, it is not consistent with the obligations of man, the purest instincts of his being, and the noblest virtues of his nature. If it is consistent with the principles of any version of religion to view with dumb indifference the errors it might correct, or the sorrows it might heal, it is not consistent with the instinctive prompting of knowledge or of natural sympathy. And if such designs, obligations and principles are consistent with the faith and practice of the Catholic Church, she is a curse to the world, at variance with the general interests of society, opposed to the most sacred rights of man, an enemy to human knowledge, to human progress, and to human sympathy. A slavery so abject, an absurdity so gross, and a despotism so monstrous, as that which she sanctions, should consign her reverence to contempt, and her holiness to the scorn and ridicule of all enlightened nations and ages.

CHAPTER V.

The Monastic Vow of Silent Contemplation.

PART FIRST.

Meditation not the Source of Knowledge.

SIMILAR in nature to the vow of seclusion and silence, and equally incompatible with a fulfilment of the obligations of reason and humanity, was the vow of silent contemplation assumed by many of the religious orders.

Meditation, abstractly considered, is neither a virtue nor a vice. It derives its merit or demerit from the objects on which it dwells, and the manner in which it employs its faculties. The mind receiving its impression from external objects, and their vividness and profundity being in proportion to the constancy with which they are contemplated, we as naturally become enlightened by what is true, expanded by what is liberal, and animated by what is pleasing, as we are misguided by what is erroneous, contracted by what is illiberal, and depressed by what is gloomy. Amid objects of reality, amid scenes of grandeur, where the subjects are the most numerous and varied, and where the faculties are awakened to their severest and most rigid scrutiny, is the great college in which the understanding is invigorated and improved; in which the fancy is ennobled and chastened; in which the mind acquires those maxims of wisdom, and that ascendency over impulse and illusion which enable it to act in conformity with the principles of happiness and of the human organism.

The process of meditation is the act of comparing facts, deducing conclusions, analyzing compounds, and tracing the chain of cause and effect. Knowledge is the material with which it works; and, in proportion to its accuracy and extent, will be the value and greatness of our elaborations.

But the processes of meditation are not adapted to the acquisition of knowledge. None are so absurd as to expect to obtain a knowledge of grammar, arithmetic, history, astronomy, or of the laws and properties of matter, by the mere exercise of the contemplative powers. To retire into solitude, and endeavor by the guess-work of meditation to acquire even a knowledge of the alphabet, would be as ridiculous as to attempt to make our feet perform the office of our hands. Not less absurd would it be, were we to immure ourselves in the gloom and silence of perpetual confinement, avoiding the objects of Nature and an intercourse with society, with the expectation that by such means, though we possessed the penetration of a Locke, the intellect of a Gibbon, or the versatility of a Voltaire, to acquire anything but profound ignorance; or any ideas but what were unnatural, distorted and misshapen.

To obtain knowledge we must exercise the perceptive faculties. The senses of seeing, hearing, smelling, tasting and touching are the only avenues by which knowledge can reach the mind. He whose observation has been the most comprehensive, and whose investigations have been the most thorough and accurate, is enabled to exercise the contemplative powers with the greatest pleasure and advantage. The distinct and graphic imagery of men, scenes, events, objects and their properties, with which he has stored his mind, will give correctness to his ideas, variety to his mental operations, comprehensiveness to his intellectual view, clearness to his judgment, and truth to his conclusions. Possessing the elements of correctness, he will also possess the elements of happiness and success. He is enabled to open the volume of Nature, and read, in her pages of rocks and stars, sublimer periods than the pen of superstition ever recorded. He stands perpetually in the vestibule of truth, opening on the fields of immensity, strewed with objects of reality, before the blaze of whose overpowering grandeur the throne and empire of fancy dwindle into insignificance. He is enabled to imbibe the fervor, inhale the inspiration, and enjoy the ecstatic delights which scientific truth alone can confer, and which in intensity and purity so far transcend the fanatic's wildest excitement. He is inducted into the secret by which science has achieved all her victories, and by which she has erected in such solid grace and grandeur those literary and philosophical structures which stand like imperishable columns amid the ruin of temples and kingdoms.

But the acquisition of these exalted attainments embraces the exercise of all the intellectual power on appropriate objects. The mental, like the corporeal powers, are various; they are differently organized and adapted to deal with objects of different natures; and, all require to be exercised judiciously, in order to be kept in a healthy tone. If any member of the body is disused, it will be deprived of its natural energy; if any faculty of the mind is disused, it will lose its natural strength. It is only when each faculty of mind and body is properly exercised that the health and vigor of the whole organism can be maintained. The physiological cause of the enervating effects of indolence, and the invigorating consequences of exercise, are found in those laws of the human organism, whereby the blood is increased in a member by exercise, and decreased by inertia, and a proportionable degree of strength imparted by one and, subtracted by the other. Now, the faculties employed in the process of meditation, comprehend but a small number of the mental powers; and if they are exclusively exercised, a superabundant volume of blood will be distributed to them, and they will absorb the aliment necessary for the subsistence of the others. The establishment of this inequality in the distribution of the blood will derange the harmonious condition of the cerebral organs; some will be overcharged, and either inflamed or constipated, and others impoverished or enervated. One class of the mental powers thus becoming over-excited, another class enfeebled, and a third paralyzed, the ideas which the mind, in this condition, is capable of elaborating, must necessarily be partial, defective, disjointed and grotesque; resembling those nightmares that flit in our sleep, or those monsters which are born without limbs, and marked with deformity and distortion. But when all the moral faculties are properly employed, they will all receive their appropriate nourishment and maintain their natural vigor. In consequence of a harmony, equality, unity and reciprocity of mental action, thus induced, all the powers will be preserved in healthy action — the perceptives in furnishing the mind with knowledge, memory in storing it up, order in classifying it, analogy in comparing it, judgment in deducing conclusions from it, taste in selecting what is most appropriate, fancy in adorning it; and all proceeding as naturally as the vital organ elaborates and vitalizes the blood, and the reproductive system transforms it into animal fluids and solids.

But the partial exercise of the mental faculties, embraced in the act of meditation, not only disproportionately develops the cerebral organs; but deranges those which it labors to keep in incessant activity. A period of rest after labor is indispensable to the maintenance of the health and vigor of the cerebral organs. Exercise increases the flow of blood to their parts; repose, by inducing the process of recuperation, not only restores their vigor but increases their healthy volume. The invigorating effect of sleep is derived from the profound slumber into which all the faculties are calmed, except those whose functions are destined to recuperate and vitalize the entire system. To labor to keep the meditative faculties in constant action is to interrupt the process of recuperation; and, consequently, to prevent them from becoming vitalized. The man who attempts to lift a weight beyond the capacity of his muscular vigor, may never afterward be enabled to raise the tenth part of what was within his former ability; and Sir Isaac Newton, whose powers of contemplation seemed almost superhuman, after he had enervated his faculties by impelling them to constant and excessive exercise, has furnished the world with an illustration of the imbecility it engendered, by his works on the prophecies.

But the principle of self-preservation inherent in the human mind, rebels against the destruction of its faculties. Habitually to exercise the contemplative faculties on one class of objects is a superhuman task. In spite of resistance the blood will pursue its natural course to the different organs of the brain, and by virtue of this fact, in conjunction with the natural condition of the system, instinct will prompt, thought intrude, emotion arise, appetite crave, passion yearn, distraction ensue; and under the external semblance of sanctity, a moral volcano will burn and heave. We may, by means of the theological subterfuge that the involuntary actions of the cerebral functions are the suggestion of impure and malignant fiends, apologize to our conscience for the intrusion of profane and worldly thoughts, but this device will not exorcise them. We shall find that in the effort to become automata, we are men; and that in the attempt to exercise one class of faculties and to concentrate them perpetually on one class of objects, we have grappled with a giant, over whom, if we triumph it will be in our death-struggle.

It is impossible to think and feel by rule. Neither particular trains of thought, nor particular kinds of emotion are at the command of the will. Belief or unbelief, the sensations of contrition, of devotion, of hope, or any other sentiment or feeling can no more be created by an act of volition, than can storms and earthquakes. There is a secret power acting on the nervous system, over which the will has no control.

The state of the atmosphere, the sanity of the system, the unconscious power of imbibed principles, the recollections of the past, the circumstances of the present, and the prospects of the future, all like unseen spirits stir the soul's depths with ideas and passions, always involuntary, and sometimes as abruptly as an electrical flash. To attempt to subject the laws by which ideas and emotions are created to the power of the will, so that they may be conjured and shaped by its mandates, is to war, not only against the constitution of the human mind, but against the powers and elements of Nature.

———o———

PART SECOND.

The Natural Effects of the Monastic Vow of Silent Contemplation.

LET us consider the character and products of the mind which the monastic vow of silent contemplation is calculated to create.

When liberal education has disciplined the intellectual powers, and study has enriched the mind with the facts and principles of science and literature, a philosopher may find in solitude an influence congenial to his high pursuits; and with his scientific instruments enlarging his field of vision, he may discover new secrets in the realms of Nature, and come forth from retirement a more useful member and a brighter ornament of society. But if with distinguished abilities, and the valuable results of an erudite industry, he should maintain perpetual silence, and continue for life in a secluded abode, he would be of no benefit to mankind, and neither win nor deserve the homage which they accord to scientific benefactors.

But the monks were very far from being philosophers. They were in general exceedingly illiterate. Some of their orders actually interdicted as profane any attempt to cultivate the intellectual powers, or to acquire either scientific or literary information. Filled with abject and obscene pilgrims, with slaves who knew of nothing but manual labor, with mechanics whose scanty wages had precluded the possibility of a rudimental education, with soldiers who had no knowledge but that of war, and who had fled before the victorious barbarian into obscurity for safety, it could not be expected that the monasteries with such material, imprisoned in solitude, deprived of social communion, enervated in mental capacity, and restricted in the exercise of their intellectual powers, could ever give birth to philosophers, or to anything but mental imbecility and moral monstrosities.

It has been alleged in favor of monastic institutions that they have originated and were sustained from a pious intention of affording the devout an asylum, where, secluded from the distractions of life, and occupied in silent contemplation on death and judgment, they might fit themselves for the society of God and angels. That such a motive has at times mingled with the causes which have induced individuals to assume the monastic vow, is undoubtedly true; but had it been in every instance the only incentive it would not have made the act less irrational, unnatural and pernicious. Such a plea, in fact, would only prove that monastic piety was identical with Pagan piety. Long before the origin of Christianity, religious orders existed in India, which sought by means of the destruction of all corporeality and intellectual activity, an incorporation with the nature of God, and the realization of a state of perfect happiness.

But an act may be absurd and pernicious, while its motive is pure; and it is always absurd when its objects are imaginary, and pernicious when they are in violation of the dictate of reason. The monastic vows and regulations were ill calculated to make men either happy, enlightened, or useful. Encaverned in solitude, the monks could not become extensively acquainted with the objects of Nature; preserving perpetual silence, they could not materially enlarge each others' information; exercising but one class of the mental organs, they could not form the numerous order of conceptions perfected only by the review of all the faculties. Isolated from human contiguity, walled up in a dungeon, or incarcerated in a monastic cell, the mind overtasked with labor, broken down by fatigue, prostrated yet urged to action, one class of the faculties paralyzed, another inflamed to frenzy, and all concentrated in silent contemplation on terrible and incomprehensible subjects, partial or complete insanity would ensue; incongruity would become tasteful, exaggerations natural, impossibilities credible, shadows realities, and visions, fiends, and angels take possession of the mind. The productions of such a mind, being a transcript of its impressions, would present nothing as real or symmetrical; but everything as disfigured, indistinct, shadowy, inharmoniously blended, or superlatively gigantic. Misshapen dwarfs, huge giants, beings that were neither men, nor beasts, nor birds, nor fishes, nor angels, nor demons, but an incongruous mixture of them all, would be its natural offspring. Men with birds' wings, beasts with human heads, women with fishes' scales, and animals variously compounded of the limbs, claws, and beaks, all in violation of the natural order of Nature, and incompatible with the laws of life, would spring in horrible profusion from the distorted imagination of the monks.

All ideas of proportion, adaptation and utility would be transgressed in their creations. They might regale credulity with an account of cities fifteen hundred miles high, with asses reproving prophets, with snakes conversing with women, with immaterial beings fluttering on ponderable pinions, and with angels whose heads reached the stars, but whose forms were so hugely disproportioned, that while one foot rested on an insignificant portion of the isle of Patmos, the other would rest on a like portion of the Mediterranean sea. The scenery, caught from the gloom of forests, caves or cloisters, would naturally wear an infernal aspect, where there would be shape, but no symmetry; color but no contrast nor harmony; where immaterial beings would be represented as tormented with the flames and suffocating effects of liquid brimstone; where they would shriek and groan without vocal organs, war and wound with material swords, and where corporeality and incorporeality would be compounded in every variety and degree of inconsistency. If in the intervals of the monk's gloomy ravings he should attempt a more cheerful picture, the scene which he would probably portray might glitter with gold and gems where they would be of no service; but it would be pervaded by an awfulness which would be depressing, and by a splendor which would be terrifying. The music might be loud enough to shake Nature to its foundation, but it would naturally be monotonous, perhaps consisting of one tone and one song, eternally sung by beings without throats, assisted by the trumpets and harps invented by mortals; and had pianos, fiddles and accordians been early enough invented, they too, would probably have chimed in the grand chorus. Beside the music of the operatic troupe, the other recreations would probably be so incompatible with the principles of human enjoyment, and make the monk's very heaven so awfully repulsive, that common sense would prudently shrink from partaking of its glory. Thus the conceptions of virtue and of vice, of perfect happiness and of perfect misery, of metaphysical and of theological dogmas, formed by the distempered brains of hermits and monks, while they might be awfully effulgent or insupportably horrible, would be conflicting in their parts, inconsistent with pure ideas of men, of phantoms, or of things; and such a strange commingling of incongruities as might remind reflections of the huts and palaces of Christian Rome, which are constructed of the tombs, altors, temples and palaces of Pagan Rome.

What reason would naturally deduce from the character of the monastic vows and rules, is amply confirmed by the facts of history. Housed with silent, ignorant and gloomy companions, the monks contemplated not the realities of truth, but the fictions of a distempered fancy; and while they scorned the first as profane, they trembled before the second as a dread reality. Conceiving the deity as a monarch, they thought of him as a tyrant; and believing their nature depraved, they punished themselves as criminals. As they imagined freedom of thought sinful, they acquired the temper of a slave; and as they were incapable of reasoning themselves, they accepted as truth whatever their ecclesiastical tyrants dictated. Impressed with the fancy that demons had taken possession of their bodies, they attempted to dislodge them by making their abode as uncomfortable as possible.

After having manacled their limbs with the heaviest chains, and lacerated their bodies in the most horrible manner, they were surprised at finding that they had not yet destroyed their constitutional principles and appetites; and regarding themselves still as objects of divine wrath, they trembled as if a fiery and bottomless pit yawned at their feet. While they labored by monastic rules and exercises to fit themselves for the society of God and angels, they rendered themselves unfit for the society of human beings. The perceptive powers uninformed, and inflamed by disease, furnishing nothing but extravagant and perverted ideas, and the fancy combining them only into monstrous and hideous shapes, the mind became perpetually filled with the most horrible images. The superabundant volume of blood consequent on overwrought excitement, distending the blood vessels of the visual and auditory organs, and causing them unnaturally to press against these organs, gave a vivid distinctness to the impressions, and so brought out the mental perspective as to give the complexion and distinctness of reality. In consequence of the condition of mind thus induced, the sights and sounds conceived by fancy were recognized as real by the perceptive organs. The senses thus recognizing visions as realities, the life of the recluse was doomed to become an incessant struggle, not only with real disease, but with imaginary demons. Less refined in their mythology than the Pagans, who regarded the earth, air and water as peopled with genii, naiads and fairies, they conceived them inhabited by malignant fiends.

The monks often fancied that they saw the misshapen forms of demons, and heard their diabolical whispers. Too illiterate or obtuse to account for natural phenomena, they supposed that they had a hand in regulating the operations of Nature; and, too unacquainted with the habits of the brute creation to understand their mechanical capacity, they regarded the contrivances of animals as the undoubted fruit of a nocturnal adventure of the infernal inhabitants. They often conceived that they saw His Satanic Majesty, with all his distinguishing appendages, such as his cloven foot, his sooty aspect, his peculiar horns, and sulphurous odor. Although his visitations were most formidable in the shape of a woman, yet they frequently had the uncommon fortitude of sustaining long conversations with him.

The more pious a monk was, the more frequently he was honored with the company of demons. This fact is not surprising, for it is certain that the more successfully he warred against nature and himself, the more diseased would become his brain, the more extravagant his conceptions, the more discordant his imagination, the more susceptible his senses to false impresions, the more frequent and terrible would apparitions appear, and the better he would be suited for the company of fiends and spirits. If in the vigorous and wholesome bustle of life, the visual organs may recognize images which have no real existence, the auditory, sounds which are imaginary, and the olfactory, odors which are the mere products of fancy, how much more vividly would analogous deceptions be likely to occur in the minds of monks and anchorites, whose condition was replete with causes calculated to create them.

Such was the melancholy condition of those monks who, aspiring after superhuman sanctification, had with sincerity of purpose assumed the monastic obligation. But there were others who, more ambitious of fame than of internal purity, had assumed the same obligations. Professedly despising pleasure and fortune, but secretly laboring to acquire their possession, they manufactured with more facility diabolical apparitions, than those whichs pontaneously psrang from the overwrought brain of the sincere.

Sanctification having become the passport to worldly honors, and its degree orthodoxly estimated by the degrees of personal familiarity with the Devil, the aspiring were too frail to resist the temptation of increasing their celebrity by multiplying the number of satanic visits; and as they could draw on an inexhaustible mine of conscienceless inventions, and deliberately adorn them with the terrific and interesting incidents of romance, they far outstripped the reputation of the sincere, and with greater facility obtained the emoluments of ecclesiastical sinecures. The sense of touch not being equally susceptible of false impressions with the other senses, while the sincere might see demons and hear their voices, they could not so well recognize them by means of contact. But the hypocritical, untrammeled by this limitation, would create by their inventive faculties any number of personal encounters and terrific battles with the armies of the infernal regions.

Although the monks sometimes relate how completely they vanquished the Devil by their eloquence and the ingenuity of their arguments, yet they oftener tell how valorously they triumphed over him after a desperate struggle with his superhuman strength; and not seldom, how alone and single-handed they encountered him in command of a battalion of fiends, inflicting on the spiritual bodies of the demons such deep gashes, and cutting up their impalpable substances in such a horrible manner that, wounded, bleeding and demoralized, they retreated in wild disorder. As the monkish cell, like the human brain, could accomodate any number of devils, it was as convenient a hall of audience in which to receive His Satanic Majesty, as it was an area for the scientific manœuvering of his legions. The crown of sanctification being awarded to the most unscrupulous inventor of pious ficitons, a hypocrite was encouraged to labor to outrival the fame of an antagonist by the boldness of his assertions, the extravagance of his fables, and the incredibleness of his fabrications. Under such circumstances we are not astonished to find that some claimed to have obtained a perfection in holiness that enabled them to see the Devil anywhere, and to look upon hell at any time.

Even at the period of the Reformation, the popular belief recognized the Devil and his imps as often visible. Martin Luther, while engaged in translating the Bible, conceived that he saw the Devil enter his study, for the purpose of embarrassing him in the execution of his useful design. Annoyed at this unceremonious and impertinent intrusion, he threw at His Satanic Majesty an inkstand, which, passing through the dusky form and striking the wall beyond, left a stain which is visible to this day.

---o---

PART THIRD.

The Ignorance and Corruption induced by the Monastic Vow of Silent Contemplation.

THE profound homage won by the monks from ignorance and superstition, gave such credit to their extravagant productions, that history has sometimes been led into the error of recording them as real events; and the craft or credulity of the church in incorporating them in her devotional books has so deepened and perpetuated reverence for them, that, even at the present day, they continue still to govern in a measure the superstition, and to contaminate the creed and ritual of reformed churches.

It has been alleged, with apparent plausibility, in favor of monastic institutions, that they were during the middle ages the protectors of learning. But, unfortunately, this noble virtue can be justly claimed for only a few of them; and for that few in but a limited sense. Some of the inmates being unfit for more remunerative employment were subjected to the drudgery of copying manuscript; sometimes the task was imposed on others as a penance. The aged and infirm of the Benedictine monks were thus employed; and, as the multiplication of manuscripts is the most efficient mode of preserving what is written on the perishable material of paper and parchment, these monks have contributed to the preservation of learning. But inveterate prejudice, obstinate bigotry, gross ignorance, and abject servitude were ill qualified to render correct versions, while they were well adapted to the perpetration of fraud and corruption. Transcribing manuscripts, not to produce accurate copies, but to consume time or do penance, and governed by the misleading principles of their order, it is not as likely that the monks would furnish authentic and reliable transcripts, as that they would mar them with errors, embellish them with fancies, and interpolate them with forgeries and wilful corruptions.

While such was the literary honesty of the religious orders, and such likely to be the character of their manuscripts, the ignorance and superstition of the age favored rather than obstructed the perpetration of any pious fraud they might contemplate. A few facts will illustrate the incredible ignorance of the Catholic clergy during the dark ages. A Jew, converted to Christianity but not to truth, having persuaded the Emperor Maximilian that the Hebrew works, the Old Testament excepted, were all of pernicious tendency, the latter, at the horrible revelatation, ordered them to to be burnt. The learned Reuchlen earnestly remonstrated against the imperial decree, and succeeded in having its execution postponed until the matter of the allegation could be critically examined. A controversy of ten years ensued. So grossly ignorant were the clergy that not one of them with whom Reuchlen debated had ever seen a Greek Testament, and as for the Hebrew Bible, they denounced its alphabetical characters as the diabolical invention of some profane sorcerer. So obstinate was their opposition to Hebrew literature that they declared their readiness to support their cause at the point of the sword. Neither the Pope nor the cardinals having sufficient learning to decide on the merits of the question, the former was induced to appoint as umpire the archbishop of Spires, whose decision happily rescued oriental literature from the flames of the stake. Pope Sylvester II., whose literary attainments were superior to those of the clergy of his age, was regarded as a magician who held unhallowed converse with infernal demons. St. Augustin, who was ignorant of the Greek tongue, and whose learning was sufficiently superficial to prepare him for canonization, pronounced the doctrine of the antipodes a blasphemous heresy; and Pope Zachariah degraded a friar for indorsing it, and excommunicated all Catholics who should believe it. The patriarch Cyrille declared that neither he, nor the Vandal clergy, nor the African clergy understood the Latin language. St. Hilary asserts from his personal knowledge that but few of the prelates in the ten provinces of Asia preserved the knowledge of the true god. (*Hilar. de Synodis.* c. 63, p. 1186). It might reasonably be supposed that the ecclesiastical councils, composed of the most influential bishops, priests and abbots, would comprehend among their members many distinguished scholars, yet according to the authority of Pope Gregory II., the councils at his time were composed of men, not only ignorant of letters, but of the scriptures. According to the testimony of Sabinus, bishop of Heraclea, the Nicene bishops were "a set of illiterate, simple creatures that understood nothing," and Cassian charges the Egyptian monks of having ignorantly preached Epicurean Paganism as the gospel of Christ. Among the crowd of slaves, soldiers, lords and priests that thronged the convents, the sign of the cross, the sign of ignorance, was a general mode of executing contracts, as all could make it, though few could write their names.

That the literary progress of the church has not kept pace with the progress of the world, will be attested by a few extracts from a work written by William Hogan, formerly a Catholic priest of Philadelphia, comprising an essay entitled, "A Synopsis of Popery, as it was and as it is," and another entitled, "Auricular Confession and Popish Nunneries," published at Hartford, by Silas Andrew and Son, in 1850 — a work that may be profitably consulted by parents who educate their daughters at nunnery schools, and by gentlemen who contemplate forming matrimonial alliances with ladies who have been accomplished at such institutions. Speaking of the ecclesiastical canons the author says: "These canons are inaccessible to the majority of the American people, even of theologians, and with the purport or meaning of them none but those who have been educated Catholic priests have much or any acquaintance. He who argues with Catholic priests must have had his education with them, he must be of them and from among them. He must know from experience that they will stop at no falsehood where the good of the church is concerned; he must know that they will scruple at no forgery when they desire to establish any point of doctrine, fundamentally or not fundamentally, which is not taught by the church; he must be aware that it is a standing rule with the Popish priests, in all their controversies with Protestants, to admit nothing and deny everything, and that if still driven into difficulty they will have recourse to the archives of the church, where they keep piles of decretals, canons, receipts, bulls, excommunications and interdicts, ready for all such emergencies, some of them dated from 300 to 1000 years before they were written or thought of, showing more clearly than perhaps anything else the extreme ignorance of mankind between the third and ninth century, when these forgeries were palmed on the world." (*Synopsis*, p. 9, 10). Again, he observes: "The majority of Catholics in this country know nothing of the religion which they profess, and for which they are willing to fight, contend, and shed the blood of their fellow beings. I am not even hazarding an assertion when I say there is not one of them that has read the gospel through, or that knows any more about the religion he professes than he does about the Koran of Mohammed. He is told by the priest that Christ established a church on earth; that it is infallible, and that he must submit implicitly to what its popes, priests and bishops teach, under pain of 'damnation.' This is all the great mass of Catholics know of religion; this is all they are required to learn; and hence it is that these people are unacquainted with the pretensions of the

Pope, the intrigues of the Jesuits, and the imposition practised on them by their bishops and priests." (*Synopsis*, p. 29). Speaking of the theological education of the priests, he says: " During the four years I spent in the college of Maynooth, they (the scriptures) formed no portion of the education of the students. It is my firm conviction, that out of the large number of students there for the ministry, there was not one who read the gospels through, nor even portions of them, except such as are found in detached passages, in works of controversy between Catholics and Protestants. Until I went to college I scarcely ever heard of a Bible. I know not of one in any parish of Munster, except it may be a Latin one, which each priest may or may not have, as he pleases. But I studied closely the holy fathers of the church; so did most of the students. We were taught to rely upon them as our sole guide in morals, and the only correct interpreters of the Bible. A right of private judgment was entirely denied us, and represented as the source of multifarious errors. The Bible, in fact, we had no veneration for. It was, in truth, but a dead letter in the college; it was a sealed book to us, though there were not an equal number of students who were obliged to study more closely the sayings, the sophistry, the metaphysics and mystic doctrines of those raving dreamers called holy fathers; many of whom, if now living would be deemed mad, and dealt with accordingly." (*Auric. Confess.*, vol. 1, p. 79, 80).

But to return to the consideration of the monks. The pen of transcribers, so generally ignorant, and so grossly superstitious, could not render authentic manuscripts even when actuated by the best intention; and when we recollect that the task which required the exercise of an enlightened and vigorous intellect was devolved on the most diseased and infirm of the religious orders, the impossibility of its effectual performance will appear without a doubt. As ignorance could not transcribe masterly, so superstition would pervert intentionally. Conscience paralyzed by bigotry, and the love of truth supplanted by a careful regard to the interests of the church, the copyists would esteem it a Christian duty to omit such parts of a manuscript as militated against the truth of their religion; to corrupt such parts as might by perversion be made to administer to its support; and to interpolate such parts with occurrences and apparent incidental allusions to events, the omission of which was fatal to its credibility; and thus by a system of typographical frauds, deliberate falsehoods and artful perversions, contrive to make it appear that all Jewish and Pagan literature concurred in establishing Catholicism.

The classics, unlike the canonical scriptures, have been subjected to the purifying process of rigid criticism, and the monkish corruptions which once perverted the meaning, are in a great measure eradicated from modern editions. Had the New Testament been subjected to a similar ordeal, such for instance as the learned Strauss, in his Life of Christ, instituted, Infidels might have fewer objections to the gospels, and the credit of these sacred books be far better sustained than it has been by voluminous commentaries, declamatory sermons and conflicting polemical works, defending the grossest frauds and the boldest interpolations.

The bigotry or fear of the church, which induced it to corrupt the works of ancient authors, led it also to wage an exterminating war against those profane productions which it could not satisfactorily answer. For this purpose the secular power was invoked, and laws were framed prescribing the severest penalty for those who should read or possess a Pagan production. The persecution against philosophers and their libraries was carried on with such pious insanity that besides its causing piles of manuscripts to be destroyed, men of letters burned their elegant libraries, lest some volume contained in them should jeopardize their lives. Young Chrysostom, happening once to find a proscribed volume, gave himself up for lost. St. Jerome, in order to deter his readers from perusing any of the heathen authors, declared he had been scourged by an angel for reading the productions of Virgil. The Orthodox Theodosius, in the destruction of the Alexandrian library, consigned to the flames the literary treasures of antiquity. The bare thought of the existence of works which baffled the talent and learning of the church to refute, irritated the sensitive piety of the monks beyond endurance. They pursued the masterly productions of Celsus and Porphery with an unscrupulousness which seemed to indicate that the annihilation of them was indispensable to the existence of Christianity. After malice had ferreted every crevice where a proscribed volume could be secreted, and vengence had not left a vestige of any of them remaining, except what was quoted or perverted in the works of Christian apologists, the Church boasted that God had not left a work of hostile literature in existence. With not less blasphemy and bigotry has the same absurdity been echoed by dishonest, ignorant theologians of all ages. So wide and unsparing was the monkish war against classic literature, that it has left no work in existence belonging to the period of Christ; and hence where knowledge is the most needed the historian finds the least; and where the facts might be expected to be the most abundant and of the clearest description, the wildest and most ridiculous fancies are presented. The necessity for this destruction proves the power of the works destroyed, and the alarm and weakness of the faith that destroyed them.

Beside the destructive hostility of the monks to the formidable literary obstacles which embarrassed the vindication of their theological subtleties, their zeal led them to perpetrate the grossest forgeries in order to manufacture historical data in their favor. Prominent among the numerous instances of this disregard to truth, are the following passages conceded by all scholars to be entire fabrications. The passage in the works of Phlegon, in which he is made to speak of a total eclipse of the sun and a simultaneous earthquake; a passage in Macrobius, which represents the author as incidentally referring to the death of a son of his as having occurred in consequence of a jealous order issued by Herod for the massacre of all children under two years old; the Epistle of Lentulus, prefect of Judæa at the time of Christ, who is represented as describing the person and character of Christ, in a governmental despatch, which according to prefectorial custom was encumbent on him, in transmitting to Rome a report of all important events occurring within the limits of his jurisdiction;

the legend of the Veronica handkerchief in which it is related how Abgarus, king of Edessa, sent ambassadors to Christ to solicit the favor of his portrait, and how wiping his face with a handkerchief, and thereby impressing his features on it, politely accommodated the legation; the Epistle of Pontius Pilate to the Emperor Tiberius, in which he is made to relate the alleged circumstances of the death and resurrection of Christ; the fabulous inscriptions on two fabulous columns, said to be situated near Tangiers, relating to a robber called Joshua, son of Nun; and all the passages found in Josephus in reference to Christ.

Origen, who wrote in the second century, complains that his own works had been altered; and the practice of this base species of dishonesty seems to have fearfully increased with the growth of the Church. The monk Jerome, in the fourth century, finding the versions of the scriptures which were received by the churches as authentic exceedingly conflicting, undertook to abate the scandal it caused, by compiling a Bible with genuine text. The product of this laborious exertion was, however, so unsatisfactory to the theological tastes of the churches, or to the results of their critical examinations, that but few of them adopted it. Although Jerome's labors were but imperfectly appreciated during his life, yet, as he had materially approximated toward furnishing a catholic desideratum, the Vulgate, which is a modification of his Bible, was declared by the Council of Trent, in 1546, to be "authentic in all lectures, disputations, sermons and expositions, and no one shall presume to reject it under any pretence whatever." But in attempting to execute this decree, the startling fact became evident that the copies of the Vulgate, in consequence of the liberty which translators had taken with the text, essentially differed from one another; that each church believed in a different Bible; that it was impossible to determine which divine book was the least corrupted; and that as the Council, inspired by the Holy Ghost, had forgotten to designate which copy of the Vulgate was the genuine one, it only increased the confusion it had attempted to remedy. If disbelief in the Bible is infidelity, the greater number of the churches were actually in a situation which made them unconscious infidel conclaves. To relieve them from this perilous predicament, the Pope appointed a learned committee to prepare a Bible which should have genuine text. But the Bible elaborated by this committee, not according with the Pope's theological fancies or secret designs, was rejected. Pope Pius IV. next tried his hand at perfecting and correcting the scriptural text; but the task exceeding his learning and ingenuity, his efforts were alike unproductive of satisfactory results. He was followed by Pope Pius V., who also labored in vain. In 1590 Pope Sixtus V. made a Bible which his judgment or prejudice pronounced to be authentic. Determined that Christendom should be reduced to the alternative of accepting his version, or having none, he anathematized all who should alter its text or reject his authority. But Pope Clement VIII., not having the fear of his infallible predecessor's anathema before his eyes, made another Bible, and promulgated it from his throne as genuine and authoritative, amid a heavy storm of Vatican thunder, in which he consigned to the care of the Devil and his angels all who should presume to correct the work of his infallible hands. A year had, however, scarcely elapsed when he was obliged to correct its glaring inconsistencies himself; incurring the vengeance of his own anathemas. Notwithstanding an incessant tinkering for ages by the ablest theologians, to mend the numerous flaws in the Catholic word of God, every well-informed Romanist admits, that while all the previously received versions of the Vulgate are too grossly corrupted to be defended, the one in present use is far from being perfect. Cardinal Bellarmine, who was deeply versed in Biblical erudition, and who in life had obtained such an eminent degree of popularity for sanctity, that when he died a guard had to be placed over his corpse, to prevent the devout from robbing it of its garments — who wished to preserve or vend them as relics — declares that the most that can be said in favor of the received version is, that it is the best that has been made.

The authorized English version of the holy scriptures, known as James' Bible, is the product of forty-seven celebrated Biblical scholars, after three years' labor. The manuscripts from which they made their translations being exceedingly corrupted and discordant, the renderings consequently were so conflicting and irreconcilable on any principle of philological or exegetical criticism, that in order to effect any agreement, and prevent the production of as many Bibles as there were translators, they put the question concerning a disagreement to vote, and decided which was the correct rendering by the authority of a majority of suffrages. But this logic was not appreciated by Dr. Smith and Bishop Belson, to whose joint scrutiny the Bible thus manufactured was afterwards submitted, and they accordingly subjected it to a further process of purification.

While philological criticism, and investigations concerning the genuineness of the sacred text, have wrung from Catholics the reluctant concession that the Vulgate needs a revision, they have equally extorted from Protestants the unwilling admission that their version is corrupted with undoubted forgeries. The doxology at the conclusion of the Lord's prayer, the story of the pool of Bethsaida, the story of the rich man and Lazarus, and the story of the adulteress, are universally conceded by scholars to be wilful fabrications. The most distinguished among Biblical scholars go further. Bretschneider, the friend and confident of Joseph II. of Austria, rejects the Gospel of St. John. Dr. Lardner rejects the Epistle to the Hebrews, the Epistle of St. James, the Second Epistle of St. Peter, the Second Epistle of St. John, the Epistle of St. Jude, and the book of Revelations. Dr. Evanson rejects the Gospel of St. Matthew, the Gospel of St. Mark, the Gospel of St. Luke, the Epistle to the Ephesians, the Epistle to the Colossians, the Epistle to the Romans, the First Epistle of St. Peter and the First Epistle of St. John.

The Greek Testament comprehends 181,253 words, yet such is the number of mistakes, perversions, forgeries and interpolations in the existing manuscripts, that in comparing the documents together 130,000 various readings are detected; showing that the manuscripts from which the New Testament is translated, are not correct in one word out of six. These discrepancies, affecting the mere spelling of a word in some instances, and, in others, the sense of a passage, are of all degrees of importance.

In Tischendorf's New Testament, published by Tauchnitz, at Leipzig, in English, and for sale by the New York booksellers, we find the following: "But the Greek text of the apostolic writings, since its origin in the first century, has suffered many a mischance at the hands of those who have used and studied it. . . . The authorized version, like Luther's, was made from a Greek text which Erasmus in 1516, and Robert Stephens in 1550, had formed from manuscripts of later date than the tenth century. . . . Since the sixteenth century Greek manuscripts have been discovered, of far greater antiquity than those of Erasmus and Stephens; as well as others in Latin, Syriac, Coptic and Gothic, into which languages the sacred text was translated, between the second and fourth centuries. . . . . Scholars are much divided in opinion as to the readings which most exactly convey the word of God." (*Introduction*, p. 1, 2).

When mistakes in a manuscript arise, from the ignorance or incompetency of the copyist, they invalidate its authority; when they arise from his carelessness, they are proofs that he entertained no reverence for it; and when they occur from a deliberate intention on his part to corrupt and to interpolate it, they are demonstrations that he did not believe in its divine inspiration. That the religious orders did not believe in the divine inspiration of the holy scriptures, is as undeniable as it is that they deliberately and intentionally marred all the Biblical manuscripts that passed through their hands. The conviction is equally irresistible that those who sanction the corruptions of the sacred text by using them as authority, and those who defend them in defiance of the irrefragable proof of their spurious character, forfeit all claim to a reputation of common honesty.

There is another class of forgeries perpetrated for the good of the Church, to which I will briefly advert. Of this description is the Decretal Epistle of Constantine the Elder, addressed to Pope Sylvester—the foundation of the Pope's claim to temporal sovereignty; and also the Creed of Athanasius, forged two hundred years after his death, and which Gennadius, Patriarch of Constantinople, upon first reading, pronounced to be the work of a drunken man. All ranks of the Church seemed to have become infatuated with an ambition to be forgers. Pope Stephen II. forged a letter, and attributed its authorship to the spirit of St. Peter. In this document, according to Gibbon, "The apostle assures his adopted sons, the King, the clergy, and the nobles of France, that dead in the flesh, he is still active in the spirit; that they now hear and must obey the voice of the founder and guardian of the Roman Church; that the virgins, the saints, and all the host of heaven, unanimously urge the request, and will confess the obligation; that riches, victory and paradise will crown their pious enterprise, and that eternal damnation will be the penalty if they suffer his tomb, his temple, and his people to fall into the hands of the perfidious Saracens. (*Dec.* vol. v., chap. xlix., p. 26.) The evidences of similar frauds are numerous. All the letters and decretals of Clementine are spurious. But few of the numerous works ascribed to Pope Gregory the Great are genuine. The First Epistle of Clement to the Corinthians is egregeously corrupted and interpolated; his second Epistle to the Corinthians, is so much mutilated that but a fragment of it remains; his autobiography, in which he is made to take a journey with St. Peter; and all his apostolic canons, are entire fabrications. The Apocalypse was rejected as spurious at the Council of Laodicea, by the seven churches to which it was addressed, and the sentence was almost universally confirmed by the churches of Christendom. Sirmund shows that the Nicene canons have been corrupted, altered, abridged, and forged to accommodate them to the designs of the church. (*Tom.* iv., p. 1–234). To establish a historical basis for some pious imposition, the the letters of bishops, decrees of councils, and bulls of Popes have been forged, distorted, marred, interpolated or destroyed. Volume after volume has been written and falsely attributed to the pen of some distinguished author, in order to obtain respect and authority for an absurd ecclesiastical claim or arbitrary usurpation. Without moral principle, and intent only on supporting the ambitious pretentions of the Pope, the religious orders, at the suggestion of interest, scrupled not to destroy the finest models of literary taste, and to perpetrate the most audacious forgeries. What could not militate against the credit of their dogmas, or obstruct the consummation of their designs, or what might, by an artful adulteration be made accessory to them, they might piously spare; but whatever was in its nature too inflexibly inimical to the success of them, they labored to annihilate. The unavoidable deduction from the existence of the monkish forgeries is, that every doctrine for which they have been fabricated to prove, is false; and that every doctrine and event for which they have been manufactured to disprove, is true. The mutilation and destruction of ancient authors by the religious orders is a positive admission that such works were fatal to their claims; the attempt to manufacture artificial proof by corrupting and interpolating them, is an acknowledgment that the successful vindication of their creed and pretensions required proof which did not exist; and the cargoes of their forgeries, each instance of which being a demonstration of these assertions, and consequently an undeniable objection to the validity of the authority upon which they rest their claims, show the vast amount of labor the monks have undergone to disprove their own doctrines, and destroy their own credibility.

In the revival of learning, inaugurated by profane genius, the monastic orders, which possessed the treasures of classic literature, took, in general, no active part. The literary fires which smouldered in their institutions cast but a sickly glare upon the darkness within, and the feeble rays could not be expected to penetrate the massive walls of these huge castles of ignorance. Resembling more a taper placed under a bushel than a light set upon a hill, they left the surrounding region enveloped in midnight gloom. The manuscripts transcribed or perverted by the monks were stowed away as useless rubbish. At length the holy charm which, for ages, had bound the church in stupid ignorance, was happily dissolved. Pope Nicholas V., catching a spark of the fire which burned in the breast of his lay associates, such as Cosmo Medici, his own, too, became ignited. Unconscious or regardless of the liberalizing tendency of classical literature, he became enthusiastic in its cause, and inaugurated a pursuit which has exposed the forgeries and legends of the Catholic Church to scorn and contempt. Whatever were his private views, his public example and assertions indicate that he had arrived at a firm conviction that the papal chair would not soon again be filled with another friend to the classics. Diligently improving the auspicious moment, he collected the dusky and mouldering manuscripts from the monasteries, while his coadjutors sent vessels to gather them from abroad. By the united labors of the Pope and his opulent laymen, respectable libraries were formed, and the world was enlightened by recovered versions of Xenophon, Diodorus, Polybius, Thuycidides and other eminent authors.

The apprehensions of Nicholas, suggested probably by his knowledge of the nature and past conduct of the church, were too well founded not to be confirmed by subsequent history. The Pagan authors of Greece and Rome, speaking in the clear tones of reason and philosophy, could not subserve the purposes of ecclesiastical fraud and intolerance. The dark conspiracy to deceive and enslave mankind, and the systematized measures to keep the world in ignorance, which constitutes a permanent feature of Catholic polity, could derive no aid from a liberal diffusion of Pagan erudition. Hence Leo X., who is ranked among the most generous of the pontifical patrons of the classics, prohibited the translation of them into the vernacular language.

But it may be alleged as an exception to the usual hatred manifested by the church to the cause of education, that the Pope did, at times, establish colleges and universities. This fact is undeniably true. Pope Sixtus IV. established several universities; but he required from each, for a charter, 10,000 ducats; and for each collegiate title and office, from 10,000 to 20,000 ducats. Pope Innocent III. also founded a university; but it was on condition that he received 50,000 scudi for its charter. He also very generously created twenty-six secretaryships, and a host of other offices, to assist the labors of education, but he sold appointments to them at very exorbitant prices. Pope Alexander VI. also founded a university, but it was in consideration of a magnificent bonus; and he even further displayed his magnanimity by nominating eighty writers of popish briefs, and selling the appointments at 850 scudi each. But after all what was the object of these institutions? Was it to advance the capacities of individual man? Was it to enlighten society at large? Not at all. Guizot says: "For the development of the clergy, for the instruction of the priesthood, she [the church] was actively alive; to promote these she had her schools, her colleges, and all other institutions which the deplorable state of society would permit. These schools and colleges, it is true, were all theological, and destined for the clergy; and, though from the intimacy between the civil and religious orders they could not but have some influence on the rest of the world, it was very slow and indirect." (*Gen. Hist. Civ.*, Sect. vi., p. 132). Guizot might have added with truth, that even for her own clergy the church never tolerated an educational institution without receiving an exorbitant pecuniary consideration, nor appointed a professor, or any other officer, without receiving pay for it.

Dens, in his "*Systematic Theology,*" reasons thus: "Because forgers of money, and other disturbers of the State, are justly punished with death, therefore also are heretics, who are forgers of the faith, and, as experience shows, greatly disturb the State." (*Dens*, 2, 88, 89). If this logic is sound, it is difficult to perceive how Popes, cardinals, monks and priests can avoid conceding justice the right of putting *them* to death, as by the universal testimony of history and the acknowledgment of the ablest Catholic authors, they have been forgers of the faith; and, as they have been greater forgers than Protestants, they may, according to their own logic, be more justly put to death. But this we should be sorry to witness.

The efforts of the church to manufacture evidence in support of gratuitous assumptions, which so clearly disproves what it asserts at every step; sinks its character and authority into such utter insignificance; and in proportion to the warmth of its zeal adds weight to the contempt it has earned, might be considered unworthy the notice of sober reason, and left to the crushing jeer of its own ludicrousness. Yet when its polluting finger presumes to touch the sacred page of history; when it would annihilate all historical authority by base interpolations, and load the shelves of libraries with its spurious trash, it has invaded a province sacred to the rights of the world; a province in which truth, reason, and human progress have a deep interest, and which must be protected against the intrusion of malignant feet.

From the monastic vows and regulations, we might be agreeably surprised if the literary productions of those who were governed by them were anything but models of absurdity and puerility. It would naturally be suspected that the ideas of the monks would be shaded by the gloom of their melancholy abode, contracted by the influence of their solitary confinement, and rendered misshapen by the habit of conversing exclusively with their own meditations; and that their literary productions would be rife with all the inventions to which bigotry and superstition could prompt, and with all the craft and unscrupulousness that could serve the purposes of unpolished and unnatural fraternities, isolated from society, absolved from the ties and obligations of humanity, and exclusively devoted to the defense and aggrandizement of an organization which aimed at monopolizing all secular rights, immunities and privileges, in order to command the dominion and luxuries of the world. This reasonable presumption we shall find too well confirmed for the credit of human nature, in those legends and theological disquisitions which have often puzzled the credulous, but much oftener curled the lips of the more enlightened into a smile of philosophical contempt. Palpably fictitious, rarely possessing the merit of ingenuity, and, in general, absolutely puerile, yet have the monkish legends been consecrated as divine in the Catholic Mass-book, enforced upon the acceptance of the obstinate by the terrors of the Inquisition, and sometimes mistaken by history for actual events.

This ludicrous mass consists in part of magnified and distorted events of true history, and in part of personages and details entirely spurious. It is elaborately ornamented, or degraded with circumstancial accounts of miracles which were never performed, with reports of debates which never took place, and with details of battles which were never fought. Faithful only in transcribing their own vitiated taste and unscrupulous conscience; and decorating their narratives with coarse scenes of blood and bigotry, of death and horror, of hell anddemons, they have furnished a record of absurdities, of a depth of hypocrisy, of an audacity in fabrication, and of a total depravity in principle unparalleled in the history of deception and imposition. Had they, like Sir Thomas Moore, in his description of Eutopia, or no place, described a people which were no people, a city which was invisible, and a river which was waterless, they could scarcely have been less imaginary, though it must be conceded that they are less entertaining and instructive.

Passing over the polemical rubbish, the absurd topics of discussion and the ludicrous logic of the monastic orders, which would be too tedious for a reader of the nineteenth century, we will briefly allude to some of their amusing legends, which have been consecrated as sacred history in the devotional books of the church. The actual sufferings and deaths of the primitive Christians, they have grotesquely magnified, and invented fanciful modes of torture, which never could have entered the more cultivated brain of a Roman emperor.

According to the story of these visionists, when a Pagan female embraced Christianity, she was often compelled to decide whether she valued her virtue higher than she did her religion; and, when the inflexibility of her faith imperiled her innocence, a divine power always interposed, and miraculously rescued her from a dangerous predicament. The male converts were subjected to similar modes of ingenious torture. A young saint, in the passion of his first love, according to their authority, was once chained naked to a bed of flowers, and in this hapless and exposed condition, wontonly assaulted by a beautiful courtezan; but he saved his chastity by biting off his tongue. St. Cecilia made a vow of perpetual virginity, but her father disregarding the unnatural obligation, betrothed her to a prince. In spite of all remonstrances to the contrary, the marriage was on the eve of being consummated, when an angel interposed, and, after satisfactorily adjusting matters between the nuptial parties, rewarded the groom for the relinquishment of his bride, and the virgin for the obstinacy of her resolution, by crowning them both with wreaths of spiritual roses and lilies, culled from heaven's flower garden. Sometime after the eventful occurences of this wedding party, Amachius, a Roman prefect, commanded Cecilia to sacrifice to the gods. Her piety obliging her to disobey the royal injunction, it was determined that the majesty of the law should be vindicated by having her boiled three days and three nights in a pot of water. The coldness of divine grace however sufficiently impregnated her body to protect it from injury. As her piety had rendered her invulnerable to the effects of boiling water, the emperor ordered the executioner to try the virtue of a ponderous axe. Accordingly she was laid upon the block; the executioner gave her neck three scientific strokes, but perceiving her head still attached by its integuments, desisted from further effort convinced that the accomplishment of the task exceeded his constitutional vigor.

7*

The miraculous feat of this saint in inventing music, a long time after all nations had acquired some proficiency, at least, in its principles, has often been the theme of pious historians, orators and poets. St. George slew a dragon (a lizard), which was about to swallow a king's daughter. St. Dennis walked two miles after his head had been cut off. St. John of God displayed so much whimsical zeal that he was supposed to be demented, and was placed in a lunatic asylum. St. Hubert went on a hunting excursion, and seeing a stag with a cross between its antlers, became converted by the vision into a bishop. He received a key from St. Peter, which is still preserved in St. Hubert's monastery, at Ardennes, and is regarded as an infallible remedy for the hydrophobia. St. Patrick found a lost boy, whom the hogs had nearly devoured. On touching the mutilated frame with his holy hand, it recovered the lost flesh which had been digested by the swine, and stood before the saint perfectly proportioned in all its parts, and without a wound. This charitable saint once fed 1,400 persons on one cow, two stags, and two wild boars. Respecting, however, the rights of property, and perceiving that to be benevolent at another's expense was a suspicious species of morality, he so adroitly contrived the management of his miracle that the cow which had been eaten up by the people, and which belonged to a poor widow, was seen the next day well and hearty, and as comfortably grazing in her usual pastures as if nothing had happened. St. Xavier, while traversing the ocean, lost overboard a crucifix. On landing, a crab brought it in his claw, and reverently laid it at his feet. The Devil, assuming the shape of a charming woman, once made indelicate proposals to him. This piece of impudence so enraged the saint that he spit into His Satanic Majesty's angelic face. The Devil, being a gentleman, was so disgusted at this coarse vulgarity, that he ever afterward shunned Xavier's society. St. Anthony of Padua, after exhausting the strength of the Catholic arguments in favor of consubstantiation, in a debate with a heretic, finally converted his antagonist by an appeal to the understanding of a horse. Holding up the host before the animal, he addressed it thus: "In virtue and in the name of thy creator, I command thee, O horse to come, and with humility adore thy God." The horse, at the request of the saint, instantly left the corn which it was eating, advanced to the host and fell upon its knees before it.

St. Andrew being assaulted by the devil with an axe, and by a company of imps with clubs, called for assistance on St. John, who responded with a regiment of angels; and capturing the devils, chained them to the ground. At this exploit St. Andrew laughed. The Emperor Maximus, having cut St. Apia Tell into ten pieces, the angel Gabriel put him together again. This contest of disintegration and recomposition was carried on with much spirit between Maximus and Gabriel. Ten times a day for ten consecutive days was the saint cut into ten pieces by the malice of the one, and put together again by the anatomical skill of the other. St. Martin of Tours, the patron saint of drunkards, whose festival was formerly celebrated by the devout with banqueting, hilarity and carousals, once, on a drunken frolic, divided his garments with a poor soldier. At night, in a dream, he beheld Christ wearing the identical garment he had given away. His mind became so impressed, probably deranged, that he turned Catholic. The face of this saint was so sanctimonious that it once paralyzed the arm of a robber, which was raised to give him a death blow. He wrought many miracles; could raise the dead to life. Clovis, after his Gothic victory, made him a rich donation; and as the hero's war steed was in the saint's stable, he proposed besides, to redeem it with the generous sum of 100 ducats, but the pious horse refused to move until the sum was doubled. St. Anthony saw a centaur in the desert. Finding the corpse of the hermit Paul in the wilderness, and being too much prostrated through fasting to bury it, two lions seeing his difficulty, politely offered their assistance; and after digging a grave and depositing in it the hermit's corpse, respectfully vanished away. St. Athanasius compliments him on account of his holy abhorence of clean water, and for not having suffered his feet to be contaminated with it except in cases of unavoidable necessity. (*Vct. Ant.*, c. 47), St. Palladus, seeing a hyena standing near his cave, addressing it, asked: "What's the matter?" "Holy father," replied the beast, "the odor of thy sanctity has reached me. I killed a sheep last night, and want to confess and get absolution." St. Beuno caused the earth to open and swallow a disappointed lover, who had cut off the head of his mistress for her having refused to marry him. He then, by saying mass over the remains of the unfortunate lady, caused her head and body to reunite, and life to reanimate her frame. St. Nepomuk, refusing to disclose the secret confessions of a queen, to her husband who suspected her of infidelity, was doomed to suffer death by drowning. This saint was canonized by Pope Innocent III., and his tomb is shown to this day. But unfortunately for the infallibility of His Holines, it has been indisputably proved that no such person as St. Nepomuk ever existed. A priest once travelling along a solitary road, heard a most harmonious sound proceeding from a beehive. On approaching it he discovered that the bees were adoring the eucharist, and singing psalms to its honor. A monk residing at the monastery of Tebenoe was visited by an angel who dictated to him a liturgy. This divine work is preferred by the learned Cassion. St. Ambrose, piously inhuman, carefully instilled into the youthful minds of Theodosius and Gratian the spirit and maxims of religious persecution. He taught them that the worship of idols was a crime against God, and that an emperor is guilty of the crime he neglects to punish. All the intolerant laws and horrible religious butcheries which disgraced the administrations of these princes, and their successors, originated in their Catholic education. The same saint justified the conduct of a bishop who had been convicted by the court of setting fire to a Jewish Synagogue. (*Tom.* ii. Epistle xl. p. 946). St. Augustine, whose most conspicuous virtue was an uncompomising hatred of heretics, warmly commended the inhuman edicts of Honorius against the Donatists, which proscribed and banished several thousands of their priests, stripped them of their possessions, deprived their laymen of the rights of citizens, distracted the land with tumult and blood, and drove a large number of them to seek relief by invoking martyrdom. The inhuman saint rejoiced at the despair and madness which shortened the lives of these unfortunate persons, as it would hereafter lessen their torments in hell. St. Jerome justly denounced the disgraceful practice of the clergy in defrauding the natural heirs out of their inheritance, and vindicated the governmental edicts to obstruct this systematic plunder. But his brother monks recriminated; charged him with being the lover of Paula, of profanely bestowing on her the title of mother-in-law of God, of assigning himself the chief place in her will, of inducing her to abandon her infant son at Rome, of exercising an undue influence on her beautiful daughter, and of inducing the mother to consecrate her to perpetual virginity, so that he might encounter no obstacles in inheriting her immense possessions, in which was comprehended the city of Necropolis. To these charges he replied that he was merely the steward of the poor. With the fortune of Paula he built four monasteries. He was bitterly opposed to St Chrysostom, who boldly denounced the corruption and licentiousness of the clergy and imperial court. Readily and maliciously he coincided with the opinion of Theophilus, that Chrysostom had delivered his soul to the Devil to be adulterated; and when zeal in the cause of virtue had brought upon the head of Chrysostom the wrath of the emperor and the court, and he was incarcerated in a dungeon, these two lights of the church had the decency to regret that some punishment more adequate to his guilt was not inflicted. St. Cyril, of Alexandria, piously lusted after temporal power, and, as the patriotic Novitians obstructed his designs, he closed their churches, took forcible possession of their sacred utensils, plundered the dwelling of Theapentus, their bishop; and then seizing on the Jewish synagogue, drove the Jews from the city and pillaged their houses. The governor interposed; but five hundred armed monks surrounded him and attempted to murder him. Hypatia, a lady celebrated for her personal charms, unblemished character, and extraordinary literary acquirements, was, on account of her Novitian proclivities, assaulted by the holy forces of St. Cyril, dragged from her carriage, and punctured to death with tiles.

The enumeration of the fables of the monks, and of the atrocious acts of canonized saints, might be continued until it filled huge volumes; but well-informed Catholics will be thankful that this notice is so brief. The Missil, the Glories of Mary and other Catholic compendia, some of which consist of fifty folio volumes, will satisfy the more curious. The profound homage paid to the monks for supposed sanctity, and the inquisitorial terrors which were brought to bear in favor of their frauds, so blunted public perception to truth that the fictitious events and personages invented by one age were believed by the succeeding, until the church became the simple dupe of its own forgeries, and self-cursed by accepting, as matters of fact, the fables and impositions with which it had humbugged former ages. Meldegg, Catholic Professor of the Theological Faculty of Freiburg, affords the following testimony in favor of what has been stated: "The old breviary," says he, "crammed full of fictitious or much-colored anecdotes of saints, with passages of indecorous import, requires a thorough revision. . . . . Some Masses are founded on stories not sufficiently proved, or palpably ficttcious, as the Mass of the *Lancea Christi*, the *Inventio Crusis*, &c."

The ludicrousness of the monastic vow of silent contemplation is visible in the misshapen ideas of the monks; its pernicious tendency, in the frauds, perversions, distortions and interpolation which it has led them to perpetrate; its bigotry, in the wide destruction of ancient literature to which it has incited them; its absurdness, in the puerile and contemptible productions which it has induced them to elaborate; and its immorality, in that coarseness and vulgarity in their literature, so offensive to a sense of propriety, and which sometimes makes an allusion to their works a matter of reluctance.

CHAPTER VI.

The Monastic Vow of Poverty.

The monachal vows which we have considered in the foregoing chapters were assumed by all the religious orders prior to the thirteenth century. At that period orders were inaugurated to assist in the administration of the public affairs of the church. As these orders assumed obligations incompatible with the observance of silence and seclusion, the vows imposing them were not enjoined. But the vow of poverty, which will be the subject of the present chapter, and the vow of celibacy and obedience, which will hereafter be considered, were assumed by all the religious orders, both antecedent and subsequent to the thirteenth century.

The vow of poverty embraced an unqualified abjuration of all right to acquire or hold individual property, but granted the privilege of owning property in a corporate capacity. This privilege was, however, variously restricted by the terms of different monastic charters. The Carmelites and the Augustines were permitted to hold such an amount of real estate as would be sufficient for their support; the Dominicans were limited to the possession of personal property; while the Franciscans were not allowed to hold either real estate or personal property.

The vow of poverty assumed by the monks was adopted either from the instigations of an artful policy, to acquire wealth with the reputation of despising it, or from a conviction that poverty was a blessing and wealth an evil. If the first hypothesis is correct, the assumption of the vow was exceedingly reprehensible; if the second, it was absolutely absurd.

A condition of poverty, abstractly considered, is a matter of neither praise nor censure. It is sometimes a source of degredation; often of crime, and always of inconvenience and embarrassment. Its general tendency is to weaken in man his inborn sense of personal independence; to debase his mind with notions of fictitious inferiority; to degrade his social dignity by inducing sycophantic and obsequious habits; and to lead him to sacrifice his conscious equality to the demands of artificial rank. The incessant toil imposed by poverty on the energies of the poor obdurates their nature; and, allowing no interval for mental culture, permits nothing to interrupt or soften its tendency. The mortifying difficulties experienced by this class of society to obtain, by honest labor, a subsistence for themselves and their natural dependents, have sometimes led them to become depredators upon society, when their constitutional principles, unwarped by indigence, would have secured their obedience to law and their labors for the public good. Graces have been lost in brothels, and talents extinguished on scaffolds, which, had tolerable means protected against the cravings of hunger, might have added lustre to the female character, and heroes, statesmen and scholars to the scroll of fame. Poverty begetting despair, and despair destroying hope, the incentive to action, the powers of genius sunk into the torpidity of stupefaction, and the strength of a lion slumbered in the inactivity of a sloth. The chill which poverty breathes over the mind is as unfriendly to the unfolding of the intellectual germs, as the icy atmosphere of winter is to the fructification of vegetable seed. The poet or philosopher, hoveled in penury, without books or scientific instruments, with spare meals and gloomy forebodings, never creates his brightest gem, nor solves his profoundest problem. However sweetly Burns may sing or Otway melt, or however importantly other sons of indigence may have contributed to the augmentation of the volume of science and literature, yet the world has never heard their sweetest song, nor read their brightest period; for the groan of penury has marred the harmony of the one, and the tear of want has dimmed the lustre of the other.

As a condition of poverty is, in the abstract, a subject of neither praise nor blame, so also is a condition of wealth. Wealth, however, is the ablest means of advancing individual and social progress, as well as the sole remedy for the evils of poverty. If it cannot be adduced as a ground of esteem or of respectability, or as an apology for the ignorance, stupidity, pomposity, vanity and vulgarity with which it may adventitiously be associated, yet, as it amplifies the means of beneficence, and protects the weakness of human nature against temptation arising from indigence, its honest acquisition is always consistent with the severest principles of rectitude; and its pursuit is recommended by the honorable pride of personal responsibility, the motives of prudence and forecast, and the consideration of every domestic and social obligation. Without its aid the world would have remained in a state of primal barbarism; the commercial intercourse of nations, the first element of civilization and the principal source of national prosperity, power and greatness, would never have been known; agricultural, manufacturing, mechanical and mining interests, unstimulated by the lucrative traffic of supplying a foreign demand for surplus domestic production, would never have been extensively developed; the knowledge, the exotic luxuries, and the improvments in the comforts and conveniences of civilized life derived from international trade, could never have been obtained; the great bond of the amity of nations, and the power created by the pecuniary advantages of exchanging with one-another the products of their different climates, and which, by dissipating mutual prejudices, suspicion, vanity and self-conceit, has united them in friendly and beneficial intercourse, would never have existed; and, as the first altars were erected for the exposure of merchandise for sale, as the first offerings were the currency by which goods were purchased, penalties satisfied, salaries paid, and amity and friendship expressed; and, as the first temples were market-houses built for the accommodation of the traffic of the caravans, and to protect the goods against plundering barbarians, who understood not the conventional rights of property, had it not been for the fact that in the pursuit of wealth, communities felt the importance of establishing convenient centres of trade and modes of exchange, the ceremonies of religion would never have been invented. (See Heeron's Historical Researches, translated by Bancroft).

As neither a condition of poverty nor a condition of wealth is a subject of praise nor censure; but, as the former inflicts on humanity its worst evils, and the latter confers on it incalculable advantages, a vow of poverty can have no innate sanctity to commend it, but must have all constituents that can render it objectionable. When it is further considered that there is a modifying reciprocity incessantly acting between the conditions of the different members of the human family, making the prosperity of one advantageous to all, and the indigence of one disadvantageous to all, we may find not only a selfish, but also a patriotic incentive in availing ourselves of any pecuniary right of our being. No one can be indigent without decreasing the wealth of another, nor opulent without contributing to the subsistence of others, nor industrious without adding to the sum of national wealth, nor indolent without consuming that for which he renders no equivalent. Now, as the vow of poverty is inconsistent with the virtues and obligations created by the mutual dependence and reciprocal influence of the condition and circumstances of mankind on each other; as it fosters all the evils that demoralize the social state; as it multiplies the number of paupers, discourages industry, sanctifies pernicious influences, and burdens society with the support of indolent and useless members, it is at variance with the interests of man and the prosperity of government.

National wealth is the aggregate of individual wealth. The greater is the amount of individual wealth in a nation, and the more equally it is distributed among the inhabitants, the less are the evils of poverty, the more independent and responsible are the citizens, the more energetically are the agricultural, mineral, manufacturing, and commercial interests developed, the more generally and intimately are the interests of the people interwoven with the fabric of the

8*

government, the greater will be the nation's prosperity, the more formidable its arms, the more peaceful its internal condition, and the more durable its prosperity.

A reformatory institution, to be efficacious, must be adapted to the nature of man and his social condition. Its principles must be his principles. Its measures must tend to aid his fullest development. To accomplish this object it must seek to abolish all restrictions on his rights, to remove whatever vitiates his sense of independence, to incite his industry by making labor honorable and its rewards certain, and to annul the immunities, exemptions, privileges and monopolies which degrade the masses by indigence and invidious distinctions, and corrupt the few by luxury and fictitious dignity. But the monachal institution, which sanctions poverty, the most prolific source of crime; which denounces individual wealth, the great element of civilization, and of individual and national improvement; which inculcates indolence, the parasite that feeds on the vitals of society; which discourages the avocations of industry, the parent of personal independence and responsibility; and which aims at a monopoly of wealth, itself the source of political inequality, of despotic government and of popular servitude— can advance no claim to a magnanimous mission. To esteem it a virtue to be poor, pleasing to infinite intelligence to renounce the best means of self-improvement, criminal to protect human integrity against the assaults originating in a condition of poverty, are ideas of such an absurd nature that the inference can scarcely be avoided, that the source whence they originated must have been utterly destitute, not only of moral principle, but of common sense.

But whenever conduct becomes enigmatical, and principles are avowed contradictory to human reason, passion and interests, an ordinary knowledge of the craft of ambition is apt to suggest a suspicion, that these singular abnegations have not sprung from a sanctity that has elevated the avowers above human nature, but from the injustice of their designs and the profundity of their dissimulation. Conscious that candor would be defeat, they have endeavored to accomplish objects by pretending to oppose them. The church never being too strongly fortified in holiness not to practise the advantageous vices of the world, has invariably been betrayed into the adoption of this crafty policy; but, always fanatical, she has never been discreet. Not only has she denied her real designs, but, in order to conceal them, has imposed vows of such an absurd and inconsistent import, as could not fail to reveal the hypocrisy and craft that dictated them. The vow of poverty was not assumed to become indigent, but to become opulent. It was a financial manœuvre, designed to facilitate the routine of business; and it proved a very efficacious means of self-emolument. It won a reputation for the holy beggars, that humbled imperial dignity at their feet. Theodosius refused sustenance until a monk who had anathematized him, nullified it by absolution. The Empress of Maximus, in her own palace, at her own table, esteemed it a high honor to be permitted to wait as a servant on St. Martin of Tours. While the assumption of unnatural vows invested the mendicant monks with the credit and importance of supernatural beings, and elevated them above the dignity of emperors and empresses, it opened to their avarice the treasures of the world, and enabled them not only to fill their coffers with the people's money, but to win their blessing in the act of defrauding them. Such was the haughty indifference of the Abbot Pambo, who seemed to imagine, with his church, that he was the owner of the wealth of the world, that when Malaria, a rich sinner, presented him a donation of plate for his monastery, and intimated that its weight was about three hundred pounds, replied : " Offer you this to me or to God ? If to God, who weighs the mountains in a balance, he need not be informed of the weight of your plate." The real design and value of the monastic vows was once forcibly expressed by a Benedictine monk, who remarked: " My vow of poverty has given me one hundred thousand crowns a year ; my vow of obedience has raised me to the rank of a sovereign prince." An incident occurred in Paris, in relation to two ecclesiastical dignitaries which illustrates the cupidity and unapostolic character of the church. Innocent IX. and St. Thomas Aquinas having met together in Paris, and a capacious plate, piled with gold, the proceeds of the sale of indulgences, being brought into the room in which they were seated, the enraptured Pope exclaimed : " Behold, the days are past when the church could say, gold and silver have I none." But the saint truthfully remarked: " The days are also past when the church could say to the paralytic, arise and walk." Prætaxtatus, a Pagan philosopher, viewing the princely revenues of the church, declared that if he could become bishop of Rome, it might even remove his scruples about believing in Christianity.

Assuming the strongest possible obligations to maintain a perpetual condition of absolute poverty, the monks yet found it compatible with the principles and teachings of the church, to convert their religious organizations into a financial corporation, and to conceal its character and design under a veil of angelic piety. The wealth which they apparently scorned, they unscrupulously amassed; the power which they scoffed at as profane, they attempted to monopolize; to whatever they seemed the most indifferent, they the most sedulously labored to acquire; and whatever they professed with their lips they violated in their practice. This consummate hypocrisy might be condemned by the profane sceptic, but the *means* crowned the *end* with too high a degree of success not to be justified by the piety of the religious orders.

The measures and designs of this false and crafty policy harmonized too well with the pretensions of the Pope, and furnished his purposes with too able and ingenious an auxiliary, not to command his fostering care and protection. Equal in duplicity and rapaciousness, he exempted the mendicant orders from all secular and ecclesiastical jurisdiction, privileged them to demand alms without restriction, invested them with the exclusive power of selling indulgences, and conferred on them the lucrative prerogative of accepting legacies under the evasive name of offerings. By this munificent lavishment of spiritual favors, the mendicant orders soon found themselves transported from an apparent condition of pauperism to a real condition of princely wealth and power; enjoying at the same time all the sympathy that indigence could excite, and all the luxury that money could purchase. Exempted from secular jurisdiction, they were empowered to plunder, ravish and murder with impunity; privileged to demand alms of all, they were the masters of the fortunes of all; endowed with the exclusive power of vending indulgences, they enjoyed a monopoly of the most lucrative trade that was ever projected; and, allowed to receive legacies, they were enabled, after having wheedled the devout out of their treasure while in health, to take advantage of their dotage, and to stand over their dying pillow, and dictate the terms of their last testament to the advantage of the church, and to the disadvantage of natural heirs.

Avarice, like the cormorant, is insatiable; the more it is gorged, the keener is its appetite; and this rapacious demon having taken complete possession of the monastic body, every dollar that its craft wrung from the devout only inflamed its greediness the more. When it had exhausted the gold of a penitent, its covetous eye became fascinated by his land; and, what avarice craved, financial sagacity quickly perceived an available method of obtaining.

The church possessing no inherent moral vitality, sank with the middle ages into barbarism; her power was then supreme, but insecurity of life and property prevailed, and under her auspices temporal power degenerated to a system of rapine and plunder. Had she been divine, she would then have beamed as a lone star on a tempestuous ocean; but being earthy, she resembled the other earthy compounds; nor could she well be distinguished from the barbarians and savages with whom she mingled, except by her imperfect notions of morality and justice, and her superior financial skill in speculating on public calamity. The barons, in the support of their interminable wars, had taxed their subjects to an extent which produced general dissatisfaction. As the monasteries enjoyed inviolability and freedom from taxation, they offered the disaffected a refuge from an oppressive taxation, if they would become lay monastic members, and convey their worldly goods to the church. A wish to inhale the supposed holy atmosphere of the monasteries, to partake of their luxuries, to enjoy the indulgence they accorded to the commission of sin, to evade an impoverishing taxation, and at the same time to retain some degree of personal freedom, induced wealthy persons of both sexes to conclude contracts with the monasteries, by which they became penniless, wholly dependent for subsistence on them, and irrevocably subjected to their despotic domination.

Beside this shrewd speculation on public calamity, the excitement and irruption of the crusades afforded the monks another opportunity for the exercise of their financial skill. With the instinctive foresight of cupidity, they had perceived the pecuniary advantages which would accrue to their order in the course of the holy war about to be inaugurated; and as they had fanned its first sparks into a general conflagration, they could hardly have any conscientious scruples in remunerating themselves, by concluding such sharp and profitable bargains as occasion presented and vows facilitated. They well knew the commercial art of bartering that which was worthless for that which was valuable ; and of advancing the market price of an article by a monopoly of it, or depressing its value by increasing the supply beyond the demand. In consequence of the public excitement real estate became greatly depressed in value, and holy war-horses, clubs, lances, battle-axes, and other sacred instruments of destruction, proportionally advanced in price. The sagacious providence of the monks having in advance accomulated vast military stores, very obligingly accommodated the devout crusader, by exchanging an inconsiderable portion of them for a very considerable tract of his land. By such operations the church obtained very extensive domains in exchange for objects of trifling value, or for very inadequate sums of money. The success of the sacerdotal financiers becoming notorious, land speculation grew into a contagious mania. Even kings came into the market to buy up the domains of their deluded vassals. The competition between monks and monarchs was as great as it was amusing; but sacerdotal craft was the more successful negotiator. The oil with which the priests had been anointed at their ordination was supposed to endow them with the power of bestowing blessings and curses at will, and the high reputation for sanctity which they had acquired by vows of absolute poverty, conferred advantages of trade on them which crowns and sceptres could not command. Kings could purchase only with money; but the monasteries had an exhaustless bank of indulgences, of parting blessings, of promised prayers, and of promised masses for departed souls. This bogus currency may provoke the levity of the profane, but it was, nevertheless, prized by the saints above the value of silver or gold, and held by the monasteries at its highest marketable price. With the command of such unlimited resources, the monasteries could successfully outbid princes, and purchase without impoverishment what monarchs could not without bankruptcy.

With an air of piety and benevolence, but with an unscrupulousness that regarded neither truth nor principle, the monks invented every fiction, and adopted every possible method of augmenting the stores of their wealth. Well aware that human piety is more easily inflamed by the prospect of gold than by the prospect of heaven, they manufactured extravagant reports of the wealth of Jerusalem; representing it as a vast storehouse of gems and precious metal. So glowing were these descriptions that the piety of the crusaders became excited into frenzy, and their devotion into irrepressible vociferousness; a delightful anticipation rapt them into heavenly ecstacies; and impatience for the glorious results of the coming combat appeared to be the only unpleasant ingredient that marred their happiness. On huts and farms, on palaces and domains, they looked down with scornful indifference; for they felt that wealth surpassing the treasures of the Indies, and palaces more gorgeous than Europe could build, would inevitably raward their pious adventure. The cool-headed priest, too well informed to partake of the general delusion, deliberately viewed the enthusiasm, and calmly calculated by what means it might be sustained and augmented, and how it could most judiciously be made to administer to the pecuniary advantage of the church. While the coldness with which the reason and conscience of priests secretly regarded the general lunacy, was well disguised, the masses, on the contrary, were all flame and fury, and wrought up to such a pitch of anxiety to wrest the holy land from the Infidels and appropriate it to themselves, that they became indifferent to the treasure and land that they already possessed. In this unhealthy state of the public mind, it was an easy task for spiritual advisers to relieve their confiding pupils of their revenues, and ultimately to become the proprietors of many of their domains.

The method by which this magnificent object was accomplished, was not only by the treachery of exchanging trumpery for valuables, but also by inducing the soldiers of the cross to devolve, during their absence, the care of their land and revenues on the monasteries, and to make them their heirs-at-law in case of death abroad. As but few of the crusaders of some of the expeditions ever returned, as many of all of them perished abroad, we must accord the credit of extraordinary shrewdness to the calculating cupidity of the monks, who could make the love, devotion, lunacy and enthusiasm of the devout, their life at home and death abroad, equally advantageous to the monastic coffers. As the infatuation, so beneficial to the church, was general; as the convulsions of the times rendered property of all descriptions exceedingly insecure; and, as many of the devout, equally frantic with the crusaders, were restrained, either by infirmity or other circumstances, from embarking in the holy enterprise, it was not difficult for the monks, amid the general frenzy, to induce such persons to become lay members of the monasteries, and to place their domains under the protection of those powerful institutions; an advantageous encumbrance which they always assumed with obliging avidity.

POVERTY.

With such money-making devices and sharp practices, and many others of a similar nature, the mendicant orders, united in an avaricious and arrogant confederacy, enjoying the protection of the Pope, and the confidence and homage of Christendom, and released from all secular and ecclesiastical jurisdiction, seemed, while abjuring the possession of property as a crime, and professing poverty as a virtue, to be rapidly monopolizing the wealth of the world—the domains of princes, the traffic of merchants, and the political power of governments. Under such circumstances monastic opulence, without the intervention of a miracle, must have prodigiously increased, and their domains augmented to provinces.

From the fifth century, in every section of Christendom, monastery after monastery continued to rise, generally constructed with stupendous proportions, and in sumptuous style; furnished with every species of luxury, and polluted by every description of vice. St. Bernard, who, by the assumption of the vow of absolute poverty, renounced a considerable private inheritance, and who subsequently scorned the proffers of lucrative dignities, could, nevertheless, by means of his monachal power and opulence erect ten monasteries, make nobles and Popes tremble at his authority, and even kings submit to his dictation.

The Jesuits, who enjoyed all the privileges of the mendicant and secular orders, excelled them both in duplicity and rapaciousnes. Animated by a crafty and unprincipled zeal for the emolument of their order, they established mission-houses among savage nations, under the pretext of civilizing them and saving their souls. But this specious pretext was but a pious mask, under which was concealed an infamous scheme of swindling the natives abroad out of property, and wheedling the devout at home out of liberal donations, and splendid legacies. Their extensive mission-houses were neither designed for temples of devotion, nor for converting idolaters; their walls less frequently witnessed the monks at devotion, than they did at plotting schemes of plunder. Like ancient temples, and more recent churches, mosques and fairs, they were designed as centres of trade to facilitate commercial transactions; and, as they were the grand resort of the people for exchange of commodities, they, like the former, gave rise to the numerous villages, towns and cities, whose names they bear. Pagan simplicity has never been a match for monkish craft; and no sooner had the gold and gems of the natives inflamed the zeal and sharpened the shrewdness of the monks, than they were wrung from them by some swindling transaction. Possessing the arts of civilized society, they were enabled to astonish the natives with miracles, and successfully to impose on their ignorance and simplicity. They boasted of having induced multitudes to embrace Christianity; but as their object was not to convert Pagans from idolatry, but to defraud them out of their land and gold, they were careful not to offend them by demanding a renunciation of the practice of idolatry, but contented themselves with entreating their converts simply to adore Christ and his mother when worshiping the images of their gods. With this ambiguous, but insinuating modification of Christianity, they made fortunes out of the devout at home and savages abroad.

In 1743, this avaricious sacerdotal order established a mission-house at the island Martinique; and so adroitly did they manage their Christianizing business operations, that in a short time they monopolized the trade of that island, and of the surrounding islands. Their success naturally excited the jealousy of the secular merchants; and as they were generally regarded as destitute of commercial honor, and unprincipled in their ambition, a formidable opposition was easily fomented against them. This opposition, apparently justified by self-preservation, and the necessity of inaugurating a more liberal and enlightened commercial policy, impaired to a considerable extent the interest and popularity of the sacerdotal establishments. At this stage of their history, a circumstance occured which culminated in their disgrace. Two valuable cargoes had been consigned to them by their French correspondents. These cargoes were captured by the English, with whom the French were at war. In conformity with maritime usage, the consignors demanded indemnity of the Jesuits. The Jesuits denied the legality of the demand, and refused to give the satisfaction asked. An appeal was consequently taken to the King of France, who, deciding in favor of the consignors, demanded the Jesuits to make the required restitution. But their presumptuous piety led them to scorn his authority in the same temper in which they had rejected the prayer of his mercantile subjects. This insolent and treasonable conduct led the king to investigate the principles of their order; and finally to abrogate it in all the states of France, as a political organization projected for the acquisition of power and riches.

By means of their Christianizing establishments in Paraguay and Uruguay, the Jesuits ruled the natives with despotic power, and acquired an immense amount of wealth. In 1750, Spain having by a commercial treaty ceded to Portugal seven districts of these domains, the monks at the head of an army of fourteen thousand men, compelled the contracting nations to annul the treaty; but an attempt being afterwards made to assassinate the King of Portugal, the government declared the order of the Jesuits to be a treasonable organization, and confiscated all their posssessions in the dominion. The order of the Catholic Knights, incorporated for the defense and propagation of the true faith, by the force of arms, like the monks, rapaciously acquired an incredible amount of riches while under the solemnest obligation to maintain a perpetual condition of absolute poverty. These holy organizations were exclusively military; the sword was the only argument they used. The Knights of St. John, with the vow of poverty on their lips, but with the sword of conquest in their hand, amassed such extensive domains, that they gave their chief an annual salary of one million guilders. The Knights Templars, while they vowed absolute poverty, acquired by arms, forced loans, donations, bequests and other means, such a prodigious amount of wealth that they erected nine thousand vast and princely palaces, each enriched with extensive territory, and all powerful enough to maintain immunity from the jurisdiction of the sovereign in whose kingdom they were located. The Teutonic Knights, while they abjured the rights of property, and swore never to allow its possession to tarnish their sanctity, wrung from Sweden all the territory that extends from the Oder along its banks to the Gulf of Finland. It is reported by travellers that the Shaggians, a barbarous tribe of Egypt, when meeting a foe, will exclaim: "Peace be with you," and thrust a lance in his heart. The wild mockery of these uncouth savages at avowed principles has been far exceeded by the conduct and profession of the monachal and military orders of the Catholic Church, whose vows were meant for imposition, and whose life was a scene of perjury.

By the aid of magnificent revenues, the various orders of the religious paupers were enabled successfully to negotiate for the most lucrative dignities of the church, and enjoyed the fairest prospects of becoming either bishops, cardinals or popes, and of obtaining the luxurious indolence, idolatrous reverence, and impious adulation they secured. The hypocritical devices of the ancient and modern Brahmins, of the Hindoo and Mohammedan monks, and of the priests and prophets of ancient Pagan nations have, in Christian countries, where no prejudice pleads in their favor, and where their origin and claims are candidly investigated, been justly exposed to the scoffs and contempt of common sense; and it is possible that under the same circumstances, the monks, priests, ceremonies and dogmas of Catholicism, which resemble them as nearly as a type can its prototype, would sink to the same level.

When we calmly reflect on the monastic institution, and observe the financial principles on which it is organized, the variety and prodigious traffic which has distinguished its career, the immense treasure and domains it has acquired by fraud and artifice, it seems like some gigantic financial corporation, projected for speculating in land, and for making money by the tricks of trade. When we call to mind the avarice by which it has been actuated, the duplicity it has practised, and the impositions of which it has been guilty, it appears to be a corporation organized to make money, regardless of every maxim of justice, and every principle of honor. When we consider how basely it has prostituted its privileges and immunities; becoming superior to law to violate the principles of rectitude; professing absolute indigence to demand, like a highwayman, a tribute of every one it chanced to meet, if not with a pistol in its hand, yet with an anathema at its disposal more dreaded by the superstitious than thousands of pistols, it looms up before the imagination as a corporation of outlaws, whose right is might, whose object is money, and whose profession is to plunder. When we reflect on its pretention of vending for gold the pardon of sin, the favor of God, immunity for guilt, and protection against the future retribution of heaven, it appears like a corporation of fiends which arrogates the prerogatives of deity, traffic in the hearts and souls of men, sport with their hopes and fears, and merchandise heaven and hell, time and eternity. And when we remember that the Roman Catholic Church has incorporated these infamous religious orders in her constitution, and has officially pronounced them to be her most useful members, and has thus sanctioned and made her own, all their duplicity, all their rapacity, all their swindling operations, all their highway robbery, and all their profanity, immorality and blasphemy, she seems like some black and midnight monster, dripping with human gore, an embodiment of every deformity, an incarnation of every loathsome, hideous and unsightly demon, and a just representation of the character and principles of the archfiend.

CHAPTER VII.

Monastic Vow of Celibacy.

NATURE has organized man for the conjugal union. She has endowed him with powers adapted to its requirements; with passions that aspire after its pleasures and benefits, and with sensibilities that can be gratified only by the performance of its obligations. By the reciprocal relations, and the amiable intercourse which it establishes between the sexes, it furnishes an attractive means of mutual improvement, refining the grossness of the sensual propensities, and developing the noblest graces of the human character. By blending masculine boldness with feminine delicacy, it takes rudeness from the one, and imparts energy to the other; and thus contributes, in an eminent degree, to the formation of that equanimity of character which is the happy medium between extremes, and of that agreeable association of strength and urbanity which is best fitted to cope with the difficulties incident to life.

By an alliance of mutual affection and interests for life, it secures their highest development, and the most complete and undisturbed enjoyment of their benefits. It identifies the honor and interests of parents and children, securing affectionate protectors for helpless infancy, faithful guardians for inexperienced youth, and interested tutors for fitting the rising generation for the useful and noble stations of society; and while it thus provides for children, it rewards the solicitude of parents with a shelter in adversity, a support in declining age, and a name in posterity.

But while such are the inducements of marriage, yet a regard to personal interest and happiness might deter a considerate person from assuming its obligations, when either a suitable companion has not been found, or pecuniary resources are insufficient to meet the domestic demands in a satisfactory manner. Pecuniary competency and similarity of taste and disposition are requisites indispensable to connubial felicity. Without them marriage would be a source of privation, difficulty and alienation; and family a painful encumbrance. When, therefore, fortune has withheld these essentials of conjugal happiness, celibacy, in either sex, is more honorable than matrimony.

But to stifle the instincts that prompt to this union, and ungraciously to spurn the incalculable benefits it proffers, unrestrained by any prudential consideration, is to violate, without motive, the laws of human happiness, and neglect the fulfilment of the most important design of the organism of man. An act so unnatural is, perhaps, seldom contemplated, except under extreme mental depression, or under the singular delusions of which religious fanaticism is so prolific. Disappointed love, reverses of fortune, or the hope of becoming insensible to the wants of humanity by acquiring supernatural perfection, has sometimes induced the weak and superstitious to assume the monastic vow of perpetual celibacy. The motive of such conduct has always originated in emotion; and though emotion is alwaya sincere, it is always fluctuating. A cloud that obscures the sun and casts a gloom over earth, soon passes away, leaving the former in its natural brightness, and the latter in its usual attractiveness. Not less ephemeral is the mental gloom which adversity or superstition may throw over the human mind. When the energies of acquisitiveness have been prostrated by repeated pecuniary misfortunes; when the warmth of ambition has been chilled by the wounds of reputation; when the currents of love have been frozen by the cold breath of disappointment; the desolated heart may feel that its struggle for subsistence is vain, that its hopes of distinction have perished, and that its ties of love are broken forever. But these despondent sensations are ephemeral; they are the results of a temporary repose of passions which are rooted in the constitution of our nature, and which can be destroyed only with our being. Though despair may for a time throw a wintry gloom over the mind, yet hope will again bud and bloom, avarice will again sigh for wealth, ambition will again thirst for distinction, love will again yearn for companionship, and every passion resuming its natural energy will again create the emotions for which it was organized, and compel us to seek its appropriate gratification in the social, conjugal, or political relations which subsist in society.

This revulsion is inevitable. It is as certain as the subsidence of a tempestuous torrent after having exhausted its energy, into its ordinary peaceful roll. As all emotions are ephemeral, so must be all the vows and resolutions which they generate. Each day brings with it new and unexpected events, which abrogate or modify the emotions and resolves which the circumstances of the preceding day had suggested; nay, more, the antithetical emotions thus created are always proportionably strong to those which they supplant. Hence vows assumed by any person under extraordinary mental excitement, will be repudiated when he is under extraordinary mental depression; and obligations assumed under either of these conditions of mind, will be found inconsistent with the ordinary obligations of life, when that usual current of thought and emotion shall set in, which always flows in harmony with human reason, philosophy and happiness, and the regular course of things. If when this condition shall supervene; if when hope shall succeed to despair, and reason and reflection to impulse and fanaticism, and when all the passions and powers of our nature shall resume their natural operation—if then, we shall have placed ourselves by any mistake, however innocently committed, in a situation where we cannot respond to the demands of our nature, we will find that we have doomed ourselves to perpetual misery.

Nor will any degree of purity or sanctity of motive arrest the evils of mistaken conduct. Nature is inexorable; she inflicts punishment on the violators of her laws without regard to the motives by which they have been actuated. She admits no apology; she knows no forgiveness. Neither tears nor penitence can mitigate her vengeance; neither pleas of conscientious motives, nor of ignorance of her ordinations, can soften the rigor of her justice. Although the desire of perfection is a natural and noble one, yet she has established laws by which alone it is to be obtained, and punishes the aggressors of them with deformity and imbecility. These laws are intelligible. Human perfection clearly comprehends the perfect development of all the physical, mental and moral powers of man. Exercise is the only means by which these faculties can be developed. The system of exercise adapted to the attainment of this end must embrace a judicious employment of every aculty belonging to the human organism; allowing none to depreciate by indolence; none to become enervated by incessant or overstrained exertion; but to maintain all in that natural and reasonable condition in which, while they are alternately relieved they are mutually strengthened. By the discipline of such a system of exercise knowledge will gradually become the foundation of reason, judgment the guide of fancy, conscience the controller of the passions, the vital organs the recuperator of the physical and mental faculties; a healthy reciprocity and modifying action will be maintained between all the powers, and that equilibrium engendered which is peace; that condensation which is energy; and that perfection which is essential to genius.

The monastic vow of perpetual celibacy is clearly unfavorable to this general exercise of the powers of human nature. It permits the exercise of only a limited number of these powers, and thereby obtrudes an insuperable obstacle to the full development of the human character. It stimulates those which it cultivates to incessant activity, and thereby distorts and deforms their organisms by an abnormal development. It fetters in inactivity the bulk of the human faculties, and thereby lessens the number and variety of the natural sources of the pleasures of life. It reduces activity in the vital system, and thereby saps the fundamental trength of the whole organization, engendering those physical and moral diseases, which render life joyless, and death often the only remedy. It prohibits the exercise of those faculties by which alone the design of the human organism can be accomplished, and permits but a few of them to be exercised in order to attain the highest degree of perfection. It would dry up the springs of a river, in order to increase the volume of its current; it would weaken the foundation of an edifice, in order to protect it against the shocks of earthquakes. But whether these ecclesiastical absurdities are more insane than idiotical, we respectfully submit to the acumen of the Œcumenical Council, whenever it shall resume its session at Rome.

The monastic vow of celibacy, is as weak in its fundamental principles, as it is absurd in its discipline. It is founded on the ascetic delusion, that the sensual passions are evils; and that human perfection and happiness consist in the attainment of a passive state of mind, untroubled by desire, thought or action. But this is a Brahminical absurdity, rusted to its core by tha abrasion of ages. Fven if the propensities were evils, yet wisdom would teach us that as they are a result of our organism, they should be regulated; especially if by a judicious regulation, they can be made to administer to the pleasures of existence. But they are not evils; on the contrary, they are unmeasurable benefits. If they are ever tormentors, it is when prudence has not regulated their gratification, or when abuse has made their cravings unnatural. If they are ever sources of disease, it is when they are exercised in violation of the laws of human nature. If they ever become impotent in the production of pleasure, it is when their possessors have become gluttons, sots, debauchees, misers, or some similar compound of human depravity. But when the animal passions are refined by knowledge, chastened by virtue, directed by reason, governed by conscience, and exercised with a considerate regard to the integrity of the other powers, they become sources of pleasure and vigor, incentives to industry and enterprise, and eminently contribute towards the advancement of the perfection and happiness of our being.

Another fundamental error of the vow of celibacy, is the delusion that man may by means of solitude and resolution arrest the natural promptings of the propensities. The propensities are constituted by nature essential portions of our being; and accordingly we must carry them with us into whatever solitude we may retire; aud as their emotions are naturally irrepressible, their powers must be felt under whatever obligation we may assume. Vows, resolutions and solitude are as incapable of arresting the progress of the passions, as they are of stopping the pulsations of the heart. Amid the deepest silence and solitude they will still yearn for expression, and yearn the more the deeper is the stillness. Amid the bustle and tumult of the world they are excited by innumerable different objects; their attention is divided among a variety of attractions; and each finds its appropriate gratification constantly offered to its taste. But in solitude there is every thing to concentrate, and nothing to divide their power; every thing to inflame, and nothing to appease their appetites; and consequently, under such circumstances, their powers must be the most ungovernable, and the torments of their craving the most unsupportable.

The foregoing observations were made on the presumption, that the vow of perpetual chastity was assumed by the Catholic orders with sincere intentions of conforming to its requirements; but this was not always the case. Whatever sincerity or sanctity may have mingled, in some cases, with the motives that prompted its assumption, neither monks nor nuns, nor priests, nor bishops, nor popes, have in general furnished a reasonable amount of evidence in favor of their chastity.

The natural and efficient regulator of the animal passions is marriage. The conjugal union, judiciously formed, is invaluable to man, but almost indispensable to woman. Her organization preeminently qualifies her for its conditions and relations. The sensitiveness peculiar to her nervous system, obliges her to shrink from the rude battle of public life; her weakness instructs her in the importance of placing herself under the guardianship of the more muscular power of man, which is noblest employed when it best protects the weak; and her characteristic instincts and capacities lead her to seek her chief employment and happiness in the modest retirement of domestic life, where she finds the temple of which she alone is priestess; the idols which excite her purest devotion; the altars on which she lavishes her choicest gifts; and where, in administering her sacred profession, in dispensing instruction to her children, care to her household, and consolation to the sick and dying, her true dignity and beauty acquires the deepest enchantment. Whatever the mental and personal charms of a female may be, the true excellence of her character can never be seen or appreciated, except in the practice of the amiable virtues which constitute the wife and the mother. This, woman knows; this she feels; and to obtain this end the rights of her nature, and the interests of society, concur in authorizing her to adopt every available means. Yet, notwithstanding these plain facts, the Catholic Church has the unpardonable presumption to pronounce a curse on her, if she should prefer a union so essential to her happiness and usefulness to a state of perpetual virginity. Every time her common sense teaches her to say that marriage is preferable to virginity, this religious monster, in the name of the Holy Trinity and all the saints and angels, answers " Let her be accursed." Every time her nature prompts her to say, that, to be joined in marriage is more blessed than to remain in a state of virginity, this monster in horror at the profane and unorthodox expressions, responds, " Let her be accursed." Hear it from the lips of the holy mother herself:

"Whosoever shall say, that the church could not institute impediments annulling marriage, or that in instituting them she has erred, let him be acursed."

"Whosoever shall say, that the marriage state is preferable to a state of virginity, or celibacy, or that it is not more blessed to remain in a state of virginity or celibacy, than to be joined in matrimony, let him be accursed."

"Whosoever shall affirm, that matrimonial causes do not belong to the ecclesiastical judges, let him be accursed." (Canon of the Council of Trent).

Atrocious as is this decree, it expresses not the full

measure of Catholic arrogance. For while with palpable inconsistency, the church solemnizes among Catholics the rites which she anathematizes them for preferring, she declares that all those whose marriage ceremonies have not been celebrated according to her fantastic requirements, are living in a state of " shameful concubinage." It would seem that by consummating the union which she holds men and women accursed for desiring, she incurs on her own soul the curse she pronounces on others. She requires no *fee* for her matrimonial services, but accepts *marriage presents*, which may perhaps have softened her malignity to this product of civilization with regard to Catholics; but non-Catholics who do not conciliate her holy aversion to it by such presents, she pronounces them profligates, their wives prostitutes, and their children bastards. Hear this from the lips of Pope Pius IX.

" Marriage cannot be given, unless there be, one and at the same time a sacrament, consequently that *any other union* between man and woman among Christians, made in virtue of what civil law soever, is nothing else than *a shameful and miserable concubinage*, so often condemned by the church." (Allocution on the State of Affairs in New Grenada).

So in the judgment of the present Pope, the non-Catholics in the United States consist of strumpets and bastards. According to the principles of the Catholic Church, thus officially enunciated, every person, the marriage rites of whose parents have not been performed by a Catholic priest, is an illegitimate offspring divested of all legal right to inherit property of his parents. If the church shall ever gain in America the numerical strength for which she is striving, what will be the consequence to non-Catholics? Will she declare them legitimate, or respect their property titles? Have not her priests made this land ring with the assertion, that Infidels and Protestants have no right where Catholicism is triumphant.

But who is she that has the audacity to proclaim such principles? A church, which has been dripping with the blood of innocence for ages, yet is thirsting for more. Who are they that prate about chastity? A body of the most corrupt, unprincipled, and licentious priests that ever disgraced the name of religion. The cold dissoluteness of the Catholic orders is not only undeniable, but it is even frightful. Had history been silent, and the real conduct of Catholic priests, and the interior of Catholic nunneries remained a profound secret, yet, an ordinary knowledge of human nature would have warranted the suspicion that the priests were not models of chastity, nor the nunneries asylums of innocence. But history has not been silent; she has spoken distinctly, and spoken often. A nun escaped from her prison-house, or a priest not yet steeled by hypocrisy to all the pleadings of virtue, or who was disgusted beyond endurance at the corruption that festers in the heart of the Catholic Church, has furnished history with startling records, and raised the sacred veil, that the superstitious might behold the horrible compound of duplicity, lust, and murder which secretly pollutes the interior of the institutions which they reverence. But these fitful revelations, although appealing to the noblest sympathies of mankind, have seldom produced an effect equal to the exigency. Like bursts of unexpected thunder, they have startled for a moment, but soon rumbled into silence and forgetfulness.

Such is the general infatuation, that people seldom question that around which the sanctions of religion are thrown, and when they do the doubt is soon obliterated. They will reverently bow to a priest without thinking it is possible that under the guise of his chaste and holy profession, avarice, lust and murder may reign supreme. They will heedlessly pass a nunnery without thinking how many broken hearts may there be hopelessly imprisoned; how many gifted and accomplished females may there be pining in anguish and despair, who, while they sought an abode of unsullied chastity, found themselves entrapped in a den of infamy, to be profaned by holy confessors! But reluctantly as charity would believe these statements, they are substantiated beyond the possibility of doubt or denial, by the records of Catholic authority of the highest order.

An insight into the mysteries of Catholicism, and the mode by which priests conceal from publicity their acts of seduction and adultery, may be learned from the following extract from Hogan's "Auricular Confession." "The secular orders," says he, "are composed chiefly of parish priests and their curates, whose duty it is to hear their parishioners. The orders of regulars are composed of friars, who are subdivided into several minor orders, and who have no particular duties to discharge, unless especially deputed to do so by the bishop, or the deputy of the diocese into which they may be divided. It is so managed by the secular priests, that whenever they fail in seducing their penitents, and are detected by them that one of those friars shall immediately be at hand to hear the confessions of all such females, and forgive their sins, on condition that they shall never reveal to moral being the thoughtless peccadillos of their parish priest, who for the moment forgot himself, and whose tears of penitence now moisten the ground on which he walks." (Auric. Confess. vol. ii. p. 168).

The adaptation of the confessional to prepare the way for seduction and adultery may be comprehended by the following extract from the 'Synopsis of Popery" by the same author. "Do any of these families," asks he, "know the questions which a priest puts to their families at the confessional? Do husbands know the questions which priests put to their wives at the confession? . . . . Fathers, mothers, guardians and husbands fancy to yourself the most indelicate, immodest, libidinous questions which the most immoral and profligate mind can conceive, — fancy those ideas put into plain language, and that by way of questions and answers, and you will then have a faint conception of the conversation which takes place between a priest and your hitherto pure daughter. If after two or three examinations, in that sacred tribunal, they still continue virtuous, they are rare examples." (Synopsis, p. 170, 171).

While the Catholic Church imposes on the priests and monks the vow of celibacy, it accords them the privilege of acting licentiously with impunity. In the life of Bishop Scipio de Ricci, written by an eminent Catholic, the practice of the church in allowing bishops and priests to keep concubines, while it forbids them to marry under pain of excommunication, is asserted and defended. The Council of Toledo passed a canon forbidding priests to keep more than one concubine in public. William Hogan asserts that every priest keeps a concubine, and every teacher in a school attached to a Catholic nunnery, has been seduced by her teacher. Chamancis says: "The adultery, obscenity and impiety of the priests are beyond description. St. Chrysostom thinks the number of them that will be saved, bears a very small proportion to those who will be damned. Cardinal Conpaggio asserts that "the priest who marries commits a more grievous sin than if he kept many concubines." Pope Paul protected houses of ill-fame, and acquired great riches by selling them licenses. The Council of Augsburg ordered that all suspected females should be driven by whips from the dwellings of the clergy, and have their hair cut off. A monk relates that he once made a contract with the Devil that if he would cease to fill his mind with lascivious ideas, he would omit some prayers to the saints whose pictures decorated the walls of his cloister, but upon communicating the substance of the agreement to the bishop, he was informed by him, that "rather than abstain from adoring Christ and mother in their holy images it would be better to enter every brothel and visit every prostitute in the city." Richard of England replied to Fulk Nuelly, the legate of Pope Innocent III., commissioned to blow the trumpet of another crusade: "You advise me to dismiss my three daughters, Pride, Avarice and Incontinence. I bequeath them to the most deserving: my pride to the Knights Templars; my avarice to the monks of Ciste; and, my incontinence to the prelates." Pope John XXIII. was deposed by the

Council of Constance for having committed seventy different sorts of crimes, among the number of which was illicit commerce with three hundred nuns. The Trappists, a menkish order of highway robbers, were constantly employed in abducting females, confining them in their monastery, and perpetrating the most atrocious rapes. At the Council of Canterbury King Edgar declared that the houses of the clergy were nothing but brothels. Petrarch laments over the fact that the clergy at the papal court were shamefully licentious. Cardinals lived openly with their concubines; and it became a question of etiquette whether a bishop's concubine should not, at the court of His Holiness, precede other ladies. Llorente, chief secretary of the Spanish Inquisition in 1789, relates that the inquisitors having granted permission to the females of a certain locality to denounce their guilty confessors, the number of priests denounced was so great that thirty secretaries were employed for sixty days in taking down depositions, and that the profligacy of the clergy so far exceeded all calculation that it was concluded to suspend investigation, and to destroy the records of the proceedings. The extent and depth of clerical depravity can never be divulged by those who know it, for St. Bernard asserts that "Bishops and priests commit acts in private which it would be scandalous to express."

From nunneries governed and visited by priests of such a character, what is the logical inference? Chamancis, an unimpeachable Catholic authority, answers this question when he says: "To veil a woman in these convents is synonymous to prostituting her." The seventh General Council of Nice prohibited the erection of double convents for the accommodation of both sexes; but the prohibition was not regarded. In Europe every nunnery has attached to it a foundling asylum; in the United States, a grave-yard. Llorente relates a curious account of Aquida, an abbess of a Carmelite nunnery at Liemo. It appears that this female had, on several occasions, professed to have become pregnant with stones, and to have retired for the purpose of giving them birth. She had often exhibited her miraculous progeny to the credulous, and pretended to be enabled, by their divine nature, to cure diseases with them. Her success in working miracles by them procured for her the reputation of a saint. But unfortunate for her eventual canonization, a rumor became current that instead of having given birth to stones, she had given birth to children, and strangled them; and that she had obliged the holy nuns under her supervision to practise the same iniquity. The informant, an inmate of the nunnery, pointed out the place where the murdered babes were buried; and subsequent excavation revealed the horrible fact, that half the tale of blood had not been told.

The following additional facts, related by William Hogan, as having transpired under his personal cognizance, afford further confirmative proof of the general character of priests and nuns, and that it remains as it has always been, in all countries, and at all periods of civilization:

"The Roman Catholics of Albany," says he, "had, about three years previous to my coming among them, three Irish priests among them, occasionally preaching, but always hearing confessions. .... As soon as I got settled in Albany I had, of course, to attend to the duty of *auricular confession*, and in less than two months found that the priests, during the time they were there, were the fathers of between sixty and one hundred children, besides having debauched many who had left the place previous to their confinement." (Auricular Confession, p. 46).

"A short time previous to my coming to this country, and soon after my being installed as confessor in the Romish Church, I became intimately acquainted with a family of great respectability. This family consisted of a widowed father and two daughters, and never in my life have I met with more interesting young ladies than the daughters were. .... In less than two months after my first visit to this family, at their peaceful and respectable breakfast table, I observed the chair which had been usually occupied by the elder of the two ladies occupied by the younger, and that of the latter to be vacant. I inquired the cause, and was informed by the father that he had just accompanied her to the coach, which had left that morning for Dublin, and that she went on a visit to the Rev. B. K. It seems that both of the daughters of whom I have spoken went to the school attached to the nunnery of the city of ——————. The confessor whose duty it was to hear the duty of the pupils of the institute, was one Rev. B. K., a friar of the Franciscan order, who, as soon as his plans were properly laid, and circumstances rendered them ripe for execution, seduced the elder lady; and finding the fact could no longer be concealed, arranged matters with a Dublin friend. .... She was confined at the house of his friend, and her illicit offspring given to the managers of the foundling hospital in Dublin. .... No sooner was this elder lady provided for, than this incarnate demon, B. K., commenced the seduction of the younger lady. He succeeded, and ruined her too. But there was no difficulty in providing for them. They both became nuns. . . . . I saw them in the convent at Mount Benedict. They were great favorites of Bishop Fenton. They were spoken of by some of the females of Boston as models of piety." (Auricular Confession. p. 100–106).

"Soon after my arrival in Philadelphia, . . . a Roman Catholic priest by the name of O. S. called on me, and showed me letters of recommendation which he had from Bishop T., of Ireland, and countersigned by the Roman Catholic bishop of New York, to Bishop England, of South Carolina. . . . . He arrived at Charleston, and was well received by Bishop England. There lived in the parish to which this reverend confessor was appointed, a gentleman of respectability and wealth. Bishop England supplied this new missionary with letters of strong recommendation to this gentleman, advising him to place his children under his charge, assuring him they would be brought up in the fear of God and love of religion. . . . . The Rev. Popish wretch seduced the eldest daughter of his benefactor, and the father becoming aware of the fact, armed himself with a case of pistols, and determined to shoot the seducer. But there was in the house a good Catholic sevant [a spy] who advised the seducer to fly. He soon arrived in Charleston; the right reverend bishop understood his case, advised him to go to confession, and absolved him from his sins; . . . . sent him on his way to New York. . . . . His victim after a little time, having given birth to a fine boy, goes to confession herself, and sends the child of sin to the Sisters of Charity residing in ———, to be taken care of as a *nullius filius*. As soon as the child was able to walk a Roman Catholic lady adopted it as her own. The real mother of the child soon removed to the city of ———, told the whole transaction to the Roman Catholic bishop of ———, who knowing that she had a handsome property, introduced her to a highly respectable Protestant gentleman, who soon married her. He (the bishop) soon after introduced the gentleman to the Sisters of Charity who had provided for the illicit offspring of the priest, concealing its parentage, and representing it as having no father living. The gentleman was pleased with the boy, and the holy bishop finally prevailed on him and his wife to adopt it as his own." (Auric. Confess. p. 111-115).

"When quite young and just emerging from childhood, I became acquainted with a Protestant family, residing in the neighborhood of my birthplace. It consisted of a mother (a widow), and three interesting children, two sons and one daughter. . . . . In the course of time the sons grew up, and their guardian in compliance with their wishes, and to gratify their ambition, procured them commissions in the army. . . . . As soon as the sons left to join their respective regiments, which were then on the Continent, the mother and daughter were much alone. . . . . There was then in the neighborhood only twenty miles from this family, a nunnery of the order of Jesuits. To this nunnery was attached a school superintended by the nuns of that order. . . . . The mother yielded, in this case, to the malign influence of fashion; . . . . sent her beautiful daughter, her earthly treasure, to the school of these nuns. . , . . Soon after the daughter was sent to school, I entered the college of Manooth as a theological student, and in due time was ordained a Catholic priest. An interval of some years passed. . . . . There was a large party given, at which among others I happened to be present; and there meeting with my friends and interchanging the usual courtesies on such occasions, she sportingly, as I then imagined, asked me whether I would preach her reception sermon, as she intended becoming a nun and taking the veil. . . . . I heard no more of the affair until about two months, when I received a note from her designating the chapel in which she expected my services. . . . . On the reception of my friend's note a cold chill crept over me, I anticipated and trembled, and felt there must be foul play. . . . . Having no connection with the convent in which she was immured, I did not see her for three months following. At the expiration of that time one of the lay sisters delivered me a note. .... I found my young friend wished to see me on something important. I of course lost no time in calling on her, and being a priest, I was immediately admitted; but never have I forgotten, never can I forget, the melancholy picture of lost beauty and fallen humanity which met my astonished gaze in the person of my once beautiful and virtuous friend. .... 'I sent for you, my friend, to see you once before my death. .... I am in the family-way and must die.'"

He then proceeds to relate, that in the course of a conversation which ensued he learned from the nun that she had been seduced by her confessor, (which fact precluded any appeal or redress), and that the lady abbess had proposed to procure an abortion, but that an inmate had informed her that the medicine which the lady abbess would give would contain poison. He promised to renew his visit within a few days; he did so, but the foul deed was done.

Fiends! Monsters! Does not the blood curdle in every vein at such recitals? Does not man and woman blush at their dishonored nature? Is there a God that can allow the use of his name to sanction such execrable depravity; that can look with indifference on women avowing chastity in his name in order to allure the purest of their sex to destruction; or that can be insensible to the imprecations of injured innocence, profaned in holy houses? Is God a fiction, or divine retribution a dream? No! While a thunderbolt leaves a monastery or a nunnery in existence, lightning has no avenging power! While either of them exists man may well doubt the existence of retributive justice in human affairs.

But it may be said, that God has delegated to society the power to punish offences committed against its moral interests, and therefore does not himself interfere in the matter. But does society exercise its authority in the matter any more visibly than deity? Society enacts laws and prescribes penalties respecting murder, rape, brothels, false imprisonment, and irregular interments. She also investigates all alleged infractions of these laws, except when they involve the honor of monastic institutions. But why are these dens exempted from the common law of the land? Why are they allowed to bar their doors against the authority which all others must respect? Why are they allowed to organize within a government an independent government, nullifying its jurisdiction over them? Why are not the interior of monastic institutions constantly and thoroughly inspected, and the authority of the common law maintained over them? Is it because they are too pious to violate the law of the land? If this were so, it would do them no harm, but much good, to have the fact week after week attested by an investigating committee composed of their opponents. But is not the contrary the fact? Do they not deprive their inmates of personal liberty? Do they not imprison them in dungeons? Do they not punish them? Do they not inflict on them barbarous chastisements? Are they not sacerdotal brothels? Has not every age and country given its testimony to show that kidnapped men and women have been imprisoned for life in their cells; that there nuns have been poisoned, abortions procured, babes murdered, women outraged by priests, and every law, human or divine violated with impunity?

Are these sensational declamations? Would for the credit of human nature they were. No! They are the true records of monastic history, alleged by kings and statesmen, proved before councils, and acknowledged by monks, nuns, priests, pishops. and popes. With such an array of evidence before society, why does it allow institutions among it where every crime *may* be committed secretly, and with impunity? Why do not grand juries, who visit other jails, penitentiaries, and asylums, inspect also the more secret and suspicious nunneries?

We have now described the nature and consequences of the monastic vow of celibacy. This obligation is opposed to the nature, and defeats the object of the human organism. It extinguishes conjugal, filial, and parental affection. It severs the ties that bind the interests of society together. It injures both the present and the future, by abrogating their mutual connection. It strikes at the root of national greatness, by arresting the tide of population. It degrades the dignity of the community, by increasing the number of illegitimate children. It wars against marriage, the noblest incentive to social refinement and civilization; the basis of woman's hope and happiness; the impulse and gratification of her pride of family, love of parental control, and desire to live in posterity. It anathematizes woman's purest aspirations, and man's holiest ties. It converts the ardor of chastity into snares for its seduction. It sanctifies prostitution and adultery. It violates the law of the land. It erects in the most magnificent parts of a city its spacious brothels, with massive walls, secret doors, false floors, guarded windows, grated cloisters, inaccessible to the inspection of law, but accessible at all hours of night or day by priests. Within these walls it allures beauty, virtue, and talent, and while pretending to fit them for the society of infinite purity, betrays them into the power of unprincipled priests, and imprisons them in eternal seclusion, where no groan can meet the public ear, where they can never tell the story of their wrong, nor appeal to a heart for sympathy, nor to a law for redress.

CHAPTER VIII.

Monastic Vow of Unconditional Obedience.

ANOTHER vow which was universally assumed by the religious orders, was the vow of unconditional obedience. By the obligation of this vow the members of the convents were subjected to the absolute authority of the superiors; the superiors to the absolute authority of the generals; the generals to the absolute authority of the pope. The authority of these holy officials strongly resembled that of the oriental despot, who, on being informed by his general that it was impossible to build the bridge over the river, as he had ordered, replied: "I inquired not of thee whether it was impossible or not; I commanded thee to build it; if thou failest thou shalt be strangled." Accordingly, at the mandate of a superior a subordinate was obliged to go on any errand, for any purpose, criminal or not, to depart on any mission, to perform any work, to undertake any enterprise, or to occupy any station that he required of him. The superior's decision was final, and from it there was no appeal. The Jesuit's general was empowered to inflict and remit punishment at option, and to expel any member of the order without the form of charge or trial. It mattered not whether the task assigned the recluse exceeded, or not, his mental or physical capacity, he was bound to obey the order immediately, and fully; to hesitate, or seem to hesitate was a crime, and by the penal code of some of the monasteries punished by the infliction of one hundred lashes.

But to reduce a human being to such an absolute servitude was no easy task. To transform an active being into a spiritless automaton; a sensitive being into a senseless machine; a rational being into an irrational brute, was not the work of a moment, but of years and discipline. In order to subdue and habituate the will to implicit and mechanical obedience, recourse had to be had to penance, to trials, to all that could stifle doubt and inquiry, debilitate the power of resistance, and degrade conscious dignity in the dust. The most menial services, the most loathsome, disgusting, and absurd offices were consequently asssigned to the probationists. They were required to suck the putrid sores of invalids, to remove enormous rocks, to walk unflinchingly into fiery furnaces, to cast their infants into ponds of water, to plant staffs in the ground and to water them until they should grow. They were never allowed to be alone, two were always to be together; the one a constant and conscious spy on the emotions of the other. The faithful son who could harden himself into a cold, cruel, and remorseless statue, was commended for his attainments in piety; but the unfaithful son who could not but betray some emotion, or remaining consciousness of the independence of his nature, in defiance of his circumspection, was doomed to suffer the torments of an excruciating penance.

The vow of solitude had stifled the social instincts; the vow of silence had paralyzed the powers of speech, and sealed up the lips of wisdom, knowledge and eloquence; the vow of contemplation had subjugated the intellectual faculties to the domination of fancy, and the bewilderments of ignorance; the vow of poverty had shackled the faculties of improvement and enterprise; the vow of celibacy had extinguished connubial and parental affection; and now the vow of unconditional obedience, by subjugating reason, conscience, and the executive powers to the absolute control of a superior, had completed the monk's slavery in the ruin of every noble and valuable attribute of his nature. Atrocious as were the other vows, the last exceeded the combined atrocity of them all. It consummated the destruction of his nature. It was the grave of his manhood; the tomb in which he buried himself alive. After its assumption his reason was not to guide him; his knowledge was not to direct him; his conscience was not to admonish him; but in defiance of them all, and even at the risk of his life, he was to tremble, and obey a spiritual despot. His perceptive faculties, his conscious independence, his love of liberty and justice, his sense of obligation and accountability, all the mental, moral, and physical powers which constitute his being, were by this vow, basely surrendered to an absolute lord, to whom he became a slave in mind and body, — and forever.

The blind obedience which the pope demands to his despotic will, is antagonistical to the Jewish religion, to the Christian religion, and to Natural religion. It is a nullification of all religion; an abrogation of the authority of the deity; a usurpation of the throne of Heaven. The Jewish and the Christian religion require unconditional obedience to God alone. In their sacred books, the pope is nowhere mentioned, nor is any power referred to analagous to what he claims. Natural religion prescribes reason and conscience as the supreme guide of man; and reason and conscience reject the papal authority as absurd and unjust. In the Hierophant of the Elysian mysteries, in the Apostolic Successor of Buddha, in the Grand Lama, in the Egyptian and Persian High Priest we may find something analagous to the claims of the Pope of Rome, but nowhere else.

The unconditional obedience required by the pope is inconsistent with all ideas of merit and demerit in human conduct. If man acts not from the independent suggestion of his reason and conscience, but from the secret orders of another, he is no more deserving of commendation for uesful acts, than a locomotive is for its obedience to the will of an engineer.

The unconditional obedience demanded by the pope is inconsistent with human accountability. It is an abrogation of all obligation, and all law. It assumes that the pope is above all authority; accountable to none; and that he is capable of nullifying all obligations between man and man, between government and subjects, between mankind and their creator. It obtrudes between man and his reason, and forbids him to listen to its voice. It obtrudes between man and his conscience, and forbids him to obey its dictates. It obtrudes between man and his civil obligations, and forbids him to obey the laws of his country. It leaves no sense of duty or obligation existing in the constitution of man. According to it, man is not accountable to reason, nor conscience, nor society, nor God, but to the pope alone. The pope is therefore " more than God," as one of his titles asserts; and God is no God or an inferior one to him.

The unconditional obedience enforced by the pope is subversive of the rights of the world. For one man, however good or great, to require the united intelligence of the human family to submit to his arbitrary dictation, is to deny their right to an independent will, reason, conscience, or principle of action, or the privilege of exercising the powers which they have inherited with their being. It is to declare that all men are abject slaves to the pope. It is to deny that any has a right above a brute that is bridled, harnessed, or yoked, to be driven by the spurs and whips of its owner. In short, it is to crush all liberty and the rights of human nature.

A claim of absolute authority is always absurd; but the papal claim of absolute dominion over human conscience and reason, surpasses all absurdity recorded in the annals of tyranny and arrogance. Even were superiors, generals, and popes as wise and virtuous as humanity permitted, yet such a degree of power entrusted to them would be detrimental to the interests of society. Parents whose welfare and honor are so intimately interwoven with the welfare and honor of their children, often regret over the mistakes which they have committed in giving counsel. For a spiritual despot, whose nature has been religiously pruned of human sensibilities, whose mind has been contracted within the bigoted circle of spiritual ideas, whose interest is antagonistical to those of his subjects, and who owns no accountability for the proper exercise of his functions, for such an inhuman monster to be entrusted with exclusive control over the reason, conscience, and interests of another, would as inevitably complete his arrogance and tyranny as it would the misery and slavery of his subordinate. Less than such a result could not be expected from the best of superiors, generals, or monks. But when the past history of these holy men has shown that they have invariably labored for their self-aggrandizement, and that as a class, they have been ignorant, immoral, cruel and intriguing, such power, in the hands of such men, would not only extinguish all virtue in the breast of the governed, but render them instruments of the most flagitious purposes. When by means of an ecclesiastical despotism, learning was governed by ignorance, wisdom by folly, virtue by vice, can we wonder that monks, superiors, generals and popes were the basest and most licentious of men; that the convents were rife with prostitution and murder; that the papal court was the most profligate in the world; and that the most prosperous period of Catholicism was the darkest age of mankind.

But the papal claim of absolute control over reason and conscience refutes itself. It suggests a strong presumption that he is conscious that he can make no successful appeal to either reason or conscience. Had it been otherwise would he have denied their authority? Were he confident that his pretensions are founded in truth, would he have prohibited investigation? Is not reason the clearest guide to truth, conscience its most powerful advocate, investigation its most formidable ally? And had these noble principles been available in supporting the pretension of the pope, would he have had the stupidity to denounce them?

If it is consistent with religion to make automata of human beings, slaves of men, a machine of the world; to harness mankind in the gears of an ecclesiastical despot, that they may be driven under his lash whithersoever his pleasure or interest may require; to obliterate the faculties that distinguish men from brutes; to deny the existence of a God by abrogating his attributes, and blaspheme Omnipotence by the ridicule of assuming his prerogatives; then the absolute, implicit, and unhesitating obedience enjoined on the religious orders by the Catholic Church is in accordance with its spirit and design. But if religion is morality in its highest development, humanity in its purest character, and reason in its freest exercise, then is the papal despotism not only subversive of religion, but destructive of the rights of man, of the obligations of virtue, and dangerous to the liberty and interests of the world.

CHAPTER IX.

Pagan Origin of the Monastic Orders. — Concluding Remarks.

WE have shown in the previous chapters that the monastic vows are in conflict, not only with the requirements of moral goodness, but with the dictates of reason, the principles of personal improvement, and the interests and progress of society. We have shown, also, that they were assumed not for the humble purpose of acquiring spiritual perfection, but for the ambitious purpose of obtaining riches, power, and dominion. From these considerations, and from the fact that the monachal orders form an elementary part of the constitution of the Catholic Church, we have inferred that she is rather a political than a religious institution; and that while politics form her nature and principles, religion is assumed as an ornament and disguise.

We will now adduce a few facts tending to show that monkish orders originated, not from Christianity; that they existed in pre-historic ages; and that so far as they constitute the Catholic Church, she is a heathen, and not a Christian institution.

It is well known that the Carmelite monks claim Elijah, the prophet, as their founder. Among the ancient personages whom they assert belonged to their order, they enumerate Pythagoras, the Gallic Druids, all the prophets and holy men mentioned in the Old and New Testament, the Apostles, the Essenes, and the ancient hermits. Although amid the wrangling of the monastic orders for preeminence, this claim has rigorously been contested, yet Pope Benedict III. allowed the Carmelites to erect in the Vatican the statue of Elijah as the founder of their order. This permission, so far as the concession of the infallible father is authority, places the antiquity of the monachal order remotely beyond that of Christianity; acknowledges its institution to have originated from Judaism; and grants that its rules and principles were adopted by ancient Pagan fraternities.

That identical institutions have flourished in Asia from the remotest historical periods, admits not of a question. The present Sufism of Arabia is but a modified form of an ancient system of pantheistical mysticism, which taught that through the observance of ascetic practices the animal passions could be destroyed, the soul purified and assimilated to God, and a beatific state attained whose tranquility nothing could disturb. The Gymnosophists, the naked philosophers of India, were an order of monks, who practised the most excruciating penance; and who, in their eagerness to become pure, sometimes burnt themselves alive. The God Fo, born in Cashmere B. C. 1027, the author of the Braminical religion, strenuously advocated monachal institutions. The different orders of the monks and hermits which originated from his allegorical and mystical teaching, assumed the vows of unconditional obedience and absolute poverty. The monks resided in monasteries, and the hermits in deserts. They both practised the most rigorous penance, professed to aspire after absolute purity, but in their conduct and principles they were grovelling, intriguing, profligate and ambitious. Buddha, born B. C. 1029, two years after Fo, founded the monastic order of the Buddhists. His convents were governed by superiors who were subject to the absolute authority of the patriarch, or, as he was officially styled, the Apostolic Successor. The functions and authority of the Buddhistic superiors were similar to those of the Catholic orders; and the pretensions and dignity of the patriarch were one and the same with those of the Pope of Rome. The monks lived in monasteries, assumed the vows of obedience, poverty and celibacy, and admitted virgins to social intercourse. Jeseus Christna, born B. C. 3,500, the incarnate redeemer of the Hindoos, whose birth, life, and miracles resemble those of Jesus Christ, (see "Bible in India,") alludes in his discourses to monks and hermits as being at his time ancient, flourishing and venerated orders. The Hindoo and Mohammedan Fakirs are classes of monks who vow obedience, poverty and celibacy, retire from the world, pass their time in silent contemplation, and acquire the veneration of the populace by the practice of absurd and cruel penance. The Essenes, who flourished in Egypt and Palestine before the Christian era, were an organization of monks who derived their theological principles from the God Theuth, the founder of the Egyptian religious ceremonies.

From the above enumerated facts the conclusion is irresistable, that the Catholic monastic orders are neither of Christian origin, nor inconsistent with the doctrines and worship of Paganism.

A Romish missionary who visited China, observing the similarity which subsisted between the Chinese and the Catholic religion, declared that the devil must have preceded him, and converted the nation to Christianity, in order to cheat the church out of the credit of the enterprise. A more learned but less pious authority concluded from the same analogy, that Catholicism did not convert Paganism, but that Paganism converted Catholicism.

We will now conclude our examination of the Catholic monastic orders, with a few general remarks.

The monastic vows are not only a bold abnegation of the authority of reason and conscience, but a crafty device to delude the credulous, and secretly to acquire riches, power and influence. Although they were assumed by the monks as perpetual obligations, yet they were evaded, modified, or abrogated as interest and policy suggested. The mendicant orders, which assumed the vow of perpetual and absolute poverty, artfully labored to amass fortunes; and soon betrayed a secret design of acquiring hierachal importance and supremacy. The Franciscans, who solemnly obligated themselves to remain forever poor, incessantly grasped after riches. When they had built nunneries, convents, and became the proprietors of extensive domains, they abrogated their vow of perpetual poverty, lest it should invalidate their title to vast possessions which they held. With equal duplicity and ambition, they assumed, upon their first organization, a vow of perpetual ignorance; abjuring the acquisition of any intellectual accomplishment, and consecrating themselves strictly to the preaching of the gospel. But becoming enchanted with the magnificence of the papal crown, and wishing to wield its immense power and lucrative patronage in behalf of their order, and perceiving that literary acquirements would facilitate the accomplishment of this object, they annulled their vow of perpetual ignorance, and began to devote themselves to the acquisition of some degree of profane erudition. Having acquired immense wealth and popularity, and removed by art or bribery every obstacle to the success of their ambition, they placed on the apostolic throne, from their own order, Nicholas V., Alexander V., Sixtus IV., and Clement XIV. The Dominicans, who were established to preach against infidels and heretics, adopted at the commencement of their career the money-making devices of the mendicant orders; but when their revenues had become so great, and their domains so extensive that they had attracted a covetous glance from the secular power, they prudently annulled the vows by which they had been acquired, lest the profane avariciousness of princes should cause their sequestration.

The Jesuits professed to have a holy abhorrence of riches, but thankfully accepted costly presents, opulent legacies, vast tracts of land, and the pecuniary means of erecting numerous stately structures. While this pious fraternity resolved not to accept any ecclesiastical dignity, it secretly and artfully labored to acquire all the privileges of the mendicant orders, all the advantages of the secular clergy, and to make the members of its order superior to those of any other, and its general next in power and importance to the pope. By hypocrisy, intrigue, and cringing sycophancy, these unscrupulous monks obtained rights and privileges enjoyed by no other ecclesiastical corporation. They not only obtained exemption from all civil and episcopal taxes, and from all amenability to any other power than that of the pope; but also the authority of absolving from all sins and ecclesiastical penalties; of changing the object of the vows of the laity; and of acquiring churches and domains without restriction. They were privileged also to suit their dress to circumstances, their conduct to peculiarities, their profession to the views of others; to be accommodating and complaisant while pursuing a political enterprise, and under the mask of any external appearance to prosecute in secret what might excite opposition if openly avowed. They were allowed to become actual merchants, mechanics, showmen, actors, and to adopt any profession calculated to facilitate the accomplishment of a design, and to throw off the mask whenever they thought expedient. Organized on the principles of deception, and unrestricted in their privileges, they secretly labored for their own aggrandizement, while they publicly professed to be sacrificing their interests to the salvation of mankind. They became professors of universities and tutors of schools, that they might select the brightest minds of the rising generation, and mould them to their purposes. They became the spiritual guides of females of rank and opulence, that they might avail themselves of their influence and control their wealth. They became the confessors of princes, that they might penetrate their intentions, ferret out their secrets, watch over their conduct, and enslave and govern their minds. They became the governors of colonies, in order to grasp secular revenues, and to exercise the political power in behalf of their interests. They established seminaries and boarding schools for both sexes, in order to acquire dominion over the young; they sought to occupy the confessional, in order to discover all domestic and governmental secrets; and they labored to monopolize the pulpit, in order to manufacture public opinion, and influence the general tone of society in their favor.

The numerous divisions into which the religious orders were divided, and their different degrees of austerity, enabled the church to suit its policy to the corruption or purity, the ignorance or learning of the nation it sought to proselyte and govern. Under its direction the monks flattered every power they were ordered to subvert, and blushed at no sycophancy that facilitated the accomplishment of an object. Governed by unnatural vows, they sacrificed freedom, the source of natural sentiment, to credulity and blind submission. The most absurd and criminal injunctions of a superior or general were obeyed without compunction or remorse. If they aspired after perfection, it was by sacrificing the virtues of life. If they strove to obtain personal purity, it was by violating the laws of their being. They sought to atone for offences by scourging their backs, ironing their limbs, chaining themselves to rocks, passing their lives in caves, in days without food, in nights without sleep, in years without speaking; subsisting without money, propagating without women, acquiring the respect of the world they despised, the riches they contemned, and the dignity they abjured. They were a palpable deception, yet an object of universal veneration. By cunning and obsequiousness they sought and obtained power; by duplicity and fraud they amassed fortunes; by luxury and tyranny they oppressed the world. Every species of absurdity, art, hypocrisy, avarice, ambition and despotism, under the guise of sanctity was embodied in their organization, and illustrated in their conduct.

The doctrines which they taught were often as pernicious as their professions were false, and their conduct crafty. As the accommodating morality of their religion allowed them to adopt any profession, or any mode of life that would favor the success of a design, so the license of their sophistry enabled them to construe the maxims of virtue according to any standard that would justify the conduct dictated by their interest or sycophancy. By the pliancy of their moral code they consecrated the basest means to pious ends. By the subterfuge of perplexing interpretations, mental reservations, and an artful ambiguity of language, they excused and sanctioned perjury and every other crime. They taught that offences were justified, if, when committed, the criminal thought differently from what he said or done; and that a mental reservation nullified the obligation of any promise, of any contract, or of any treaty. The perversions of the maxims of virtue by which they sought to justify the crimes of others, they applied to their own conduct in the broadest sense. In 1809, when the papal archives were brought to France, the startling fact became public that the holy fathers had been in the habit of availing themselves of pious subterfuges. It then appeared that while they had made contracts, and issued bulls in conformity with the demands of temporal princes, they had at the same time nullified, by virtue of mental reservations, such of them as were obnoxious.

The absurdities and perniciousness of their moral code were not exceeded by those of their penal code. According to the doctrines of Catholicity the guilt of every crime may be expiated by the performance of penance. To regulate the priest in prescribing this mode of punishment, the church furnished him with an ecclesiastical body of laws, which he as carefully as prudently concealed from the eyes of the intelligent. All priests were enabled, by the use of this code, to understand the true orthodox degree of punishment which had been authoratively decided should be inflicted on penitents, for the commission of any offence of word, thought or deed ; and a uniformity in the administration of penal prescriptions was maintained, which harmonized with the divine inspiration by which the confessor pretended to be guided in the matter. Fasts, prayers, self-torture, abstinence from business, were, by the authority of the ecclesiastical code, declared to be the divinely appointed methods of expiating the guilt of rape, of fornication, of adultery, of robbery, of murder, and of every degree and species of crime. These offences being very henious in their nature, and very frequently committed by those who believed in the ability of the church to absolve them from their guilt, and time being required for the performance of the atoning penance, it is easy to see that an ordinary Catholic sinner was in eminent danger of incurring a debt which would require several centuries of penance to liquidate. Here was a dilemma. Long fasting would starve him ; long abstinence from business would empoverish him ; and either expedient would prevent him from being a source of revenue to the church ; and, in fact, defeat the object of the holy sacrament of penance. To obviate this difficulty the ingenious method of indulgences was adopted. By this happy expedient provision was made for the relief of all criminals at stipulated prices, graduated according to their pecuniary circumstances. A penance imposed on a rich sinner for one year's indulgence in the commission of a particular offence, was, by this crafty device, allowed to be cancelled by the payment of twenty shillings to the priest; and if the sinner was poor, by the payment of nine shillings. Yet even by this indulgence and charitable discrimination, as every separate offence required the atonement of a separate penance, few sinners escaped incurring less than a debt of three hundred years, or of two hundred pounds sterling. The liquidation of such an obligation during the dark ages would consume a small fortune; but the expansive benevolence of the church, touched at the sorrows of her contrite members, graciously accepted their land after she had exhausted their purse.

As crime had its degrees of turpitude, the ecclesiastical code prescribed degrees of severity in punishing it. Whoever could not pay with their purse had to pay with their body. Three thousand lashes, and the repetition of a portion of the Psalter, were prescribed as an indispensable satisfaction for any crime whose penance required a year to discharge; and fifteen thousand lashes and the repetition of the whole Psalter, for any crime whose penance required five years to discharge. A year's penance was taxed at three thousand lashes, a century's at three hundred thousand lashes, and five centuries at fifteen hundred thousand lashes.

These scourgings were always sanctified by the repetition of psalms. As vicarious flagellation did not impair the revenues of the church, it was not objected to; and a sinner would often expiate his guilt by vigorously laying the stripes it demanded on the back of an accommodating friend. The skill and hardihood of St. Dominic was able to discharge the penitential lashes of a century in six days; and his pious example was attempted to be imitated even by ladies of fashion and quality.

The monasteries were ambiguous, oppressive corporations. If they have at times preserved the literary treasures of the ancients, they have impaired their authority by numerous corruptions and interpolations. If they have sometimes established institutions for the education of youth, they have generally usurped the fortunes of their patrons. If they have ever been places of refuge for the proscribed, they have always been the means of oppressing industry, and restricting freedom. If they have been schools for the correction of error, and improvement in virtue, yet the absurdities and immoralities taught within their sanctuaries, and the crimes notoriously practised therein, have inflicted deeper injury on the cause of truth, and on the interest of public morals, than can be atoned for by any usefulness or virtue which they could possess, or can pretend to claim. Their virtues were accidents; their vices natural offsprings. They were financial institutions. The labor performed by their inmates as a penance, was made a lucrative source of revenue. The articles which they manufactured were represented as capable of imparting a peculiar blessing to the purchaser, making them cheap at any price. A simple badge of a religious order, to which were ascribed divine virtue, and an unlimited amount of indulgences, was sold to lay members at the price of a respectable fortune. The tutors with which the monasteries furnished schools, the professors which they gave to colleges, the confessors with which they supplied princes, and the spiritual guides with which they provided the affluent of both sexes, were benevolently granted upon the payment of exorbitant sums of money. Gold being the source of power and luxury, it became the governing principle of the church. For it she granted indulgences to violate the laws of heaven and earth; threatened and repealed excommunications; and merchandised every spiritual blessing, all the prerogatives of heaven, and all the privileges of earth. Gold supplied the place of contrition, atoned for the offences of criminals, released sinners from purgatory, and opened to guilt the gates of Paradise. As it more ably than any thing else increased the power and dominion of the church, it was a more adorable object than the deity, a more precious savior than Christ, a more sanctifying possession than the Holy Ghost. As all had sinned, all had to pay; and as all were totally depraved, all had to be liberal. The confessor was judge; and as he was interested in the amount, he was likely to be exorbitant in the demand. The sin of total depravity, which all had inherited from the forbidden fruit which Adam had eaten, empowered a priest to demand of a penitent the surrender of the whole of his fortune.

With extraordinary financial ingenuity, the church converted not only the crimes of her members, but the virtues of her departed saints, into a lucrative source of revenue. Happily conceiving that the saints, some of whom had been executed as malefactors, had performed more good works than was necessary for the salvation of their souls, she inferred that the superabundant quantity of their goodness might be dealt out to the destitute without detriment to the owners. With more cupidity than reason, the church laid claim to these works of supererogation, and began to vend them at exorbitant prices. The exhaustlessness of the store, and the scarcity of the article among her members, made the enterprise a very profitable speculation.

After disposing of a great portion of heaven, and finding it exceedingly remunerative, her inveterate disposition to traffic led her to examine the saints more carefully, and see if they had not other disposable material for the exercise of her commercial ingenuity. She was not long in discovering that the bones of the saints were likely to be deemed as valuable as their virtues had been, and might prove as marketable. This discovery induced an industrious search for their graves, and a careful excavation of them. The bones of Samuel, the judge of Isreal, which had slept for five hundred years in Palestine, were exhumed and transported to Rome. St. Stephen having appeared in a dream to a pious man, and informed him where his corpse reposed, the locality was immediately examined by bishops and priests in company with the dreamer. Unmistakable proofs appeared as to the existence of a grave, but some honest doubts arose as to it being the identical one in which St. Stephen had been deposited; yet they all vanished upon opening the coffin, for such celestial odors arose from the corpse, and such devout reverence was manifested by the trees and rocks in the vicinity, that the most sceptical was satisfied of the genuineness of the relics. A saint's tomb being equal in value to a gold mine, it was natural for the church to seek for it with great eagerness. But the deep earnestness of her enthusiasm blunted the acuteness of her judgment. It sometimes led her to mistake the bones of cats, of dogs, and of jackals for those of saints; and as there is no difference between the bones of thieves and murderers and those of saints, and as both classes have often been regarded by law as synonymous, and interred together in the same field, the former were frequently gathered up in mistake for the latter. But however mortifying were such errors, they did not prove as unfortunate as might have been expected; for until anatomy and history had rectified them, the bones of pigs, of jackals, and of malefactors, brought as good prices as the veritable bones of saints, were as eagerly sought after; and what is very remarkable, performed as many and as great miracles.

We do not pretend to assert that the religious orders, even the most objectionable of them, did not in some instances render valuable aid to the cause of education and humanity. The sanctity and disinterestedness with which their profession was invested, though generally assumed, were sometimes real. But the corrupt and pernicious principles which entered into their constitution, were too self-evident to be concealed from the eyes of mankind; and too revolting to escape the animadversion of some of the more noble and courageous members of their fraternity. Some of the clergy, and many of the learned men of the age boldly complained of their base immorality. Their aversion to reform, and the worldly policy which characterized their religious profession, sunk them in the estimation of the enlightened and philanthropic. Their pernicious intermeddling in political affairs, their cunning and obsequiousness, their busy and intriguing spirit, and the powerful confederacy of their orders, made them objects of suspicion to jurists and statesmen. The numerous exemptions which they enjoyed under the protection of the laws, their privileges nullifying the jurisdiction of the civil authority over them, their overgrown power, and the base accommodation of principle to circumstances, by which they labored to advance the pope's pretension to supreme dominion, rendered their existence in a government a political solecism. But notwithstanding these palpable facts, the force of habit and of education, the deep-rooted reverence which existed in the public mind for the spiritual guides, the superstitious dread of their anathemas, and the servile temper which monarchical government engenders in the minds of subjects, all conspired to conciliate Christendom to the deep degradation inflicted on society by the monastic orders, until their arrogant conduct towards some powerful monarch had surpassed the limits of his forbearance. It was then that the discontent and indignation which their outrageous conduct had created in the public mind, but which superstition had held in check, broke forth in bold and explicit demands for reformation. Reforms, consequently, were not only projected, but peremptorily enforced. The temporal and spiritual powers of the monastic orders were restricted by the abolishment of their exemptions. Sovreigns appropriated many of their rich estates to education and charitable purposes; and sometimes to their own use. Even Catholic princes obliged the monks to submit to unpleasant restrictions, or to purchase exemption at an enormous rate. The different orders, one after the other, were abrogated on account of some intolerable conduct. The Jesuists were abolished in England on account of the political plotting of its members; in Holland for having caused the assassination of Maurice de Nassau; in Portugal for an attempt to murder Joseph I.; in Spain, and its colonies, for conspiring against the government; in Italy for licentiousness; and in France, as the decree expresses, because "Their doctrine destroys the law of nature, that rule of morals which God has inscribed on the heart of man. Their dogmas break all bounds of civil society, authorizing theft, perjury, falsehood, the most inordinate and criminal impiety, and generally all passions and wickedness; teaching the nefarious principle of secret compensation, equivocation and mental reservation; extirpating every sentiment of humanity in their sanction of homicide and parracide; subverting the authority of government, and, in fine, overthrowing the practice and foundation of religion, and substituting in their stead all sorts of superstition, with magic, blasphemy, and adultery." That their conduct and principles are of the most execrable description, the history of all nations affords melancholy evidence. They attempted to dethrone Queen Elizabeth, but defeated in that, sought to murder her. They caused the assassination of the Prince of Orange. They endeavored to poison Maximillion I., King of Austria. They attempted to murder Henry IV., and Louis XV. They poisoned Pope Clement XIII., for having attempted to abolish them, and Pope Clement XIX., for having abrogated their order, although he did it with mental reservations. Loaded with the crimes of ages, and the curses of nations, they were abolished with different limitations in every part of Europe; and as they were the most powerful of the monastic orders, the others rapidly incurred the sentence of the same degradation.

But notwithstanding all this, the Jesuistical order, so execrable in its principles, so dangerous to public peace and morals, and so justly reprobated by all enlightened men and governments, was restored by Pope Pius VII., who intimated that it would reappear in the same authority in which it fell. Again these monks are traversing the world, arresting the progress of science, demoralizing society, and plotting treason and rebellion in the advancement of the pope's claims to supreme temporal and spiritual dominion, until the foundation of independent government begins to quake; until the pillars of constitutional liberty begin to totter; until despotism dares insult the ears of freemen with the boldness of its prophecies; and until statesmen and patriots turn pale as they view the portentous vapors darkling the political horizon, which may gather into a storm, whose rain will be the blood of nations, and whose thunder will shake governments to atoms.

CHAPTER X.

Popes, their Pretensions, Elections, Character. and Administrations.

That we may not commit the error of attributing to the holy mother absurdities which she repudiates, we will inquire what are her pretensions before arraigning her reason or justice in making them. An unequivocal answer to this inquiry may be obtained from the import of her titles, from the bulls of her popes, from the canons of her councils, and from the assertions of her acknowledged authorities. Some of the pope's accredited titles are the following: "The Father of all Fathers;" "The Chief High Priest and Prince of God;" "The Regent of the House of the Lord;" "The Oracle of Religion;" "Our Most Holy Lord God;" "Our Lord God the Pope;" "The Divine Majesty;" "The Victorious God and Man in the See of Rome;" "The Lamb of God that taketh away the sins of the world;" "The Bearer of Eternal Life;" "The Most Holy Father;" "Priest of the World;" "God's Vicar General on Earth;" "The Most High and Mighty God on Earth;" "More than God," &c., &c.

"Pius V., our reigning pope, is prince over all nations and kingdoms, and he has power to pluck up, scatter, plant, ruin and build."—*Canon of the Council of Trent.*

"All mortals are judged by the pope, and the pope by nobody."—*Lateran Canon.*

"It is necessary to salvation that all Christians be subject to the pope."—*Pope Boniface VIII.*

"Ireland, and all the isles on which Christ, the holy sun of righteousness hath shone, do belong to the patrimony of St. Peter and the holy Catholic Church"—*Bull of Pope Adrian.*

"He (the pope) alone has the right to assume empire. All nations must kiss his feet. His name is the only one to be uttered in the churches. It is the only name in the world. He has the right to depose emperors. No council can call itself general without the consent of the pope. No chapter, no book can be reputed canonical without his authority. No one can invalidate his sentence; he can abrogate those of all others. He cannot be judged by any. All persons whatsoever are forbidden to condemn him who is called to the apostolic chair. The Church of Rome is never wrong, and will never fall into error. Every Roman pontiff when ordained becomes holy."—*Bull of Gregory VII.*

"The pope is supreme over all the world, may impose taxes, and destroy crowns and castles for the preservation of Christianity."—*St. Thomas Aquinas.*

"The supremacy of the pope over all persons and things is the main substance of Christianity."—*Bellarmine.*

"The pope is crowned with a triple crown, and is constituted over his (God's) hand to regulate concerning all inferiors; he opens heaven, sends the guilty to hell, confirms emperors, and orders the clerical orders."—*Antonius of Florence, Dist. 40, Si Papa.*

"The pope is the only Vicar of God; his power is over all the world, Pagan as well as Christian, the only Vicar of God, who has supreme power and empire over all princes and kings of the earth."—*Blarcus*, *De Rom. Eccl.*, *Art.* 5, *sec.* 19.

"The pope has supreme power over kings and Christian princes; he may remove them from office, and in their place put others."—*Brovius*, *De Rom. Pontiff*, *Cap.* 46, *p.* 62.

"The pope is the Lord of the whole world. The pope has temporal power; his temporal power is most eminent. All other powers depend on the pope."—*Marcinus*, *Jure Princep. Rom.*, *Lib.* 2, *cap.* 1, 2.

"The pope is divine monarch, supreme emperor and king. Hence the pope is crowned with a triple crown, as king of heaven, of earth, and of hell. He is also above angels; so that if it were possible that angels could err from the faith, they could be judged and excommunicated by the pope."—*Feraris in Papa*, *Art.* 11, *No.* 10.

"The vicar of God in the place of God, remits to man the debt of a plighted promise."—*Dens.* 4, 134.

"The pope can do all things that he wishes to do, and is empowered by God to do all things that he himself can."—*Tiba*.

"The pope can transubstantiate sin into duty, and duty into sin."—*Durand*.

"The bishop of Rome cannot even sin without being praised."—*Moscovius*.

"God's tribunal and the pope's tribunal are the same."—*Moscovius*.

From the loftiness of these pretensions, we are involuntarily impelled to look to the holy fathers for corresponding principles, character and conduct. If they possess the moral attributes of the deity, they must possess also his physical attributes; and if they possess his physical attributes, they can much easier create some world out of nothing over which to domineer, than they can create a claim to all the crowns, riches, and territory of the earth, out of the patrimony of St. Peter, who was never worth a cent. If, indeed, the pope's tribunal and God's tribunal are the same; if he above all in heaven would be the proper judge, and anathematizer of angels, should any of them fall; if he can annul the obligation of any oath which man is under to his maker, then he must be the associate judge of God Almighty, equal to him in dignity, superior to him in jurisdiction, and supereminent to him in authority. If the pope can transubstantiate sin into duty and duty into sin, he can annihilate all distinction between right and wrong, and convert the worship of God into a sin, and the adoration of himself into a duty. But these extraordinary pretensions, if unsupported by irrefragable proofs of divine power and virtue; if the administrative abilities of the popes have not transcended those of infinite wisdom and goodness; and if their monarchy is not such a just embodiment of unquestionable and universally accepted principles as has produced and maintained among their subjects on earth a degree of peace, order, and concord superior to that which subsists among the angels in heaven, then are their pretensions not only presumptous but ridiculous, not only arrogant but blasphemous; denying the existence of God by claiming equality with him, contemning his authority by usurping his prerogatives, and trampling under foot his name and character, by presuming to exercise a superior degree of executive and judicial authority.

In selecting a person among mortals capable of filling a throne so exalted above the thrones of earth and heaven, we perceive the great embarrassment under which those must have labored on whom the difficult task was devolved. They claim, however to have succeeded by the aid of divine inspiration, although it cannot be denied that the persons whom they have selected were in general the weakest and most corrupt men of their age.

In the course of time and experience it became the custom of the bishops, on the demise of a pope, to recommend to the suffrages of the college of cardinals a suitable person for his successor. As the populace claimed and enjoyed the prerogative of confirming or rejecting the choice of the bishops, and as nobles, from selfish and ambitious motives, often interfered in the proceedings, the papal elections were always scenes of excitement, and sometimes of disorder. The jealousy of emperors interfered in the matter, also, claiming the right to arbitrate between rival candidates, to interdict the consecration of any pope elect until the forms of his election should be inspected by their deputies, and approved by themselves, and to convene synods for the purpose of trying any of the holy fathers who should be charged with criminal conduct, and to punishing such of them as should be found guilty. But the despotism of the church, naturally increasing with her power, enabled her eventually to relieve herself of these unpleasant restrictions, to assert independence of the secular powers, and to maintain it by force of arms. This papal triumph removing the wholesome check which had hitherto restrained and softened the

14

violence of episcopal ambition, left the claims of rival candidates for the vicarship of Christ to be disputed by the anathemas of the clergy and the frenzy of the mob. The knell of a pope's death became the tocsin of war, and the election of his successor a bloody struggle for political interest. Rival aspirants appeared in the ecclesiastical arena; acrimonious contests ensued; adherents were bought; competitors insulted; votes extorted by threats; Rome polluted with blood; and the peace of Christendom endangered. To defeat a hostile or elect a friendly candidate, nobles and princes would appeal to the passions of the mob, and excite them to ungovernable fury. Emperors would interpose not only in the election, but in the administration of a pope. They often obliged the inspired college to select such a candidate as suited their interest; sometimes they prevented, and at other times anticipated its action. Through the influence and intrigues of two royal harlots, Theodora and Marozia, the chair of St. Peter was filled with their lovers. Pope John XII., when he was eighteen years old, and Pope Benedict IX., when he was twelve years, were, through the wealth and power of those prostitutes, elevated to the papal dignity. Pope John XII was deposed for ingratitude and treachery by the Emperor Otho I., who caused the inspired college to elect Leo VII., and placed him by military force on the apostolic throne. Pope John XIII. was elected by the inspired college at the command of Otho II., Pope Clement II. at the command of Henry III., and Pope Clement III. at the Command of Henry IV. Clement II. was elected to displace Benedict IX., Clement III. to displace Gregory VII., Boniface I. to displace Dioscorus, and Martin V. to displace John XXII., Gregory XII. and Benedict XII. three cotemporaneous holy fathers. The antagonistical popes would mutually denounce each other as anti-popes, and tax their ingenuity to effect each other's destruction. Benedict XII. disposed of his rival by violence; John XIV. incarcerated his in a dungeon, in which he starved to death.

Besides the rivalship which infuriated opposing candidates, and the intermeddling of princes in their elections in order to secure a pliant instrument for their political designs, the inspired college itself was often rent into revengeful and irreconcilable factions. So violent sometimes were these conflicts, that the college became divided into two parties, each of which proceeded to separate churches, and electing its favorite, presented him to the people as having been chosen by divine inspiration. Two antagonistical popes thus being elected in accordance with papal usages, divine inspiration, and canonical law, it became difficult, without the aid of another inspired college, to determine which of the two popes was the genuine holy father. Sometimes this question was decided by priority in the moment of an election; sometimes popular sanction or imperial preference resolved the difficulty; and at other times different sections of Christendom arriving at opposite conclusions, supported different popes. At one period two popes divided the patrimony of St. Peter, the one reigning over one portion of it, and the other over another; and at another time three popes asserted jurisdiction over it. These rival holy fathers would incessantly encounter one another with bulls, anathemas, and swords; and invoking foreign arms in their support would distract, not only Rome, but all Europe, with their irreconcilable controversies.

In order to abate the calamity of the papal elections, Pope Alexander III., chosen in 1179, abolished the mode of electing a pope in which the clergy and people participated, and invested the sole right in the college of cardinals. This expedient prevented the frequency of double elections, and their tumultuous and bloody schisms. But still the disorderly elements which shook the church could not be entirely eradicated without the abolishment of the papal throne. The passions and private interests of the members of the sacred college; their wish to secure the honors and emoluments of an independent reign; their insidious machinations to become popes themselves; often deprived the church, under the new electoral method, of the benefits of a holy father. An interregnum of months, sometimes of years, would ensue between the death of a pope and the election of his successor, while disgraceful negotiations were always visible. Pope Clement IV. promised the crown of both of the Sicilies to Charles of Anjou, on condition that he would use his influence with the inspired college in favor of his election to the papal throne; and Pope Boniface VIII., after expending large sums of money on an election, excommunicated the obstinate cardinals who had refused to vote for him.

The ambition and corruption of the cardinals having kept the papal throne vacant for three years previous to the election of Gregory X., he issued a bull in 1265, requiring the members of the college to assemble in Rome nine days after the demise of a pope, and after taking an oath to abjure all previous understanding, to retire with a single attendant into a common apartment, and to remain there until they should be able to agree on a choice. If within three days the influence of the Holy Ghost should not be sufficiently powerful to enable them to arrive at a canonical agreement, the luxury of their repast was to be abridged to a single dish at dinner and supper; and if within eight days these privations should still be insufficient to quicken the divine influence on the grossness of human nature, the cardinals were then condemned to subsist on a small allowance of bread, water and wine. The stimulus of this regimen has seldom failed to produce a speedy and harmonious agreement.

But the corruption of the Holy See was the growth of ages, and had carefully been systematized by the hand of experienced craft. It could not therefore be entirely eradicated by any modification in the papal electoral forms; although improvements might be introduced, making them the occasion of less scandal. The fact that an attendant on a cardinal during the session of an electoral college is worth an independent fortune, is significant of the corrupt machinations by which the holy fathers continue still to be elected. The bull of Pope Gregory X. has, ineed, prevented the former frequency of schisms, but it was insufficient to prevent one of seventy years' duration, which occurred on the death of Pope Benedict XI, in 1348. The inspired college having assembled in accordance with the requirements of the canon, sworn to abjure all previous understanding, became, nevertheless, divided on the question whether **a Frenchman** or an Italian should be elected as the vicar of Christ. Two-thirds of the cardinals were in favor of a Frenchman, but a mob of thirty thousand Romans preferred an Italian. "Death or an Italian Pope," shouted an infuriated crowd, as it gathered around the Vatican, and made preparations for burning any of the inspired college who should vote for a French candidate; while the cathedral bells, in harmony with the discordant clamor of the mob, pealed forth an ominous warning. Under the terror of these intimidations, the inspired college submitted to the wishes of the mob; and electing Urban VI., an Italian, and presenting him to the populace declared, according to usage, that they had been inspired to choose him through the influence of the Holy Ghost. The disappointed cardinals disguised their mortification under the warmest congratulations to the newly elected pope, but gratified their secret malice by entering into clandestine negotiation with Philip IV., King of France, and stipulating with him to accommodate his interest by electing a pope in the place of Urban, who should conform to his wishes in all things. After having by flattery, and professions of friendship and allegiance, sufficiently deceived the vicar of Christ, they retired to Fundi, and, excommunicating him, elected Pope Clement in his place. The papal monarchy hence became divided into two antagonistical bodies, the one having its capitol at Rome, the other at Avignon in France.

The aspirants to the dignity of the vicarship of Christ endeavored, in general, to obtain its holy honors by the employment of artifice and intrigue. They were ready to flatter any power, assume any semblance, agree to any terms. and profess any sentiment that promised to favor their design. At the council of Constance, Pope Martin V. advocated the most liberal ecclesiastical reforms, but recanted his heresy as soon as he obtained the triple crown. Pope Alexander VI. was elected by bribing Cardinals Cibo, Spozza and Rearis. Pope Alexander VII., while a cardinal, assumed the semblance of great humility and sanctity, but no sooner had he become a successor of St. Peter, than he threw off the cumbrous mask by which he gained the honor, and openly began a course of dissipation and luxurious indulgence. Sixtus VI. played a deep and crafty game to win the papal crown. In order to deceive the cardinals he assumed the appearance of an infirm old man, deaf, blind, and scarcely able to hobble on a crutch; and who desired nothing but obscurity, devotion and repose. By the agency of the confessional he correctly informed himself of the wishes of princes and the secret designs of cardinals. Under a mask of profound dissimulation he gained the confidence of kings and nobles, and evaded the scrutiny of cardinals. Having transformed himself into the semblance of such a convenient tool as the members of the college desired to place on the apostolic throne, they chose him unanimously; but repented of it unanimously immediately afterwards. No sooner had the electoral formalities been conconcluded than, in the presence of the cardinals, he raised himself from his former stooping position, contemptuously threw away his crutch, and with a bounding and vigorous step displayed to the horror consternation of the sacred college that it had chosen for a holy father, not a pliant simpleton, but a man of authority, determination, and sagacity. Pope Celestine was elected solely on account of his ignorance and mental imbecility. For twenty-seven months the disputes of the cardinals had kept the papal throne without an incumbent. To conciliate their differences they finally agreed to elect Celestine, who was celebrated for his intellectual deficiency and profound ignorance of the world. When this holy father entered Apulea after his consecration, he symbolically rode upon an ass. But his incapability of transacting the ordinary business the Holy See, obliged the sacred college to reassemble, and endeavor by the aid of the Holy Ghost to select a more suitable vicar of Christ. It succeeded in electing Boniface VIII., who possessed more business capacity, but less moral integrity; and who, standing in mortal dread of his simple and unaspiring predecessor, and fearing the instability of the apostolic throne while he was at large, pusillanimously imprisoned him for life.

It is a singular fact that while distant potentates trembled at the thunders of the Vatican, the subjects of Rome scoffed with impunity at its insolent pretensions. The tyranny and corruption of the holy fathers have frequently been met with contempt and insurrection by the populace. The cardinals have at times been stripped, beaten, and trodden under foot. The priests have been caught by mobs, which, after digging out their eyes, and crowning their heads with ludicrous mitres, have sent them as admonitions to the pope. The sacred processions, headed by the holy fathers, have been saluted with showers of stones. The vice-gerents of God, while on the apostolic throne, have been seized by the throat, rudely buffeted, torn from their chair and incarcerated in dungeons. Laudislaus, King of Naples, whom the pope had entitled "*General of the Church*," in consideration of services rendered, thrice afterwards entered Rome as a master, profaned the churches, violated the virgins, plundered the citizens, and worshipped at the shrine of St. Peter. The holy fathers, assailed by subjects at home and princes abroad, were constantly fleeing from the insecure patrimony of St. Peter to find refuge in France, Anangni, Perugia, Viterbo, or some other locality. Sometimes they retaliated the insults of their Catholic subjects, and levied armies to chastise them; and, on one occasion they had, in a friendly conference, eleven deputies of the people murdered in cold blood, and their bodies cast into the streets.

When the Holy See was transplanted from Rome to Avignon, the vices, corruption, and tumults which were characteristic were transplanted along with it. The same popular insubordination and papal insecurity prevailed; the people were seditious and the popes insulted. A Catholic freebooter at the head of his band, once entered Avignon, plundered the people and churches, compelled the pope and cardinals to ransom themselves by the payment of an enormous sum of gold, and to absolve him and his fellow robbers from the guilt of the transaction, and from all their crime.

Notwithstanding the ostentatious sanctity and gorgeous show with which the church invests her external form, her throne has never been occupied by a distinguised paragon of virtue; nor has it, notwithstanding her liberal indulgence to moral turpiturd, often been graced by those whom she dared to canonize for the purity of their conduct. High principled and lofty minded men have scorned to aspire to her dignities; and had they not, they still could not have stooped to the dishonorable means by which they are to be obtained. With pretensions demoralizing her officials by destroying their sense of moral accountability, fostering their vanity, pride and superciliousness, and dissolving all restraints on the instigations of malice, revenge, cupidity, licentiousness, duplicity and tyranny, it would be absurdity to expect to find in their character any exalted degree of moral excellence. Look at those whom the inspired college has chosen vicegerent of God. Where we might expect to see the Solons, Cimons, and Catos of the age, we always see despotism, generally duplicity, and often profligacy and cruelty. Look at Pope Gregory, the Great. Was he not an aspiring and unscrupulous despot? While pretending to wish to be unknown, did he not employ every device to become the most notorious man of his age. To pave his way to the pontifical throne, he devoted his patrimony to the use of convents, and immured himself in them. By seeming to resist, he secured his election; and by addressing an artful remonstrance against its confirmation to the emperor, he removed every obstacle in the way of his consecration. To disguise more deeply his ambition, he solicited a merchant, whom he knew could not accommodate him, to convey him secretly from Rome; and, finally, overacted his part by secreting himself in a wilderness, and building a fire that his retreat might be discovered. His financial skill was unquestioned. He induced Recared, King of

Spain, to exchange a great amount of gold and a valuable collection of jewels for a few hairs of St. John the Baptist, a piece of the true cross, a key which, it was alleged, contained some grains of a chain with which St. Peter had been shackled while in a dungeon. He also sanctified the most atrocious assassination that was, perhaps, ever perpetrated. The Roman legions having become demoralized, the Emperor Maurice attempted to reduce them to order by the enforcement of rigorous military discipline. This effort produced a general dissatisfaction among the troops, which culminated in the election of Phocus, an obscure soldier, in the place of Maurice. The emperor, desirous of restoring tranquility to the nation, magnanimously abdicated the purple. Never having heard of the name of Phocus before, he inquired of his general who he was. "Alas," replied he, "a great coward, and I fear will be a murderer." This prophecy was soon fulfilled. Phocus sent to the private dwelling of Maurice assassins, who, before the eyes of their father coldly butchered his five sons, and then consummated the horrible tragedy with the murder of the emperor himself. After this barbarous act had been perpetrated, Pope Gregory, although he owed his elevation to the indulgence of Maurice, complimented Phocus on his good fortune, and rejoiced that his piety and benignity had raised him to the imperial throne.

From this model pope let us turn to Pope John XII., elected in 956. In ambition unprincipled, in cruelty inexorable, in dissoluteness cold and calculating; the annals of history scarcely furnish an equal compound of moral deformity. Elevated to the papal throne through the influence of a prostitute, he made the principles of his patroness the maxims of his conduct. He was a drunkard, a profligate, a blasphemer, and a murderer. He passed his time in hunting and gambling. He swore by the Pagan Gods and Goddesses. He lived in public adultery with Roman matrons. He converted the papal palace into a brothel, and made it a school for education in the arts of prostitution. His rapes of widows, wives, and virgins were so frequent, that female pilgrims were deterred from visiting the tomb of St. Peter, for fear of being violated by the holy father while kneeling at his shrine, to invoke his aid in the practice of chastity and piety.

Now advert to Gregory VII., elected in 1075, and see what baseness, trickery, avarice, and insolence have been consecrated as holy in the character of a vicar of Christ. Protected from reproach by his claim to infallibility, he presumed to outrage the sense of common decency by living with the Countess Matilda under suspicious circumstances; and conceiting that he was endowed with supreme power over all kings and governments, and that if they resist his authority he must punish them, he undertook to dethrone Henry IV., Emperor of Germany and Italy, because that prince had exercised the right of investiture contrary to the interdiction of the papal bulls. For this insolent proceedure the emperor determined to depose him, and drive him from Rome. Penetrating the emperor's design, he attempted to defeat it by buying the adherence of the Italian populace; but this movement was effectually counterpoised by the emperor's purchasing the support of the Italian nobility. He also convened a council at by which Gregory was deposed; and another at Brisen at which Clement III. was elected. To place Clement in possession of the papal dignity, Henry formed a coalition with the Emperor Alexius: to defeat this project Gregory formed an alliance with Robert Guiscard, Duke of Apulia. The arms of Robert were victorious, and Gregory was delivered from his perilous situation. But victory sometimes is as disastrous as defeat. The formidable allies of the holy father, which success had introduced into the city of Rome, comprehended a numerous band of Saracens who hated the Christian name and capital, although they had for money and the license of war been induced to take up arms in defence of the sacerdotal monarch. A furious sedition happening to arise in the city among the inhabitants, the Saracens eagerly availed themselves of the occasion to gratify their hatred of Rome and of Christianity. They commenced murdering the citizens, plundering dwellings, profaning churches, and firing buildings; nor was their revenge satiated until they had, not only depopulated the city, but reduced the greater portion of it to ashes. This catastrophe completed the disgrace of Gregory. Finding himself universally detested as its author, he had to flee for safety to Salerno, leaving Henry to consummate, without opposition, his design of placing Clement III. upon the apostolic throne.

From the conduct of this crafty and talented sacerdotal despot, let us turn a glance at pope Innocent II., elected in 1130. The elevation of this Pope was the tocsin of a war which, during his administration, kept Rome and Italy in a state of violent convulsion. The sacred college not being able canonically to concur in his election, became divided into two obstinate factions, each of which elected a vicegerent of God; the one being Pope Innocent II., and the other Pope Anaclitus. Two implacable despots being thus authorized to claim the papal throne, a furious holy war was inevitable. Anaclitus having the heavier artillery drove Innocent from Rome; but France and Germany espousing the cause of the fugitive, enabled him to secure a sufficient army to effect his return. He was, nevertheless, obliged to limit his papal jurisdiction to one portion of the city; his antagonist being too strongly entrenched in the other to be dislodged. But even from this limited domain he was again driven by the arms of his formidable rival, and again reinstated by the forces of the temporal power. The two holy fathers continued to hate, persecute and anathematize each other, until death settled the sanguinary controversy by the removal of Anaclitus. Relieved of the terrors of a powerful adversary, Innocent II. convoked the Lateran Council, in which one thousand bishops condemned the soul of Anaclitus, and excommunicated Rogers of Sicily for having supported the schismatic. On account of this papal insolence, Robert declared war against Pope Innocent; and taking him prisoner, obliged him to absolve him from the sentence of the excommunication, and to invest him with the papal provinces of Apulia, Capua, and Calibria.

Let us now direct a moment's attention to Pope Innocent III, elected in 1198, who, when receiving the triple crown exclaimed: "The church has given me a crown as a symbol of temporalities she has conferred on me a mitre in token of spiritual power;—a mitre for the priesthood; a crown for the kingdom; making me the vicar of him who bears on his garments and thighs, 'THE KING OF KINGS, AND LORD OF LORDS.'" Inflated with this popular conceit he imagined that he was supreme prince over all nations and kingdoms, and that he had a divine right to pluck up, destroy, scatter, ruin, plant and build whenever a notion happened to inspire his presumptuous brain. He arbitrarily obliged the prefect of Rome to swear allegiance to him, demanded royal homage of Marguard of Romagna, and upon the refusal of that prince to compromise his sovreignty by submitting to such unwarrantable dictations, deprived him of the duchy of Mark Ancona. With a despotic hand he wrung Spoleto from Duke Conrad. He excommunicated Philip of France for having repudiated his wife, and obliged him to sue for mercy at his feet. He deposed King John, of England, for refusing to confirm the election of a bishop; instigated France to declare war against him, obliged him to resign his kingdom to the See of Rome, to pay large sums of money for absolution, and to hold his throne as a papal fief. He exercised an oppressive despotism over the temporal provinces of Christendom, established inqisisitorial tribunals, suspended religious worship by interdicts, and urged the cruel persecution of the Albigenses. When his military forces were ready for combat, he is said to have exclaimed: "Sword, sword, whet thyself for vengeance."

Turn from this ornament of the papal throne, and consider the character and administration of Pope Boniface VIII., elected in 1295. Pliable and revengeful, presumptuous and ambitious, he sought to make tools of

princes, and slaves of subjects. On his way to the
Lateran palace, after his election, the King of Hungary
and the King of Sicily, in token of their inferior rank,
held the bridle of his horse; and with crowns on their
heads waited on him at table as menials. He boldly
excommunicated Philip IV., of France, but cowardly
sought to escape the penalty by taking refuge in the
fortress of Anangni. While luxuriating in this sumpuous retreat, in fancied security, William of Nosgeret surrounded the palace with three hundred horse, and a
scuffle ensued in which the vicegerent of God was
rudely seized by the throat, severely kicked and cuffed,
and cast into prison. A mob, however, soon released
him from confinement. In view of his flagitious and
undeniable acts of duplicity, simony, usurpation and
profligacy, King Philip had resolved to summon a council at Lyons for the purpose of deposing him; but the
chastisement of incarceration which he had undergone
so mortified his pride, that within three days after his
liberation he died in a paroxysm of rage and fury.

Look at the character of Pope Alexander III., elected
in 1159, who, demoralized and misled by papal pretensions, distracted all Europe, and kept the Holy See in a
state of perpetual insurrection. Under the protection
of Frederic I. the anti-popes Victor III., Pascal III.,
and Calaxtus III., successively arose against him; repeatedly driving him from Rome; sometimes to France;
sometimes to Anangni; and sometimes to Venice. But
fortune eventually favoring him, he wreaked the heaviest vengeance on the heads of his antagonists. He
obliged Frederic to kiss his feet, and to hold the stirrup
of his horse. He laid Scotland under an interdict.

He restored the thrones of England and Germany on conditions that augmented his power. And in the exercise of his apostolic authority gave the world calamitous proof that ecclesiastical supremacy is incompatible with the peace of the world.

Regard for an instant the character of Pope Alexander VI., elected in 1523, who perfected in his papal character the dissipation which had disgraced his youth. His policy, both domestic and foreign, was base, treacherous and execrable. He undertook to seize on the Italian provinces by the most cruel and dishonorable methods. He attempted to extort money from the different sections of Christendom by fraud and force. He seduced his own daughter; and gave notorious evidence of the profligacy of his life by five illegitimate children. He conspired with his son, Cardinal Cæsar Borgia, to poison four cardinals, but the conspirators drinking the poison themselves, became the victims of their own treachery.

Look at Pope Julius II., elected in 1505, and mark his savage, ferocious, and warlike character. Ambitious of military renown, he commanded his army in person, and without regard to the rights of nations or individuals gratified his lust of power and dominion. In the prosecution of the interests of the Holy See, he excommunicated the Duke of Ferrara, gave Navara to Spain, besieged Muandolo, colleagued against the republic of Venice, and made war upon Louis XII., King of France.

Behold Clement V., elected in 1305, and mark the gross simony, nepotism, and arrogance which disgraced his administration. Hear him excommunicating Henry

VII. of Germany, and his allies, for his refusing to mediate between him and Robert; and hear him pronouncing a curse on the Venitians for their refusing to submit to his dictation; declaring them infamous, confiscating their gold and war vessels, abolishing their governmental offices, and absolving the subjects from obedience to the laws.

Turn to John XXII., elected in 1410, and see if any vice, public or private, debarred a candidate from the papal throne. In his youth a pirate, the sanctity of his pontifical character neither restrained nor concealed the precocious viciousness which he had manifested. Although he may have amused himself with the popish conceit that a holy father cannot sin without being praised, yet the Council of Constance, on the testimony of thirty-seven good Catholic witnesses, found seventy indictments against him, and degraded him from the papal dignity. Among the crimes for which he was deposed were simony, murder, rape, sodomy, and illicit intercourse with his brother's wife, and with three hundred nuns. This holy father died in jail.

Look at Julius III., elected in 1550, whose unnatural licentiousness transcending all bounds of decency, sought its gratification with boys, men, and even cardinals. Hear Sixtus V., in the college of cardinals, pronouncing a eulogy on the assassinators of Henry III. King of France, and comparing them with Judith and Eleazer. Hear Alexander I., as he placed his foot on Frederic, King of Denmark, exclaim: "Thus shalt thou tread upon the lion and the adder." Hear Pius V., as he excommunicated Queen Elizabeth, exclaim: "I have this day set thee over the nations, over the kingdoms, to root out, to pull down, to destroy, to build up and to throw down." Witness Pope Leo III. abruptly crowning Charlemagne, and to the astonishment of the worl investing him with all the titles, honors, and regal ornaments of the Cæsars. Witness Gregory IV. fomenting discord between Charlemagne and his sons, then between the sons themselves, then tampering with the officers of the imperial army, then absolving them from their oath of allegiance, then uttering to Louis I., son and successor of Charlemagne, that arrogant assertion : " Know my chair is above the emperor's throne;" and ultimately see the design of these atrocious acts, in the claim of the subsequent popes to the dominion of the Cæsars, by virtue of the donation of Charlemagne.

Look at the two hundred and ninety-seven popes that have filled the papal chair: Twenty-four of them were anti-popes; twenty-six were deposed; nineteen were compelled to abandon Rome; twenty-eight were kept on their throne only by foreign intervention ; fifty-four were obliged to rule over foreign parts ; sixty-four died by violence; eighteen were poisoned; one was shut up in a cage ; one was strangled; one smothered ; one died by having nails driven in his temples ; one by a noose around his neck; and only one hundred and fifty-three out of the whole number have proved themselves at all worthy. Read the papal annals; hear the frequent and atrocious anathemas of the popes; mark the vices that have continued century after century to disgrace the administrations of the holy fathers, and say if prrofane history affords a catalogue of monarchs so black with crime, so unprincipled in ambition, so remorseless in revenge. Their pretensions were made not from conscious right, but to justify intended usurpations. They claimed to be endowed with power to do whatever God himself could do, in order to forge a plea for governing the world as despots. They claimed the prerogative of absolving subjects from their oaths of allegiance, that they might rule kings with absolute authority. They claimed that they could not sin without being praised, that they might commit any crime without being censured. They claimed the ability of transubstantiating sin into duty, and duty into sin, that they might justify themselves in adopting any means to obtain an end. They claimed all the authority and holiness of heaven, that they might be worshipped and feared as Gods. But while they had the audacity to prefer these claims, it is not a supposable case that the dullest of them was such a stupendous fool as to believe in the validity of his own pretensions. With a triple crown on their heads, with the keys of heaven and hell in their hands, with an assertion on their lips that they are the king of kings, and the proprietors of all the thrones, domains, revenues, gold and gems of the earth, they seriously pretend that they are the successors of St. Peter, an humble fisherman, who like his master, had not where to lay his head, and whose patrimony, which they claim to inherit, must have consisted at most of but an empty purse, a staff, a suit of unfashionable garments, and, perhaps, some old fishing nets. And while they have been elected by emperors, by mobs, by arms and clubs, by bribery, and by every species of corruption, they affirm that they have been chosen by the inspiration of the Holy Ghost.

The papal monarchy was neither designed nor calculated to foster the growth of either truth, reason or virtue. The policy and measures which it adopted were never intended to correct vice, but to make it administer to the importance of its power, and the wealth of its coffers. Its design has always been to reign supreme; and in conformity with a policy dictated by this design, it has destroyed every virtue that obtruded an obstacle to the accomplishment of its purposes, and protected every vice that appeared to favor their success.

Such being the principles of the papal government, it could not be hoped that the holy fathers would be the friends of truth and reform. In fact they must have been conscious that a rigid system of reform would have swept them from their thrones, and doomed many of them to confinement in the dungeons of a penitentiary. Accordingly we see that while temporal princes, some clergymen, and numerous laymen loudly demanded reform in the head and body of the church, the popes strenuously opposed the project as a dangerous innovation. When summons had been issued by temporal princes for the assembling of councils for purposes of reformation, the pontiffs frequently forbid obedience to them. When circumstances have obliged popes to issue orders for the convocation of such assemblages, they have rendered them nugatory by neglecting to fix the time and place to their meeting. When compelled to be more definite in their conduct and language, they have endeavored, by changing the time and place for holding a proposed council, to defeat the object which they were obliged to sanction. When their cautious vacillations have been summarily arrested, and all the obstacles they had obtruded removed, and a council for reform had been assembled, they edeavored by base and corrupt means to control its action, and defeat its usefulness. When in defiance of papal remonstrances, threats and intrigues, reformatory decrees have been passed by councils, the popes have, nevertheless, attempted to nullify them by evasion, trickery or neglect.

Pope Gregory declared that a council could be useful only under a Catholic prince. Pius II. forbid an appeal to a council. Julius II. interdicted the assembling of one after it had been summoned. When the united voice of princes and subjects compelled Pius VII. to call a council, he nullified his own summons by neglecting to fit the time for its meeting. When a critical state of public affairs had led Pope Paul to imagine that he could shape the proceedings of an inspired council according to his private interest, he convoked the Council of Trent; but finding his intrigues inadequate to his ambition, he induced his legates to exhaust its time in frivolous ceremonies and useless excursions. When the Council of Pisa obliged Alexander VII. to pledge his word to prosecute certain specified reforms, he adopted no measure in compliance with his word. When the Council of Basle enacted decrees of reform, the artifice of Pope Eugenius rendered them of no avail. When the Council of Constance, after deposing three rival popes, elected Martin V. in consideration of the zeal with which he had advocated church reform, it was soon apparent that his zeal for reform was his ambition to be elevated to the papal throne, and that it all had expired as soon as his election was secure. Pope Pius denounced the reforms which Joseph II., of Austria, proposed to introduce into his kingdom, and adopted every expedient to counteract them. When the tyranny and profligacy of the monastic orders had awakened the indignation of all Christendom, the vicar of Christ, by means of bulls, anathemas and intrigues, defended them with ferocious zeal. When the Jesuists were banished from England for treasonable machinations, from Italy for profligacy, from Portugal for attempts at assassination, and from the other parts of Europe for execrable conduct, the popes not only defended, but recommended them as the most pious and useful members of the church. When the papal throne was restored by England, a heretic, and Russia, a schismatic, in conjunction with the Catholic powers, after it had been abolished by France, the pope, in defiance of the wishes and resolutions of his liberators, and in violation of the obligations of honor and gratitude, restored the barbarous inquisition, the obnoxious order of the Jesuists, and the superstitious practices of the dark ages.

The holy mother, indeed, has given birth to little besides monstosities. The features and principles of her offspring cast a dark suspicion on her chastity. They usually wear the lineament, if not the cloven foot of the arch-fiend. Ambition, duplicity, treachery, viciousness, and immorality are deeply featured in their countenances, and some of them seem to be an incarnation of every crime that could entitle a human being to be considered as the offspring and heir of hell. If there were some honorable exceptions, they were like stars on a stormy night, obscured by the heavy mist through which they shone. Some popes, it is true, have been great governors; men of great foresight and enterprise; men who, looking beyond their age, have prepared measures that have successfully met future exegencies; but their sagacity has been quickened by ambition and avarice; and their great talents have been wasted on duplicity and intrigue. The less exceptionable of them have acknowledged and deplored the corruption of the Holy See; but they seem to think it is incurable, for their hopes of the future are always darkened by the recollection of the past. Hence we hear Nicholas V., as he bestowed an office on the worthy, say: "Take this, you will not always have a Nicholas to bestow a gift on the ground of merit."

CHAPTER XI.

THE PAPAL MONARCHY.

SECTION ONE.

The Papal Crown—Banner—Cabinet—Court—Decrees—Jurisprudence—Coinage—Army and Navy—Revenues—Oaths—and Spies.

WHATEVER plausibility the creed and ritual of the Catholic church may throw around her religious pretensions, the fact is undeniable that she is a temporal power, claiming to be the only legitimate sovereignty on earth, and the right to reduce all governments, by fair or foul means, under her absolute authority. The pope, the head of this unlimited monarchy, is a political prince; his capital is the city of Rome, and his domains, until recently, were the States of the Church. According to a practice observed at the coronation of princes, the pope is invested with national authority by ascending the Chair of State, and receiving a headdress emblematical of temporal sovereignty. These symbolical headdresses were originally garlands, invented by Prometheus in imitation of the chains which he had worn for the redemption of mankind, but which in the course of time became applied, by the Uranian priestesses to decorate themselves and their altars; by lovers, to adorn the doors of their mistressees: by the devout, to deck the animals which they devoted to sacrifice; by slave owners, to attract attention to the slaves whom the exposed for sale; by relatives, to embellish the corpse of a deceased friend; and finally, in the dark ages, when they were transformed into a variety of fantastical shapes, profusely decorated with gold, gems and pearls, and had become associated with ideas of greatness, power and authority, they were exclusively appropriated by kings to symbolize the regal authority. In the ninth century, this practice having become fashionable among the royal classes, Pope Alexander III., who was elected in 1159, aspiring to be considered rather as the successor of kings than of a fisherman, ventured to encircle his sacerdotal mitre with a regal diadem, emblematical of universal spiritual sovereignty. To this crown Pope Boniface VIII., elected in 1295, added a second, to symbolize the pope's universal temporal power; and to this crown Pope Urban V., elected in 1363, added a third, to denote the pope's supreme spiritual and temporal power over Europe, Asia and Africa. The adoption of these regal emblems by the holy fathers may seem in the eyes of the profane to represent not their rights, but their ambition. They claim, however, to have been moved by the Holy Ghost in adopting their head decorations; but if this pretension absolves them from the vice of ambition, it limits at the same time their authority to Europe, Asia and Africa. The Holy Ghost not having intimated the existence of America in his social intercourse with the papal monarchs, nor prescribed to them the adoption of a fourth crown to symbolize their authority over it, it is rational to infer from these facts that he intended to infer by his silence, that the popes have no right whatever of exercising any jurisdiction over its territory. If the pope's regalia have any significance, it is that his government is restricted to Europe, Asia and Africa; and that he has no right to exercise either temporal or spiritual authority over any church, society or institution, on the American continent. But in sight of the pope's monarchical palace, triple crown, and regal ornaments, the statue of St. Peter, erected in the seventh century, wearing a simple mitre, stands scoffing at them in eternal derision.

The pope as an independent sovereign has not only a temporal crown, but a political banner. This ensign consists of a white flag with a device of cross-keys; its white color may signify peace; the cross-keys the possession of earth and heaven; and, conjointly, these emblems may intimate that there is to be no peace until the claims of the pope to universal spiritual and temporal sovereignty is acknowledged by all nations. Apollo, the symbol of the rising sun, and Pluto, the symbol of the closing day, are represented with keys in their hands, to denote their office of opening and shutting the gates of day. It is thought by some that the idea of the papal keys was borrowed from these emblems of the Pagan Gods. But it was the custom of a conquered city to present to the victor the keys of its gates, through its officials, in token of the submission of the inhabitants to his authority. In conformity with this ancient custom, it is affirmed by the popes that Pepin, King of France, after he had wrested the Exarcate from the possession of the Lombards, presented the keys of the subjugated cities to the Holy See on the tomb of St. Peter. They assert also, that

Charlemagne presented the pope with a banner, and authorized him to unfurl it in the cause of the church. But if the story of Pepin's gift is as empty as the tomb of St. Peter, at Rome, is and always has been, of the corpse of the apostle; and if Charlemagne's donation of cities, most of which he never pessessed, and the remainder of which he governed as his own with the most jealous scrupulosity until the day of his death, it is difficult to perceive how the popes, by virtue of these gifts, can have any claim to either keys or banners.

The pope, as an independent sovereign, has also a national cabinet. His privy council is the college of cardinals; his minister of internal and foreign affairs is the cardinal secretary; his viceroys are the legates and nuncios which he accredits to foreign powers; his governors and lieutenant-governors are the Catholic bishops and archbishops, which are located in different parts of the world; and his ministers of finance and police are the priests of different grades and orders. The civil offices of the papal monarchy have always been filled by members of the sacerdotal orders, and disposed of by the holy father for money.

As an independent sovereign the pope has an imperial court. In the grades of this court he himself enjoys the first rank, being placed on an equality with God, and in some respects above him. The cardinals stand next to princes; they wear a purple mantle, the emblem of royalty; formerly they ranked in Christendom equal with kings, preceded princes of blood, and sat on the right of kings, or near the throne. The generals of the Catholic orders, the abbots, archbishops, bishops and priests, consider their titles as royal, and maintain that in consideration of them they should be exempted from the jurisdiction of civil magistrates.

As an independent sovereign the pope has the power to issue absolute decrees. The papal bulls, apostolic briefs, and encyclical letters, are the exercise of sovereign power. From the despotic tone of these documents, sometimes moderated by fear, but never from inclination, the pope evidently claims the right of interfering not only in the ecclesiastical, but also in the political affairs of all nations.

As an independent sovereign the pope has a system of jurisprudence and administrative justice. The canonical law by which he governs his monarchy consists of the *Concordantia Discordantium* or *Decretium Gratiani;* the *Decratales Gregorii Noni;* the *Liber Sextus*, by Boniface VIII; the *Extravagantes Johannis XXII;* the *Extravagantes Communes*, and the *Clementinus;* all of which are known under the general name of *Corpus Juris Canonica;* and all except the *Extravagantes* have the full authority of law. The papal system of administrative justice consists of a chief court, a civil court, and an apostolical court. The apostolical court regulates the pope's domains and collects the taxes. The members of the court are always bishops, and the presiding officer is generally a cardinal.

As an independent sovereign the pope has exercised the governmental prerogative of coining money. The papal coins have various devices. They all have the cross-keys; most of them the triple crown; and some of them are inscribed with the word *Dominus*.

As an independent sovereign the pope has always maintained, when possible, an army and a navy. Pope

Clement VIII. elected in 1523, raised an army of regulars and volunteers of thirty thousand foot and three thousand cavalry. Pope Leo IX. commanded an army consisting of Italian volunteers, several bands of robbers, and seven hundred Suabians. Pope Alexander VI. at the head of a powerful army conquered Bologna, Ancona, Ravenna and Ferrara. After the return of the pope to Rome from Avignon, in 1577, a standing army was formed consisting of cavalry and infantry.

The papal military organizations have been of the most formidable description. The Dominican Knights, the Teutonic Knights, the Knights of St. John, and the Knight Templars, instituted for the defence and propagation of Catholicism by the force of arms, were skilfully organized and rigorously disciplined. They assumed the vows of celibacy, poverty and unconditional obedience. They were interdicted, by the terms of their charter, from acknowledging any protector but the pope, and were made independent of any other authority. Upon becoming initiated into their orders, the pope absolved them from all human obligations, and they were required to sunder all human ties. They enjoyed all the immunities and privileges of the religious orders; and in conjunction with them formed a standing army of three hundred thousand men, fully equipped for war, exclusively devoted to the pope's interest, and ready at his call to serve him by land or sea.

As an independent sovereign the pope has a national revenue. This revenue is domestic and foreign. From official reports the pope's domestic revenue, in 1853, amounted to 13,000,000 florins; his foreign revenue is not publicly known. In the dark ages half of the ecclesiastical revenues of Europe flowed into the church treasury at Rome; but at present the various streams of wealth destined for the church, are diverted to convenient localities, situated in different parts of the world, to be disbursed according to regulations prescribed by the holy father. As the subject is somewhat curious, we are tempted to inquire into some of the sources of the papal revenue.

One source of the pope's revenue is the sale of indulgences. St. Peter's Church, at Rome, which cost 45,000,000 crowns, was chiefly built from the proceeds of this species of traffic. William Hogau furnishes some singular facts respecting this ingenious device, by which the church accommodates the wishes of the members in the commission of sin, to her pecuniary advantage. He says:

"They (the pope and the propagandi) resolved that indulgences should, in the future, be called *scapulus*, and thus piously enable all Catholic priests and bishops to swear on the Holy Evangelists that no indulgences were sold in the United States. . . . . The scapula costs the purchaser one dollar. The priest who sells it tells him that in order to make it thoroughly efficacious, it is necessary that he should cause some masses to be said. . . . . I may safely say that, on an average, every scapula sold in the United States costs at least five dollars."—*Synopsis, pp.* 176, 177.

The number of Catholics in the world is computed, by Catholic authority, at 150,000,000. Some of the papal subjects would not, perhaps, purchase a scapula in a year, while others might purchase a hundred; but at the moderate estimate of one scapula annually to each Catholic, the pope would derive from this source an annual revenue of 750,000,000 dollars. The sale of the scapula would, of course, be in proportion to the wickedness of the church members; the more virtuous they were the less would they be necessitated to contribute to the coffers of the church; and as merchants and traders always scheme to create a demand for their goods, it is not reasonable that either the pope or his priests would encourage their Catholic subjects in conduct that would render them of no value to them; and that would injure the sale and lessen the demand of their articles of trade, by which their treasure and luxuries are so much augmented.

Another source of the pope's revenue are the masses which the church requires to be said for the deliverance of the souls of deceased Catholics out of purgatory. These masses were sold before the rebellion at fifty cents a piece; whether they have since risen in value in proportion to other articles, I have not the means of ascertaining. What number of masses are requisite for conjuring a Cotholic layman's soul up from purgatory, I am not informed; but there is a will of a priest recorded in Towsontown, Md.. which bequeaths to a brother priest the sum of one hundred dollars to pay for two hundred masses, " to be said for the benefit of his poor soul." If the church will not release the soul of a priest from purgatory for less than one hundred dollars, how much does she demand of a layman for a similar purpose? It would seem that the sanctity of a priest ought enable her to get him out of the purgatorial fire, and release him from the clutches of the devil for a much less sum of money than would be requisite for the same purpose in the case of an unanointed layman. This traffic in the souls of dead men by the church, has been prosecuted in such an oppressive manner that her members have sometimes been provoked to remonstrate. I once knew of a young Catholic who charged his priest with having forged a will in order to swindle him out of a great portion of his maternal inheritance. The pretext on which this pious fraud was attempted to be based was a plea that the mother of the youth had bequeathed to the priest a house of hers, in payment of a sufficient number of masses for the release of her soul from purgatory. The annual revenue derived by the pope for his service in opening the gates of purgatory to the devout must be prodigious; but the secrecy with which it is veiled renders a reliable computation exceedingly difficult. If we consider the number of Catholics that are in the world, and the probable annual number of deaths that occur among them, and calculate the sum of money which would be necessary to deliver the average number that die yearly out of the flames of purgatory, we may form some conception of the vastness of this resource of papal revenue. Wars, pestilence, bereavements of friends, which are calamities to families and nations, are pecuniary advantages to the church; and in proportion to the mortality of her members, she has cause to rejoice over the improvement of her finances.

Another source of the pope's revenue are the proceeds derived from the sale of crosses, amulets, relics, pictures, beads, and articles made by monks and nuns. These articles of pious merchandise are blest by the bishop, and sold sometimes privately, and sometimes at Catholic fairs. They are supposed by the purchaser to insure him good luck, and to keep evil from his dwelling; and although they are often an unsightly set of trumpery; yet as they are consecrated by the bishop's blessing, which, however, rather depreciates their intrinsic value, they are prized by the cajoled Catholics as exceeding in value either gold or gems. We have no data enabling us to calculate the amount of revenue derived by the pope from this source of income; but we may be allowed to conclude from the fact that, as the church has availed herself of its advantages in all countries and ages, it has proved exceedingly remunerative.

Another source of the papal revenue are the contributions extorted from laborers, female servants, and others of the industrial classes. I know of a servant girl who paid one dollar every autumn towards furnishing the church with winter fuel. What fuel costs the church, I do not know; perhaps little or nothing. The number of Catholics in the United States are computed by Catholic authority to amount to 10,000,0000; and if each one contributes one dollar annually for the benefit he derives from the church furnaces, (and I am credibly informed he does), the pope receives from this source an annual income of 10,000,000 dollars. But this is not the only method by which the laboring classes are filched out of their honest gains by the holy mother. On the regular monthly pay-day of contractors for public works, and of mining, manufacturing and mechanical companies, the priest makes his appearance, and exacts a dollar a month from each of the faithful.

If there are non-Catholics among the employes, who hesitate to contribute the monthly donation, they are insulted, intimidated, and their life threatened to such a degree that they consider it prudent to yield to the demand, or seek employment elsewhere. This system of extortion is engineered among the workmen by some favorite of the Catholic priest, who makes it his business to see that he is not disappointed in getting his dollar a month. An engineer of this description, employed on the Baltimore and Ohio railroad, in his avidity to accommodate the priesthood narrowly escaped being victimized by a secular sharper. A stranger, professing to be a Catholic priest, solicited in behalf of his necessities, his charity and influence. Promptly heading a subscription list with the generous sum of two dollars and fifty cents, he was soon enabled to exult in the subscription of a very respectable amount by his fellow workmen. The list was, in accordance with usage, handed to the cashier of the establishment; but before any money was paid on its account it was discovered that the priest was a spurious one, and that the money he solicited was not intended for the treasury of the pope, but for the pocket of an unconsecrated impostor. Catholic periodicals, with commendable regard to their patrons' interest, have frequently published instances in which pretended priests and monks have successfully gulled the faithful. When we consider the vast proportion of poor to rich Catholics in the world, it seems evident that this branch of the pope's financial machinery, by which he wins a dollar a month from each of the industrial classes of the Catholic church, must furnish his coffers with an annual revenue exceeding that of any other government.

Another source of the pope's revenue are alms collected by an order of lay mendicants. The church, instructed by the practice of mendication among all nations and classes, at all periods of history, and under all circumstances, has been enabled to perfect a system of extraordinary comprehensiveness, sharpness and efficiency. Organ grinders, bead counters, children, mothers with babes in their arms, men without legs, the blind, the deaf, the cripple, any object that can touch the tender or religious sympathies of the community, are employed as beggars for the pope of Rome. This description of medicants sometimes openly solicit alms for the holy father, but at other times endeavor to conceal their mission under a mask of profound dissimulation. The eloquence of broken noses, distorted forms, mutilated limbs, and tattered garments, are made to plead with touching pathos in behalf of the papal monarch. The revenue which he derives from his numerous crowd of professional beggars, is one of the secrets of the Holy See; but from the liberality with which Catholics respond, from a sense of religious duty, and Protestants from prudential motives, it may reasonably be presumed that it is not inconsiderable.

Another source of the pope's revenue is derived from his foreign possessions. These possessions consist of churches, monasteries, nunneries, mission houses, edifices for schools, colleges, hospitals, asylums, private dwellings, tracts of land, and every other species of property. The papal foreign property is sometimes held in the name of the pope, sometimes in that of a priest, and sometimes in that of a corporation, real or pretended. Every priest coming to the United States, in order that he may legally be qualified to hold property for the benefit of the church, is required to take the oath of allegiance, whether he considers it consistent or not with his ordination oath. (See Hogan's Synopsis, p. 36). In 1822 the pope claiming to be the proprietor of St. Mary's Church at Philadelphia, leased it to a foreign priest, and sent him over to take charge of it. The trustees, and William Hogan, the recognized encumbent, refusing to obey the order of the pope's agents, a suit of ejectment was brought against them in the Supreme Court of Pensylvania. Judge Tilghman presided at the trial. He decided that the pope could legally hold no property in the United States, and sustained the action of the defendants. (See Hogan's Synopsis, pp. 113, 114). In a suit brought by the brothers of the order of Hermits of St. Augustine, against the county of Philadelphia, for the destruction of St. Augustine's Church by a mob of the American party, it was discovered that the alleged corporation was entirely spurious. The pretended corporators consisted of Micheal Hurly, pastor of St. Augustine's Church at Philadelphia, Prince Gallager, pastor at Bedford, Pa., Lewis de Barth, pastor of St. Mary's Church at Philadelphia, Patrick Henry, pastor at Coffee Run, Chester County, Pa., and J. B. Holland, pastor at Lancaster, Pa. So profoundly secret was the existence of this company kept, that no laymen or priest outside of the pretended corporators had ever heard of it before the trial, and as the public documents contained no enrolment of it in accordance with the requirement of law, it was pronounced entirely spurious and invalid. The value of the property held in the name of this pretended corporation, in evasion of the laws of the United States, was computed at 5,000,000 dollars. Even in cities where the Catholic population is deemed numerically insignificant, millions worth of property of which the inhabitants have not the slightest conception, is owned by the pope, under cover of fictitious names or otherwise. (See Hogan's Auric. Confess., vol. 2, p. 204, &c). Whenever the church has obtained sufficient power she has made a bequest to the coffers of the church a condition to the validity of a will; and where she has failed to acquire this power, she has still exacted a compliance with it from her members, under pain of her penalties. Splendid palaces and gorgeous church edifices alone are not adequate to satisfy the cravings of her avarice, she must have lands and every species of wealth. Wherever her priests have effected a pious entering wedge in a block of buildings, by means of a church or an asylum, they must scheme to work out the other proprietors, and monopolize the whole themselves. Their covetous eye is always fixed on some magnificent farm, and their active speculation, or deeper craft, has enabled them to become in possession of very desirable tracts of land. I know of a priest who netted ten thousand dollars by a single land speculation. The priests, by means of the confessional, become accurately acquainted with all secrets, with every contemplative movement in the general or State government, or in financial corporations, that can effect the market value of lands or stocks; and it would be exceedingly astonishing if, with this advantage, their speculations should not invariably be successful. In possession of such means, the church has in every age accumulated prodigious wealth. Before the secularization of the monastic property in Europe, the ecclesiastical domains and revenues were so great that the benefices were bestowed by kings on royal heirs. In California and Mexico, previous to the revolution that caused the sequestration of the church domains, her mission-houses owned nearly all the territory of the State. In China, even at this day, there are three bishoprics endowed by the crown of Portugal, which hold seven provinces; and the bishops of the Apostolic Vicars hold several others. The possessions of the Catholic priests render them the wealthiest citizens of the country in which they reside; and as no heir can inherit their estates, each succeeding generation is destined to see them augmented until every bishopric, however poor now, has become a princely domain, with a princely revenue, governed by a titled priest.

Every Catholic edifice in the world, and every description of property held by a priest, belongs to the pope; the real title, as lord paramount, being vested in him, whatever ostensible title policy or necessity may have induced the church to adopt. Over these possessions he exercises supreme, despotic dominion, sometimes directly, and sometimes indirectly.

We have now enumerated some of the sources of the pope's revenue; but we have mentioned but a few of them. In fact the rites of the Catholic church partake so plainly of a financial character, that they seem to have been instituted for purposes of ecclesiastical revenue. With a fiscal system principally based on them, extending over Christendom, rigorous in its exactions on all classes, the church unites a rapacity so unprincipled, measures so oppressive and unjustifiable, deeds so horrible and arrogations so presumptuous, that were it not for her religious aspect she might be mistaken for the demon of avarice. While rolling in opulence and luxury, she stoops to the basest trickery to filch from laborers and servant girls their wages; to disinherit lawful heirs; taking advantage of ignorance and superstition, and pretending to regulate the condition of the soul in the eternal world. The immense sum of gold which she has, by means of her fiscal system, been piling up in her coffers for ages, has had no visible outlet except what has been expended in the support of her officials, and on bribery, corruption, and political intrigue. The policy that dictates the accumulation and reservation of this vast amount of treasure, must contemplate the undertaking of some gigantic enterprise; and the world may yet be startled from its slumber by the martial assertion of the church to her pretensions of supreme dominion over the world; and by the fact that she is better organized for war, and better furnished with its sinews than any other power.

As an independent sovereign the pope has oaths of allegiance which he prescribes to such of his subjects as he judges proper. According to the authority of William Hogan, the consecration oath of the Jesuistical bishops is as follows:

"Therefore, to the utmost of my power I shall and
"will defend this doctrine, and his holiness's rights and
"customs against all usurpers, and heretical and Pro-
"testant authority whatsoever; especially against the
"new pretended authority of the Church of England,

"and all adherents, in regard that they and she be
"usurpal and heretical, opposing the true mother church
"of Rome. I do renounce and disown my allegiance
"as due to any heretical king, prince, or State named
"Protestant, or of obedience to any of their inferior
"magistrates or officers. I do further declare the doc-
"trine of the Church of England, and of Calvinists,
"Huguenots, and of the other named Potestants to be
"damnable, and they themselves are damned, and to be
"damned, that will not forsake them. I do further de-
"clare that I will help, assist, advise all wherever I
"shall be, in England, Scotland, Ireland, or in any
"other kingdom I shall come to, and do my best to ex-
"tirpate the heretical Protestant doctrines, and destroy
"all their pretending powers, regal or otherwise. I
"do further promise and declare, that notwithstanding
"I am dispensed with, to assume any other religion
"heretical for the propagation of the mother church's
"interest, to keep secret and private all her agent's
"councils from time to time, as they entrust me, and
"not to divulge, directly or indirectly, by word, writ-
"ing, or circumstance whatever, but to execute all
"that shall be proposed, given in charge, or discovered
"unto me, by you my ghostly father, or by any of his
"sacred convents. All which I, A. B. do swear by the
"blessed Trinity, and blessed Sacraments which I am
"now to receive, to perform, and on my part to keep
"inviolably, and do call all the heavenly and glorious
"hosts to witness these my real intentions to keep this
"my oath."

The consecration oath of a Catholic bishop is as follows:

"I do solemnly swear on the Holy Evangelists, and
"before Almighty God, to defend the domains of St.
"Peter against every aggressor; to preserve, augment
"and extend the rights, honors, and privileges of the
"Lord Pope and his successors; to observe, and with all

"my might to enforce his decrees, ordinances, reserva-
"tions, provisions, and all dispositions whatsoever;
"to persecute and combat, to the last extremity
"heretics and schismatics, and all who will not pay
"the sovereign Pope all the obedience which he shall
"require."

The remainder of this oath is similar to the foregoing Jesuistical oath.

The priests of Maynooth, who form the vast majority of Catholic priests in this country, assume the following obligation to the church:

"I, A. B., do declare not to act or conduct any mat-
"ter or thing prejudicial to her, in her sacred orders,
"doctrines, tenets, or commands, without leave of its
"supreme power, or its authority under her appoint-
"ment; being so permitted, then to act, and further
"her interests, more than my own earthly good and
"earthly pleasures; as she and her head, His Holiness
"and his successors, have, or ought to have, the su-
"premacy over all kings, princes, estates, or powers
"whatsoever, either to deprive them of their crowns,
"or governments, or to set up others in lieu thereof,
"they dissenting from the mother church and her com-
"mands."

It is said that by rescript of Pope Pius VII., in 1818, the clause relating to "heretics" in the bishop's oath, is omitted by the bishops subject to the British crown. It is also omitted in the following oath, published by the Nashville *American Union*, April 6, 1856:

"I, N., elect of the church N., shall be from this
"hour henceforward obedient to Blessed Peter the
"Apostle, and to the holy Roman Catholic Church, and
"to the most blessed father Pope N., and to his succes-
"sors canonically chosen. I shall assist them to retain
"and defend, against any man whatever, the Roman

"Popedom, without prejudice to my rank; and shall take care to preserve, defend and promote the rights, honors, privileges, and authority of the holy Roman Church, of the Pope, and his successors aforesaid. With my whole strength I shall observe, and cause to be observed by others, the rules of the Holy Fathers, the decrees, ordinances, or dispositions and mandates of the Apostolic See."

The next clause declares the willingness of the bishop to attend synods, give an account to the pope of every thing appertaining to the church and his flock, and obey such apostolic mandate as he shall receive. The oath concludes thus:

"I shall not sell, nor give away, nor mortgage, enfeoff anew, nor in any way alienate the possessions belonging to my table, without the leave of the Roman Pontiff. And should I proceed to any alienation of them, I am willing to contract, by the very fact, the penalties specified in the constitutions published on this subject."

The Sanfideste's oath, exacted by Pope Gregory of his military forces, was as follows:

"I swear to elevate the altar and the throne upon the infamous Liberals, and to exterminate them without pity for the cries of their children, or the tears of their old men."

William Hogan, speaking of the instructions given him previous to his embarkation for America, by his bishop, describes it as follows:

"Let it be your first duty to extirpate heretics, but be cautious as to the manner of doing it. Do nothing without consulting the bishop of the diocese in which you may be located, and if there be no bishop there, advise with the metropolitan bishop. He has instructions from Rome, and he understands the character of the people. Be sure not to permit the members of the holy church who may be under your charge to read the Bible. It is the source of all heresy. Wherever you see an opportunity of building a church, make it known to your bishop. Let the land be purchased for the Pope, and his successors in office. Never yield or give up the divine right which the head of the church has, by virtue of the keys, to the command of North America, as well as every other country. The confessional will enable you to know the people by degrees; with the aid of that holy tribunal, and the bishops, who are guided by the spirit of God, we may expect at no distant day, to bring over North America to our holy church."—*Synopsis, pp.* 110, 111.

The atrocious doctrine that it is proper to equivocate, to dissimulate, and to deceive by mental reservations, is boldly defended by the highest authorities of the Catholic church. Dens says: "Notwithstanding it is not lawful to lie, or to feign what is not, however, it is lawful to dissemble what is, or to cover the truth with words, or other ambiguous or doubtful signs, for a just cause, and when there is not a necessity of confessing."—(Theol., vol. 2, p. 116). Again, he says: "The Vicar of God, in the place of God, remits to man the debt of a plighted promise."—(*Ib.*, 4: 134, 135). St. Liqnori says: "It is certain, and a common opinion among all divines, that for a just cause it is lawful to use equivocation, and to confirm it with an oath."—(Less. 1, 2, ch. 41, n. 47).

The obligation of all oaths of allegiance in conflict with the papal clerical oaths, or the interests of the pope, are declared by the universal authority of the church to be null and void. Dens says: "All the faithful, also bishops and patriarchs, are bound to obey the Roman pontiff. The pope hath also not only directive, but coactive power over the faithful."—(De Eccles. No. 94, p. 439). Pope Urban, elected in 1087, says: "Subjects are not bound to observe the fealty which they swear to a Christian prince, who withstands God and the saints, and condemns the precepts."—(Pithon, p. 260). Pope Gregory IX says: "The fealty which subjects have sworn to a Christian king, who opposes God and his saints, they are not bound by any authority to perform."—Decret., vol. 1, p. 648). Again he says: "An oath contrary to the utility of the church is not to be observed."—Vol. 2, p. 358.) And again he asserts: "You are not bound by an oath of this kind, but on the contrary you are freely bid Good-speed in standing against kings for the rights and honors of that very church, and even in legislatively defending your own peculiar privileges."—Vol. 2., p. 360). Bronson, speaking of the church says: "As the guardian and judge of law she must have power to take cognizance of the State, and to judge whether or not it does conform to the condition and requirement of its trust, and to pronounce sentence accordingly."—(Rev. Jan. 1854). Pope Pius V., in relation to Queen Elizabeth, said: "We do declare her to be deprived of her pretended right to the kingdom, and of all dominion whatsoever; and also the subjects sworn to her to be forever dissolved from any such oath." Pope Innocent III., elected in 1198, "Freed all that were bound to those who had fallen into heresy, from all fealty, homage, and obedience."—(Pithon, p. 241). Bronson says: "Rome divided her British territory into dioceses, and sends cardinals to London, notwithstanding the laws that England shall not thus be divided."—Rev., April, 1854). The trustees of the church of St. Louis, at Buffalo, N. Y., having refused to comply with the canons of the Council of Trent in violating the trust laws of the State of New York, the bishop proceeded to excommunicate them. In consequence of this conduct, the legislature of 1855 passed an act defining ecclesiastical tenure. In a letter of Bishop Hughes, dated March 28th, 1855, and published in the *Freeman's Journal*, respecting this law, he says : " Now in this it seems to meddle with our religion, as well as our civil rights; and we shall find twenty ways outside the intricate web of its prohibitions for doing, and doing more largely still, the very thing it wishes us not to do."

A curious and very objectionable feature of the papal monarchy is, a system of searching espionage which it attempts to establish over society. In addition to the confessors and spiritual guides by which the pope seeks to discover the thoughts, and direct the conduct of his Catholic subjects, he employs a set of men and women who, in the capacity of servants scrutinize the domestic affairs of non-Catholics, mark their conversation, and communicate all important facts through their superior, to him at Rome. As an illustration of the disrespectful inquisitiveness, and base incivility of this department of the papal government, we submit the following facts furnished by William Hogan :

" Soon after my arrival in Philadelphia," says he, " I became acqainted with a Protestant family. I had the pleasure of dining occasionally with them, and could not help noticing a seemingly delicate young man, who waited at the table. . . . . Not long after this a messenger called at my room to say that Theodore was taken ill, and wished to see me. I was then officiating as a Romish priest, and calling to see him was shown up stairs to a garret room, into which, after a loud rap, and announcement of my name, I was admitted. . . . . He deliberately turned out of his bed, locked the door, and very respectfully handed me a chair, and asked me to sit down as he had something very important to tell me. . . . . 'Sir, you have taken me for a young man, but you are mistaken; I am a girl, but not so young as I appeared in my boy's dress. I sent for you because I want to get a character, and confess to you before I leave the city.' I answered, 'You must explain yourself more fully before you can do either.' I moved my chair farther from the bed, and tightened my grasp on a sword-cane which I carried in my hand. 'Feel no alarm,' said the now young woman, 'I am armed as well as you are,' taking from under her jacket an elegant poignard. 'I will not hurt you. I am a lay sister belonging to the order of Jesuists in Stonyhurst, England, and wear this dagger to protect myself. There was no longer any mystery in the matter. I knew now where I was, and the character of the being that stood before me. I discovered from her that she had arrived in New Orleans some time previous, with all due recommendation to the priests and nuns of that city. . . . . They received her with all due caution as far as could be seen by the public; but privately in the warmest manner. Jesuists are active and diligent in the discharge of duties to their superiors., and of course this lay sister, who was chosen from among many for her zeal and craft, lost no time in entering on her mission. The Sisters of Charity took immediate charge of her, recommended her as a chambermaid to one of the most respectable Protestant families in that city, and having clothed her in an appropriate dress, she entered on her employment. . . . . So great a favorite did she become in the family, that in a short time she became acquainted with all the circumstances and secrets, from those of the father to those of the smallest child.

"According to the custom universally in vogue, she kept notes of every circumstance which may tend to elucidate the character of the family, never carrying them about her, but depositing them with the mother abbess especially deputed to take charge of them. . . . . Thus did this lay sister continue to go from place to place, from family to family, until she became better acquainted with the politics, the pecuniary means, religious opinions, and whether favorable or not to the propagation of popery in this country, than even the very individuls with whom she associated. . . . . This lay sistr, this excellent chambermaid, or lay Jesuist sister, wished to come North to a better climate. . . . . . Americans can be gulled. The *Sisters of Charity* have always in readiness some friend to supply them with the means of performing *corporeal acts of mercy*. This friend went around to the American families where this chambermaid had lived from time to time, told them she wanted to come as far as Baltimore, that it was a pity to have her travel as a steerage passenger; a person of her virtue and correct deportment should not be placed in a situation where she might be liable to insult and rude treatment. . . . . A handsome purse was soon made up, a cabin passage was engaged, and the young ladies on whom she waited made her presents of every article of dress necessary for her comfort and convenience. She was the depository of all their love stories; she knew the names of their lovers, . . . and if there were secrets among them they were known to her; and, having made herself acquainted with the secrets of New Orleans, she arrived in Baltimore. . . . She took possession of a place as soon as convenient, and spent several months in that city. . . . Having now become acquainted with the secret circumstances of almost every Protestant family of note in Baltimore, and made her report to the mother abbess of the nunnery of her order in that city, she returned to the District of Columbia, and after advising with the mother abbess of the convent, she determined to change her apparent character and apparel.

"By advice of this venerable lady and holy prioress, on whom many of the wives of our national representatives, and even grave senators, looked as an example of piety and chastity, she cut her hair, dressed her in a smart looking waiter's jacket and trowsers, and with the best recommendations for intelligence and capacity, applied for a situation as Waiter in Gadsby's Hotel, in Washington city. This smart and tidy looking young man got instant employment. . . . . Those senators on whom he waited, not suspecting that he had the ordinary curiosity of servants in general, were entirely thrown off their guard, and in their conversations with one another seemed to forget their usual caution. Such, in short, was their confidence in him, that their most important papers and letters were left loose upon the table, satisfied by saying, as they went out: 'Theodore, take care of my room and papers.' . . . . Now it was known whether Henry Clay was a gambler; whether Daniel Webster was a libertine; whether John C. Calhoun was an honest but credulous man. . . . . In fact this lay sister in male uniform, but a waiter in Gadsby's Hotel, was enabled to give more correct information of the actual state of things in this country, through the general of the Jesuist order in Rome, than the whole corpse of diplomats from foreign countries then residing at our seat of government. . . . . 'I want a written character from you. You must state in it that I have complied with my duty, and as it is necessary that I should wear a cap for a while, you must say that you visited me in my sick room, that I confessed to you, received the *viaticum*, and had just recovered from a violent fever. My business is not done yet. I must go to New York, where the Sisters of Charity will find a place for me as a waiting maid."—*Auricular Confession, volume* 2: *pp.* 99-108.

Through the instrumentality of this execrable system of espionage, the pope becomes acquainted with the character, intentions, and acts of every important private and public personage; with the nature and object of every secret society; with the private intentions of every government; with the incipiency and progress of every seditious and treasonable project; and is prepared at all times, by the accuracy and comprehensiveness of his information, to instruct his generals in the actual state of affairs existing in any part of the world, and to direct their conduct in the advancement of his interest, by the most prudent and enlightened council.

THE PAPAL MONARCHY.

SECTION TWO.

The Pope's Direct Authority—His Opposition to Marriage— To Slavery—His Claim to Temporal Power on the forged Decretal Letter of Constantine—On the Fictitious Gift of Pepin—On the Pretended Donation of Charlemagne—on the Disputed Bequest of Matilda, Duchess of Tuscany—The Title of Pope a Usurpation—The Papal Artful Policy—The State of Italy under the Papal Government.

WE have now sketched the pope's temporal monarchy, which has its seat in Rome, and its subjects in every part of the world. He claims to be invested by divine right with supreme sovereignty over earth, heaven and hell. To question the legitimacy of this claim is condemned, and has been punished as blasphemous by his authority. Joseph Wolf, of Halle, a Jew who had been converted to the Catholic faith, was, while studying divinity at the *Seminarium Romanum*, imprisoned for blasphemy for having expressed a doubt of the pope's infallibility. Fra Paola, who had expressed in a private letter that so far from coveting the dignities of Rome he held them in abomination, and who had advocated liberty in a dispute which had occurred between the pope and the Venitian government, was summoned to Rome to answer for his criminal assertions and conduct; and though acquitted of the allegations preferred against him, narrowly escaped the assassin's dagger

But the "More than God," the Pope, is a very jealous "more than God." He allows no master to stand between him and his subjects. His authority over mind and body must be direct, and all influences or institutions that obstruct it must be annihilated. Hence Cardinal Ballarmine, the distinguished papal controvesialist, who was so devout a Catholic that when he died he bequeathed one half of his soul to Jesus Christ and the other half to the Virgin Mary, provoked the censure of the holy father by asserting in a publication that the pope's influence in temporal matters was not direct but indirect. As husbands obstruct the direct influence of popes on wives, parents on children, and friends on friends, he would nullify the conjugal, parental, filial and social relations. Hence in a canon of the Council of Trent, he pronounces a curse on all who say that marriage is preferable to celibacy. Should the prompting of the social instincts be too strong to be repressed by the terrors of canonical anathemas, and should they in natural indifference to them still create the bonds, connections, and institutions of friendship and families, he has a clerical machinery skilfully adapted to moderate their influences and reciprocities, and to maintain the predominence of his direct authority. Michelet, the philosophical historian and celebrated controversialist, in a work entitled "Priests, Women and Children," has explained the ingenious method by which this object is effected. By separating as much as possible the husband from the wife, and the children from their parents, the direct papal influence, through the priest, is exerted on the isolated husband abroad, on the lonely wife at home, and the defenceless children in nunnery schools and Catholic asylums. Examples of a similar policy are portrayed by Eugene Sue, a Catholic, in his "Wandering Jew." The logical consequence of the dogma of the pope's direct authority has, in fact, made the Catholic church a "free love" institution. Chastity and marriage she tolerates because she cannot do otherwise; but in the lives of her monks, her priests, her popes, and her saints, she as practically ignores as she consistently hates them.

The jealous claim of the pope to a direct influence on the mind of his subjects, has unavoidably made the church an inveterate enemy of human slavery. The pope hates slavery, not because he wishes men free, but because he wishes to exercise a direct authority over their minds. The master nullifies the pope's influence on the slave, and therefore he wishes him removed. No influence is equal to that of a master. The whip he holds over the back of his slave, and the power he has over his life, annihilates all other influences. Hence the Catholic church has always been opposed to slavery. Guizot remarks, respecting feudal slavery: "It cannot be denied, however, that the church has used its influence to restrain it; the clergy in general, and especially several popes, enforced the manumission of slaves as a duty incumbent on laymen, and loudly enveighed against keeping Christians in bondage."—(Gen. Hist., Lect. VI., p. 132). Pope Pius II., in 1462, in a letter addressed to the bishops of Rubi; Pope Paul III., in 1537, in his apostolic letter to the cardinal bishops of Toledo; Pope Urban VII., in 1590, in an apostolic letter

18*

to the Collector Jurium of the apostolic churches of Portugal; Pope Benedict XIV., in 1731, in his apostolic letter to the clergy of Brazil; and Pope Pius VII., in his official address to his clergy, all denounced the traffic in blacks, and demanded that every species of slavery should cease among Christians. Pope Gregory, in his apostolic letter of 1839 says: "We, then, by virtue of our apostolic authority, censure all the aforesaid practices as unworthy the Christian name, and by that same authority we strictly prohibit and interdict any ecclesiastic or layman from presuming to uphold, under any pretext or color whatever, that same traffic in blacks, as if it were lawful in its nature, or otherwise to preach, or in any way whatever publicly or privately to teach in opposition to these things which we have made the subject of our admonition in this our apostolic letter." We are aware that African slavery owes its origin to a Catholic priest, who, perceiving that the demand for laborers in the West India was likely to subject the Indians to bondage, suggested as a less wrong that negroes should be purchased of the Portuguese settlements in Africa, and held as slaves for life; but whatever were his private opinions respecting the propriety of African slavery, his church has never recognized it as legal.

The perversion of public opinion by the Catholic church, and the practical beguilement of her warmest friends, effected by the consummate craft with which she plots to achieve her objects, have presented fresh evidence to the world in the singular fact, that while she is radically the most efficient abolition society that ever was projected, and that while in her official mandates to the clergy she has invariably denounced the traffic in human beings as infamous, yet has she commanded the homage of the American slave-holder for her friendly disposition towards the Southern institution; and induced her members, while using them as instruments in the accomplishment of her projects for the abolishment of slavery, to hate, denounce, and to anathematize the North for its abolition proclivities.

But there were other considerations which probably stimulated the humanity of the church in her labors for the abolition of slavery. The condition of the slave precludes the possibility of his serving her in the capacity of a spy on the opinions and conduct of his master; and as he received no wages she could not assess him for her benefit. The perfection of the pope's system of espionage, and the augmentation of his revenue, were both connected with the slave's disenthralment. These advantages could not be undesirable to the church, and the avidity with which she has improved them, shows how clearly she foresaw them. Through accident or Jesuistical craft, it has happened, that colored servants have been supplanted to an incredible extent by white Catholic servants, who as serviceable spies far excel them. I regret not the abolishment of the revolting traffic in human beings, nor do I censure the Catholic church for the important aid she rendered in its achievement; but I hope American freemen will not want the vigilance to prevent her from improving the new condition of things, so much to her advantage as to endanger the liberty of the country.

But the "Lord God, the Pope," who claims by divine right to be lord paramount of the world, has unwarily invalidated his title even to the "patrimony of St. Peter," by an attempt to establish it by forged decretal letters. Forgeries are criminal acts, and punished by all nations as high misdemeanors. They are prejudicial to the ground of action of a claimant, and as evident proof of an intent to swindle, as they are of a base and contemptible origin. When successful, they may overhang the mind for a while, as clouds in a dead still atmosphere do the earth; but at the slightest breeze they are dissipated, and the superstructure based upon them, though gorgeous as the setting sun, will, like its areal enchantment, break up and dissolve away. Yet of such base and flimsy material are the pope's claim to temporal power constructed. Innumerable bulls, decretals, receipts, briefs, canons, letters, interdicts, and other documents, have been forged, altered and interpolated by the holy brotherhood, to furnish a legal basis for the pope's temporal power. These documents were prepared between the third and ninth centuries, and carefully treasured up in the papal archives, ready for use as occasion might require. One of the boldest of these pious forgeries is the decretal letter attributed to Constantine the Great, forged probably by Benedict of Mentz, in the ninth century. It reads as follows:

"We attribute to the Chair of St. Peter all imperial dignity, and power and glory. We give to Pope Sylvester, and to his successors, our palace of Lateran, one of the finest in the world; we give to him our crown, our mitre, our diadem, all our imperial vestments. We give to the Holy Pontiff as a free gift the city of Rome, and all the cities of Western Italy, as well as all the cities of other countries. To make room for him we abdicate our authority over these provinces, transferring the seat of our empire to Byzantium, since it is not just that a temporal emperor shall retain any power where God has set the head of his church."

The reason assigned for the bestowal of this magnificent donation was gratitude on the part of Constantine, for having been cured of leprosy through the administration of the rite of baptism at the hands of Pope Sylvester. But it is historically established that Constantine did not receive the rite of baptism until a late hour in his last sickness; that when he did receive it, it did not cure his malady; and that the rite was administered, not by the Pope of Rome, but by an Arian bishop. Whatever donations of crowns, kingdoms and cities were bestowed on the bishop who officiated on the occasion, were unquestionably granted to a heretical sectary; and if Rome does not wish to confess herself an Arian, she cannot consistently claim their gifts. But even had the case been otherwise, how could Constantine bestow on the pope all the cities of Western Italy, and of all other countries, when he did not possess them himself? As the gift of a donor is worthless unless he has an actual right in what he bestows, the pretensions of the pope on the ground of Constantine's gift, are an actual nullification of all his claims to temporal sovereignty. It is generally conceded that Constantine allowed the pope the use of some buildings in Rome; but it is denied that he ever invested him with a title to them as lord paramount. This limited indulgence was the pope's precedent for holding real estate, and formed the basis of his claim to all the crowns and kingdoms of the world. But like the rapacious dog, who, with his mouth full of meat, lost all he had by snapping at the shadow of more in a river, the pope, by attempting through forged documents to grasp at all the world, has lost his title to any part of it.

Although the decretal letter attributed to Constantine was palpably spurious, yet such was the general ignorance of the times, the respect for the sanctity and infallibility of the pope, and the danger of provoking the wrath of the inquisition by questioning a dogma of the church, that its validity was not called into question. At length, however, in a legal proceedings of a monastery at Sabine, its fraudulent character was attempted to be substantiated. The bold criticisms of Laurentius Valla, in the fifteenth century, gave the first decisive blow to its credibility, and in the succeeding age it sunk into public contempt, beneath the scorn of historians, the ridicule of poets, and the concessions of theologians. But notwithstanding its universally acknowledged spurious character, such is the reluctance of the popes to yield a point, that it still continues to remain a portion of the canon law of the holy Catholic church.

The alleged gift of Pepin to the Roman See forms another pretext by which the popes have endeavored to lay a basis for their claim to the right of temporal sovereignty. Pope Gregory excited a rebellion against the authority of the Emperor Leo III., in the course of which the Italian Exarcate was dismembered from the empire. It was decided by the victors that the government should be administered by two Consuls, in which the pope should participate, not in a secular, but in a paternal capacity. For a monarch claiming the world as a just inheritance, and all princes and governors as his menials, to accept such a humble concession to his unlimited authority, and such an ambiguous office, is the most remarkable instance on record of a monarchial condescension. He, however, not only accepted it, but what is still more surprising, accepted it with eagerness and gratitude; and even intrigued to obtain it. But during the administration of Pope Stephen II. the victorious sword of the Lombards wrung the Exercate from the Consular government of Rome. The pope, to retrieve his fortunes applied to Pepin, Mayor of France, who, responding with an adequate force, reconquered the Exercate, and expelled the barbarians. Grateful for the martial services of Pepin, the pope solicited of the civil authority the privilege of appointing him Patriarch of Rome, a title which was borne by the former Exarchs; and by this innocent method initiated a precedent which soon ripened into a prerogative of appointing civil magistrates. Having thus advanced the interests of the Holy See by complimenting its deliverer, he next ventured to anoint his head with oil, in hopes that in thus imitating the example of Samuel in anointing kings, future popes might have a pretext for usurping his prerogatives in acknowledging their right to reign. Pepin, who ruled france under the title of Mayor, wished to imprison the heir to the throne and usurp the government, and the pope gave him his opinion that it was best for him to do so. In grateful consideration of these extraordinary favors, it is alleged by the popes that Pepin bestowed the conquered domains, consisting of the Exercate and the Pentopolis (five cities) on the

See of Rome, as supreme absolute lord. It is, nevertheless, certain, that Pepin's donations to the Holy See were on condition of its vassalage to the Frankish power, and that during his life he exercised absolute sovereignty over Rome, and over all his conquests, and allowed no pope to be either elected or consecrated without his permission.

The right of the monarch of the world to temporal power, which was first founded upon the usurpation of Constantine, and next upon the conquests of Pepin, was annihilated by the conquests of the Lombards. Desiderious, their king, wrested the Exercate from Rome; and wishing to subjugate Charlemagne under his authority, proposed to Pope Adrian I. that he should excite the subjects of that prince to rebellion, declare him a usurper, and crown his nephews in his place. Adrian listened to these overtures with seeming friendship, but with malignant delight, and secretly communicating their substance to Charlemagne, the sword of the latter was immediately drawn in behalf of the church; the pope revenged; Desiderius imprisoned for life in a monastery; and all Italy, except the Duchy of Benevento and the lower Italian republics, were reconquered. Upon this signal success of his arms, it is alleged by the popes that the blood-stained warrior, to purchase masses for the benefit of his soul, confirmed the Holy See in the absolute possession of the former grants of Pepin. The only copy ever known of these pretended donations is one received by Cancio, the pope's chamberlain, in the twelfth century. The undeniable historical fact that Charlemagne asserted, and maintained during his whole life, a jealous and inalianable right to Rome, and to every other portion of his dominions, casts a dark shade of suspicion upon the genuineness of these documents. Even were they authenticated, yet as the right of a monarch to annul is equal to his right to grant, and as his practice is the evidence of what he surrenders or annuls, the exclusive sovereignty which Charlemagne maintained over his Italian conquests, until the day of his death, is a complete nullification of any grant that he had made to the pope, and positive proof that any right or title to Rome, or to temporal power, constructed upon them by the holy fathers, is as invalid, futile and ludicrous, as if they were based on a grant from the man in the moon; in whose place of abode a traveller, according to Ariosto, once found some of the lost documents upon which the popes base their claim to temporal dominion.

Besides these laborious but ineffectual efforts to fabricate historical data in support of the papal pretension to temporal sovereignty, Gregory VII., in 1075 asserted that Matilda, Duchess of Tuscany, had bequeathed to the church her domains. These possessions consisted of Tuscany, a part of Umbria, a part of Mark Ancona, and the Duchies of Spoleto and Verona. The validity of these bequests was disputed by the natural heirs; the contest lasted three hundred years, during which Italy was distracted, and Germany depopulated. Frederic I., in vindication of his claims against the pretensions of the pope, invaded Italy on three different occasions. Henry IV. emperor of Germany, thrice crossed the Alps to chastise the popes for aggressions on the Germanic possessions in Italy. During the first campaign pope Paschal was made a prisoner; but on the approach of the imperial army a second time he fled from Rome. Yet amid the disputes of the Germanic succession, and during the minority of Frederic II., the arms and intrigues of the pope won the concession of Europe to his claim of Matilda's estates.

The spurious character of the pope's title to temporal power has been exposed by the ablest Catholic authors, and rejected with impatient contempt by history. But the arguments which have converted a world, have never been able to convert the popes. They still maintain that the reputed donations of Constantine, of Pepin, of Charlemagne and of Matilda, are real and valid. This assertion may appear incredible, but in 1822 Marino Malini, the pope's chamberlain, endeavored to establish the genuineness of the fictitious charters of Louis-de-Debonnaire, of Otho I., and of Henry II., in vindication of the pope's titles of the alleged grants to the See of Rome.

If the apostolic chair of St. Peter is endowed with a divine title to universal temporal sovereignty, a human title is supefluous. The indefatigable exertions of the popes to establish a human title to their temporal possessions, is a concession that they have no divine title to them, and that a human title is necessary to the validity of their claim. But as they have based their title on the authority of forged documents, and endeavored to fortify and maintain it by successive fabrications of the same nature, it is evident that they are fully and alarmingly conscious that they have no title, either by virtue of their office, or by that of any donation whatever, to temporal possession or authority.

Not only is the holy father's temporal power a usurpation, but so is also his exclusive claim to the use of the title of pope. Every bishop, and even some laymen, in the first centuries of Christianity, bore this title. In the ancient Greek church it was bestowed upon every clergyman. At the General Council of Constantinople, in 869, its adoption was first limited to the four patriarchs. And in the course of the usurpations of the holy fathers, pope Gregory VII., by authority of an Italian Council, finally assumed it as the exclusive title of the bishops of Rome.

The popes, the monarchs of the world, in vindicating their title to the States of the Church, had to maintain a long, bloody and desperate struggle, during which their domains were abridged or enlarged, lost or won, according to the varying fortunes of their arms and intrigues. But as these warlike enterprises of the holy fathers were intimately connected with the convulsions and revolutions of Europe, it will prevent repetition by deferring further allusion to them until we arrive at the subsequent chapters, in which we shall consider the papal political intrigues in general.

The papal monarchy is certainly one of the most crafty, demoralizing, and oppressive despotisms that has ever disgraced the name of government. Its ambition is insatiable, its duplicity inscrutible, and its policy and measures are disgraceful and unprincipled. The popes have converted the courteous indulgence of friendship into inviolable rights, and from the feeblest concession have manufactured the most exorbitant claim. Pretending to be spiritual advisers, they became temporal despots. Soon as they had acquired the right of owning a farm, they asserted the right of owning a kingdom; and when the right was conceded of owning a single kingdom, they claimed the right of owning all the kingdoms of the earth. A church, a mission-house, an acre of land they construed into an implication that they had a right to all power, temporal or spiritual, for which their capacious maw could crave. They first founded mission-houses in different parts of the world; next they claimed absolute jurisdiction over them. Disputes respecting property arising between the citizens of Rome and these foreign mission-houses of the church, the popes claimed the exlusive right to arbitrate between them. The right to arbitrate gave them the power to judge, and the opportunity of adjusting disputes according to their advantage. As ecclesiastical litigation conduced to the extension of their authority, pontiffs were not always too honorable to discourage the causes which favored their mediatorial interposition. From the right to arbitrate between churches, they next claimed the right to arbitrate between subjects, then between cities, then between nobles, and then between monarchs. As their mediation in church or state affairs enabled them to adjust disputes according to their policy, they insidiously labored to multiply the causes which favored their friendly intervention.

By a succession of forgeries, usurpations, and skilful manœuvres the papal government advanced, in the progress of events, from an obscure origin to supreme secular and spiritual jurisdiction. By gradual steps the popes acquired the right to decide on ecclesiastical and matrimonial questions; to dispose of church dignities and benefices; to protect their temporal acquisitions from alianation by the interdiction of the marriage of the clergy; to abridge the investiture of bishoprics by the princes; to reduce the clergy to absolute dependence on their favor by dissolving all bonds of interest which subsisted between the bishops and the princes; to convene at option synods and councils, and to exercise the prerogative of ratifying their decrees; to command the concession of their infallibility; to enforce confessors on princes and statesmen; to introduce the inquisition into kingdoms; and to regulate and superintend schools and colleges. The attainment of these objects was the work of centuries. Conceiving a desire in one age, they plotted for its accomplishment through the events and discords of succeeding ages; and when machinations had matured their plan, they consummated their wishes by usurpation. The pretensions to the alleged donation of Pepin, of Charlemagne, of Matilda, and of the Gothic princes, were not asserted until long after the death of the pretended donors, nor until art and intrigue had prepared the way for it. The alleged grant of Constantine was first announced in 765 by Pope Adrian I., in an epistle to Charlemagne. The claim to the estates of Matilda was first made by Pope Paschal, on the ground that they were granted to the Holy See as a fief; and next by pope Innocent II., on the ground that they had been granted to it as lord paramount. The participation of Pope Leo III. in the Consular government of Rome, in a paternal capacity, was the first instance of a pope's exercising temporal authority. The anointing of Pepin by Pope Adrian I., in imitation of the example of Samuel, was the first

19*

semblance of the pope's usurpation of the prerogatives of that official in acknowledging the right of kings. The victory of Nicholas I. over the Emperor Lothair, was the first papal triumph over the secular authority. The coronation of Charles the Bold, in 875, by Pope John VIII., was the first act of the papal monarch in disposing of crowns. The conquests of Robert Guiscard, instigated by promises of the popes, furnished the first ground of their feudal claims. The fear of the terrible consequences of their anathemas and interdictions, the ill regulated constitution of the European States, the imperfection of domestic and international law, and the efficient operation of the papal machinery, enabled them to render kingdom after kingdom tributary to the Holy See. England, from the period of the introduction of the Catholic church into her realm; Belgaria and Aragon, from the eleventh century; Poland and Hungary from the thirteenth century; and the kingdom of the two Sicilies, from 1265, had been reduced to dependency on the sacerdotal monarchy; and had the crusades been successful, favored by the confusion which it had universally produced with regard to the rights of citizens and the titles of property, it would have, under the pretext of a zeal to wrest the sepulchre of Christ from the possession of the Infidels, reduced the world to a state of vassalage. The success of the political measures and intrigues of the Holy See having, at the time of Gregory VII., raised it to a high degree of power and importance, he attempted to convert it into a theocratical government, with the pope for its head, the priests for its officials, the people for its subjects, and the world for its dominion. Under Innocent III., elected in 1195, it acquired almost unlimited spiritual and temporal authority. Under Sixtus V., in 1585, it contemplated the subjugation of Russia and Egypt, but the death of Bathore, Duke of Tuscany, frustrated the design. But under Pope Clement XII., in 1652, its power began to decline. He was obliged to cede Naples to Germany, the quarters of the pope's embassadors in Venice to the Venitian government, and the right of investiture in Savoy to the secular authority. Pope Pius VI., elected in 1775, beheld the church property in France confiscated, and the religious orders suppressed; in Naples the abolition of the customary tribute of a horse; in Germany the interdiction of the nunciature; in Italy the dismemberment of Romagna, Bologna and Ferrara; and finally, the French troops entering Rome and declaring it a republic.

It is evident from the facts that have been adduced, that the Catholic church, or the papal monarchy, designates an institution which has politics for its principles, monarchy for its object, and religion for its garb. It is not only political in its nature and design, but it is a political despotism, insulting in its pretensions to the common sense of mankind, and dangerous in its principles to the rights of independent governments. When we consider the monarchial principles with which it is constituted; its blasphemous arrogation of the attributes and prerogatives of the deity; its presumptuous claim to supreme jurisdiction over all other governments; the base forgeries which it has committed in the support of its arbitrary pretensions; its impious scoff at secular promises, contracts, laws, oaths and constitutions; its atrocious sanctions of prevarication, of evasion, and of mental reservation; its disgraceful system of espionage; its system of finance, by which it wrings from beggars their pittance, from the laborer the reward of his toil, from the dying the inheritance of heirs; that it may pile the wealth of the world in secret coffers, to be lavished on bribery, on corruption, on political intermeddling, on fomenting sedition and conspiracies, and ultimately, through the means of their disorganizing agencies, for the subjugation of all governments under its absolute authority. When we behold the blood-stained sword which it has drawn in the support of its frauds and usurpations; the frequent convulsions with which its unprincipled ambition has shaken the world; its triumphs over science, freedom and human right; the rapine, devastated fields, and burning cities which has marked the progress of its career; or when we turn our eyes to its late condition in Italy, and see, in the nineteenth century, under its authority, the inquisition at its bloody work; the study of philosophy banished from universities; no book allowed to be published, or imported, except such as meet the approval of bigoted censors; the government sustained only by suppressing insurrection; the prisons crowded with heretics; political offenders cruelly put to death; the nation struggling for freedom, but bound in the fetters of despotism—good heavens! what a scourge is it, and has it been to mankind. Bigotry and superstition may chaunt its victories; but a land once prosperous, now choaked up and oppressed with the ruins of its former greatness; fields once fertile now turned into barren wastes; a people once the most valiant, polished and civilized, now the most debased, rude and imbecile—with ancestors that governed the world, now not able to govern themselves; a commonwealth of kings, now a commonwealth of slaves; where for liberty Cicero plead, Brutus stabbed and Cato died, now a pope curses, an inquisition murders, and prisons reverberate with the groans of patriots and freemen. These, oh patriots! are the eternal monuments that commemorate the progress and achievements of the papal monarchy. The usurper of all rights, the sanctifier of all wrongs, the shrine of bigotry, the model of despotism : the church now stands reaffirming the crimes and errors of centuries, and is thirsting for an opportunity of repeating its past horrible history. Such is the papal monarchy; such is the Catholic church; such is the political institution which she claims the divine authority to obtrude, by any means, on the world; and such are the demoralizing, seditious and treasonable principles which she carries in her bosom, scatters in her pathway, and is laboring to implant in the American republic, in order that she may overthrow its structure, that monarchy may supplant its liberal principles, despotic decrees its legislative enactments, arbitrary appointments its popular elections, aristocracy its equality, slavery its freedom, usurpation its guarantees of natural rights, and bigotry, violence, and superstition its tolerance, order and science.

CHAPTER XII.

PAPAL POLITICAL INTRIGUES IN ENGLAND.

Papal Political Machinery—Papal Political Intrigues in England, under the Reigns of Henry II.—of King John—of Henry VII.—of Charles I.—of Charles II.—of James II.—of William and Mary.

THE design of ruling nations was clearly indicated by the principles upon which the monastic orders were founded. Regarding supremacy to the pope as the main substance of Christianity, and obedience to his will as necessary to salvation, their doctrines harmonized with his claim to supreme temporal and spiritual power; and their organization, based strictly on monarchial principles, skilfully adapted to secure unity and concentration of action, formed, together with the military knights, a political machinery in the advancement of the papal interests, which was capable of intimidating the boldest antagonist, and of shaking the power of the strongest government. With the knowledge of this fact we may perceive the origin of some of those mysterious seditions and rebellions which have arisen apparently from trifling causes, and which, from insignificant beginnings have gained such strength and dimensions as to dismay the valor of disciplined arms, and distract every section of the land, and every department of the government. We may also perceive from the same fact, why the struggle of civil and religious liberty has been such a long, bloody, and interminable conflict. That rational beings should trample upon their rights, surrender up their personal sovereignty, kneel in adoration at the feet of a despot, deliberately rivet on their own limbs the irons of slavery, crucify their champions, and deify their enemies, is certainly strange; and without the supposition of the intervention of some secret power by which reason was unseated in such instances, it is not conceivable. But that the pope, by means of his political machinery, is capable of producing identical extraordinary effects, is a fact supported by the irrefragable testimony of history; and that he has never scrupled to exercise his terrible power whenever his ambitious projects required it, unawed by the magnitude of the public calamity which it threatened to entail, is a fact written with the blood and tears of nations. The secrecy, extent, and irresistible energy of his power, have sometimes led his unsuspecting subjects to regard him as a magician; and sometimes they have been the cause of his arraignment before councils on the charge of practising magic, and of having dealings with the devil. But although the effects which he produced were as malignant and surprising as those which have been ascribed to the supernatural power of the arch-fiend, yet the only magic he ever had the necessity of using was his political machinery; through which he could charm like the poisonous adder; mislead like the fabled sirens; pervert the public judgment; calm or distract a nation; excite it to rebel against its best governor, or to enthrone in power its bitterest foe.

From the hour when first the Catholic church planted her foot on the soil of England until the present moment, her emissaries have labored as far as practicable, by every available means, under every garb, in all departments of the government, and at all periods of its history, to subject the nation to the despotism of Rome. For a long period the priests were the instructors of her princes, the advisers of her kings, and under the semblance of spiritual guides, the spies on their thoughts and actions.

Passing by the numerous instances of papal political intrigue in the history of England, we will glance at a few of those which have taken place since the coronation of Henry II., in 1154. The most accomplished prince of his time, and celebrated for the acuteness of his judgment and the equitableness of his decisions, he received at the hands of his regal cotemporaries the distinguished honor of being chosen by them as their arbiter, to settle their matters of dispute. He received also, from the policy or generosity of Pope Adrian IV., a gift of the kingdom of Ireland. The following extract from Adrian's bull on that occasion will explain the nature and object of the donation: " No one doubts, and you know the fact yourself, that Ireland, and all the isles that have received the Christian faith belong to the church of Rome. And you have signified to us that you wish to enter this island, in order to subject the people to the laws, and extirpate their vices; to make them pay to St. Peter a penny a year for each house, and preserve in all things the rights of the church; which we grant to you with pleasure for the increase of the Christian religion."—(Labb. 13, 14, 15). At the dictation of the pope, the Irish clergy met at Waterford and took the oath of allegiance to Henry and his successors. Thus by a pretended prerogative of popery, "Ireland was blotted from the map, and consigned to the loss of freedom, without a tribunal and without a crime."—(McGeoghegan, 1: 440). But notwithstanding the munificent bounty of the pope, yet the growing weight of the ecclesiastical establishments—so oppressive to the industry and enterprize of the people—and the continual and insidious encroachments of the clergy on the prerogatives of the crown, determined Henry, under the administration of Pope Alexander III., to summon a council of nobles and clergy at Clarendon, to frame such a constitution as would be adequate for the protection of the prerogatives of the crown and the rights of the subjects. The principles of this constitution, like seeds sown among thorns and brambles, were in danger of being oppressed in their early growth by a heavy encumbrance of Catholic ignorance and superstition; and not until intelligence and public spirit had removed the obstruction did they show their native benificent vigor. Under the stormy reign of Henry II. they were checked, thwarted, and at times almost extirpated; but under that of King John they produced the "Magna Charta," under that of Charles II. the "Habeas Corpus," and under those of succeding princes the various liberal acts which constitute English liberty.

Although this liberal and judicious constitution had received the sanction of the Council of Clarendon, yet it was violently opposed by Thomas-a-Becket, the oracle of the pope, and the chief engineer of his political machinery in England. Denouncing it as a profane infraction of the privileges and immunities of the church, he proceeded to excommunicate all persons who had acquired, or should acquire ecclesiastical property under the authority of its provisions. In savage zeal in behalf of the pope, he had violated his oath of allegiance to the king; and thus imprudently furnished his antagonists with legal authority to retaliate the mischief of revenge by the confiscation of all his property. Chagrined at the triumph of his foes, and exasperated at the loss of his temporal possessions, he sought to solace his wounded pride, and vent the ebullitions of his despair and rage in excommunicating the principal officers of the crown, and all who should presume to violate the church prerogatives. But duly impressed with the intrinsic impotence of his own curses, and that neither their sanctity nor potency could protect his insolent tongue from punishment even while uttering them, he fled to France, that he might exercise with impunity his sacred functions in cursing his foes. By the mandates of his anathema the papal machinery was, of course, set in violent operation to destroy the king for the benefit of the church, and to invoke in its cause the insidious but formidable aid of scandal, vituperation and defamation. The brilliant qualities of Henry were unfortunately overshaded with the dark vice of unchastity. As greater rakes are often horrified at the peccadillos of lesser ones, so in this case, the more profligate clergy became exceedingly exasperated upon discovering in the conduct of Henry the practice of their own irregularities, modified by less grossness and more refinement. Not possessing that charity which covereth a multitude of sins, but that religion which magnifies, distorts and publishes them, they soon managed to startle the sobriety of every hamlet with whispers of the king's incredible depravity. To secure the visitation of divine justice on the head of Henry, they profaned the sanctity of his domestic circle by the dissemination of treacherous and extravagant inventions, until the queen was frenzied with jealousy, and Geoffry and Richard, two sons of Henry, were incited to rebellion. The prudence and martial abilities of the king enabled him, however, soon to suppress these afflictive and unnatural seditions. But the papal machinery, more tremendous and pestiferious than the fabled monsters of antiquity, with their poisonous breath, their hundred heads and thousand hands, was still in action in every part of the empire. Hence Henry's son Louis, whom he had crowned as his successor, was induced to demand of him the surrender of the diadem. In anticipation of this demand papal intrigue had secured the support of France and Scotland in its favor; and consequently England was suddenly involved in the horrors of a civil and a foreign war. But the coolness and extraordinary military genius of Henry was adequate to the terrible emergency. After a desperate contest he repelled the invaders, and restored order to his kingdom. But the moral effluvia which was produced by the action of the papal political machinery, continued still to generate those noxious vapors which had so frequently overclouded the atmosphere of England, and broke in storms of pestilence, blood and death. The peace of his kingdom was consequently again disturbed by the discovery of a conspiracy, at the head of which was Richard, Henry's third son, and complicated with which was John, his favorite and youngest son. Upon the disclosure of this mortifying fact, the king pronounced a curse upon his rebellious children, which was more properly merited by the pope and the father confessors of the princes, to whom the first conception of their treason was known; and if they did not originate, might have blasted it in its bud. But Henry was unconsciously dealing with an invisible monster, that in the garb of a holy father was commanding his homage and reverence, while it was profaning his domestic hearth, exciting his subjects to sedition, his children to rebellion, and at the same time inducing him to attribute to his family and subjects the dreadful calamities that had been conjured by the machinations of the monster himself. Had Henry had the sagacity to penetrate the secrets of the Holy See, and had he been able, in defiance of a papal alliance with the united crowned heads of Christendom, to have annulled the authority of the pope in his relm, and broken up the machinery of his treasonable machinations, how effectually might he have suppressed the rebellion of his sons, and the disorders of his kingdom; and what a blessing he would have been to England and to mankind. Freedom will, however, ever be grateful to the king, who laid the foundation of England's liberty. The cost at which he purchased this invaluable legacy for posterity was as tremendous as are the obligations of gratitude which it imposes. His family converted into a nest of venomous reptiles; his sons, around whom his fondest hopes had clustered, transformed into treacherous foes; his laborious efforts to elevate the importance and improve the condition of his subjects, converted into sources of the deepest of misfortunes; these were the papal demands, outweighing the wealth of worlds, which were imposed on him for having served the cause of justice, of humanity, and of his country; and under the rigorous exactions of these demands, three days after the disclosure of the last conspiracy of his sons, he sunk into an unconsecrated grave, ruined and broken hearted.

The Papal See governed by an unscrupulous ambition to realize the success of its projects for acquiring unbounded territorial aggrandizement, has, with equal craft and baseness, endeavored to make the vices as well as the power of princes administer to its interests. This policy is illustrated in the schemes of papal policy and intrigue concocted under the reign of King John, youngest son of Henry II., who on the decease of his father in 1199 ascended the English throne. This prince had conspired against the most indulgent of fathers, had warred against his brother Richard, had murdered his brother Arthur, had repudiated his wives, and had exercised regal authority with insolence and tyranny, without provoking the maledictions or interference of the Holy See. But as these enormities deprived him of the affections of his subjects, a ruler's chief support; exhausted his coffers, the sinews of war and opposition; made him more dependent on the favor of Rome, more entangled in the network of its policy, and admirably prepared the way for the accomplishment of its ulterior designs, its indulgence, and perhaps connivance may be reasonably accounted for. But after a war with France exhausted the resources of John, rendered him less popular, and more irascible and impatient, Pope Innocent III. improved the flattering opportunity which crime and misfortune had presented, to provoke a collision with him favorable to the success of the papal designs. John claimed the right of investiture; and in making this claim seems to have been supported by the cooperation of the papal political machinery. The See of Canterbury having become vacant, the pope appointed Cardinal Langston to fill the vacancy. This act John resisted as an unjustifiable encroachment on the prerogatives of the crown. But the arts of the pope had involved the king in a snare; and now having fairly entangled him, proceeded to prepare the way for realizing his temporal project by exercising his spiritual functions. Accordingly he suspended the performance of religious worship in the king's dominions, excommunicated him, and absolved his subjects from their allegiance to him. The papal political machinery acting in harmony with the maledictions of the pope, the wildest disorders were excited among the people; anarchy suspended all law; the army refused to obey the king's orders; his friends deserted him; and he found himself without domestics, without alliances, and without the means of resistance. It is an invariable practice of the holy fathers, who claim a right to all the world by virtue of their office, to endeavor to supersede the necessity of this title by acquiring a legal one. Hence, Innocent III., seeing the helpless condition to which he had reduced John, and touched at the cruel misfortunes in which he had involved him, now graciously proposed to mitigate the rigors of his adversities, and to restore him to his former authority, if he would cede his kingdom to the Pope of Rome, and consent to rule it as a vassal of the pope. Divested of adherents, arms or alliances, the king submitted unconditionally to the terms dictated by the sacerdotal despot. The design of the papal See of reducing England to a state of vassalage, conceived in ambition, pursued by craft and cruelty, was thus consummated by the most execrable tyranny. This empty title to England and Ireland, so full of trick and fraud, is nevertheless still mentioned by the Holy See as valid and indisputable.

But the benefits of the statesmanship, and of the divinely inspired council of the holy father, by which John was bound in future to be governed in the administration of his kingdom, did not prevent him from exciting the indignation of his subjects, by encroachments on their rights; nor restrain him from the perpetration of such unwarrantable acts as created a popular hatred of him, which finally culminated in open resistance to his authority. So violent were the conflicts that arose between him and his subjects, that in order to save his crown he had to yield to their demand the act of the "Magna Charta." The pope, however, the natural foe of all constitutional guarantees of popular right and liberty, benevolently interposed in behalf of the imbecile and overawed prince, and absolved him from all obligations to comply with any of the unpleasant concessions which he had made; declaring the Magna Charta antagonistical to the Catholic religion; forbidding the king to observe any of its provisions; and pronouncing sentence of excommunication on all who should obey, or attempt to enforce the heretical act. Again the papal machinery was set in violent operation. Spies watched, confessors reported, abbots schemed, bishops predicted, priests thundered, monks prowled and assassins murdered, until every city, village and house, was distracted with alarm. In the midst of the consternation which stupefied the public mind the king, through the instrumentality of the papal machinery, suddenly appeared at the head of a formidable army; and as if he were a foreign enemy, commenced butchering his subjects, firing their dwellings and carrying terror and devastation through his own kingdom. So profoundly secret were the papal machinations carried on, and so suddenly and unexpectedly had John appeared with an army fully equipped for war that—no suspicion of such a design having been excited in the minds of the military barons— no preparations were made to meet the emergency. As suddenly, mysteriously, and adroitly as King John's army had sprung into existence, so did the barons resolve, in order to defeat its object, to tender the crown of the realm to France; which proffer being accepted, the intrigues of the pope were thwarted, and Philip of France became sovereign of England.

The popes claim the divine attribute of infallibility, yet in changing their policy and practice to suit the variations of time, place and circumstance, they seem generally to have descended to the common level of humanity. In order, however, to reconcile the irreconcilable, while they profess to have had communicated to them the incommunicable, they claim to have been endowed with power to change the unchangeable. Should a prince resolve to do that which the pope's infallible holiness has declared to be criminal, and should that prince happen to be too powerful to be intimidated, and too dangerous to be provoked into rebellion, in such delicate cases the pope, with his facilities to accommodate all difficulties, grants a dispensation, whereby the applicant is empowered to violate all the infallible laws of the church without incurring any of their penalties.

In the reign of Henry VII., who became king of England in 1485, we find an illustration of this policy. That sovereign had married Arthur, his eldest son, to Catherine, daughter of Ferdinand, king of Arragon. On the decease of Arthur, the king, with the view of retaining the opulent Spanish dowery in his family, desired to marry the widow of Arthur to his next son. The young prince Henry, but fifteen years old, protested against marrying a lady for whom he had no affection, and who was so much his senior. Besides this difficulty the contemplated alliance was in violation of the laws of consanguinity, so solemnly established by the authority of the infallible church, and so terrifically armed with all the terrors of anathemas and excommunication. To silence the objection of his son, and the thunders of the Vatican, Henry applied to the pope for permission to execute his purposes, in violation of the established laws of the church; and the pope, not deeming it prudent to offend so powerful a potentate, granted his request. But vain are the pope's pretensions to be able to change the moral law of heaven unless he can also change the natural course of events. In this attempt to accommodate principle to interest, and the infallible laws of the church to the changing whim of an avaricious monarch, he laid the foundation for the final separation of the kingdom of England from the See of Rome.

After the death of Henry VII. his son, under the title of Henry VIII., succeeded to the British throne. Frank and vain, he became at an early period of his life an object of the subtle policy of Rome. Naturally generous, his indomitable love of power and dominion often led him to violate the obligations of humanity; and impetuous in passion, and impatient of restraint, he was tempted to annihilate the constitutional restraints which conflicted with his designs, and to make the forms of justice subservient to the gratification of his ambition and interest.

Happening to become enamored of Anne Bolyne, he began to suspect the legality of his marriage with Catherine; and though he had recognized its obligations by a union of twenty years, yet the oftener he saw his mistress the stronger became his convictions of the heterodoxy and unlawfulness of his matrimonial relations, and the more scrupulous he became about his chastity. The want of male issue, and the disparity of years between him and his wife mingled reflections with these legal and religious scruples, and made them so pungent that Henry, in order to get rid of the torment thus inflicted, finally applied to the pope for a divorce. The pope promised to grant his request; but the fear of offending Charles V., Catherine's nephew, produced strange vacillation in the mind of the infallible holy father. Two powerful and crafty princes dictated to him opposite courses; to offend either would be disastrous; he therefore pretended to favor the wishes of both. Aware of papal artifice, however, Henry became imperious in his demands. The pope appeared to yield, and to soothe the impatient prince with a semblance of compliance, but a means of procrastination, he commissioned Cardinals Wolsey and Campaggio to adjust the difficulty. They cited the queen to appear before them; she appealed to the pope; they declared her contumacious. By these proceedings the controversy becoming more embarrassed than before, and less capable of a speedy solution, Henry peremptorily decided the matter by consummating his marriage with Anne Bolyne. This act astonished the pope, and enraged Charles V. To gratify Charles, and to punish Henry, the holy father proceeded to excommunicate the latter. The despotic character of Henry, however, had too much overawed his subjects to allow the papal machinery to give much efficacy to the manifestos of its prime engineer; and placing himself at the head of the Catholic church in England, he released his subjects from allegiance to the See of Rome, effected a separation from it, and nullified its temporal authority over his dominions.

Discarding the dogma of the pope's temporal power, Henry still strictly adhered to the standard of Catholic theology in all other respects; and the pope, at the same time, through the medium of Cardinal Wolsey, continued to exert considerable indirect influence on his mind. This prelate who, while he was a preacher at Limington was put into the stocks for disorderly conduct in a drunken frolic; who afterwards was made domestic chaplain by Dean, Archbishop of Canterbury, and who was finally created cardinal by the pope, obtained such unlimited power over the mind of Henry that the pope pensioned him to keep him in his interest. It is not a matter of much surprise that Henry's aversion to the reformers, inflamed by the arts of such a vicious counsellor, should have brought so many of them to the stake; nor that the bigotry and intolerance of Catholicism should have survived the destruction of its political engine. Henry VIII. condemned to death Lambert, a school teacher, for denying the real presence At intervals during his reign he rigorously persecuted the Protestants Catherine Parr, his last wife, barely escaped execution for having encouraged the reformers. A warrant had been wrung from the king by the Bishop of Winchester, for her committal to the Tower on the charge of heretical opinions; but having become secretly apprised of the fact in time she sought the king, and satisfied him that when she had objected to his opinions it was from a desire to become enlightened by his superior knowledge and intelligence. While he employed violent means to enforce conformity to the Catholic theology, he visited equal vengeance on those who advocated the pope's temporal authority. When he discovered that the monks and friars were guilty of defending the obnoxious heresy of the pope's temporal power, he suppressed their houses; but not wishing to destroy the monastic orders, he applied the sequestered funds to the establishment of other similar institutions; but on perceiving these also to be secretly engaged in machinations to restore the pope's temporal authority, he abolished the religious orders altogether. Even Cardinal Wolsey fell under his suspicion, and was executed for treason by his order. After he had beheaded his wife, Catherine Howard for unchastity, his severity against those who advocated the pope's temporal sovereignty, and against those who denied the Romish theology, was cruel in the highest degree.

What papal rapaciousness cannot boldly grasp, it will secretly plot to obtain. Kings who control nations, women who may perhaps control kings, and children who are presumptive heirs of empires, are powerful instruments in the accomplishment of political designs, and especial objects of papal intrigue.

The inveterate opposition to Catholics in England rendered it almost impossible for a Catholic to ascend the throne, and eventually interdicted it by positive enactments. To counteract the consequences of this spirit, a scheme was projected by papal craft to have the heirs of the throne educated by Catholic mothers, so that future kings might rule as Protestants with Catholic proclivities, and in course of time, through the demoralization, dissatisfaction, discord and blood effected by the cooperation of its adherents, the supremacy of the pope might be reestablished in England. James I., who on the death of Elizabeth succeeded to the crown of England and Scotland, a ruler devoid of statesmen-like abilities, without firmness or stability, and bloated up with fanciful notions of royal prerogatives, was the pliant instrument of this subtle policy. An amorous flame having been kindled in him and in Henrietta Maria, daughter of Henry IV., of France, it was stipulated that the union should be consummated, on condition that the heirs which should issue should be subject to the exclusive control of their mother until they were thirteen years of age. This contract secured a Catholic education to the heirs of the British throne, and laid the foundations for the dreadful calamities which afflicted the nation during the reigns of Charles II. and James II.

The abolition of papal despotism over the English mind giving freedom to thought and inquiry, could not but enlarge its conceptions of civil and religious liberty. The old system of prerogatives sunk into contempt, and the new system of representative government became more popular as the mind became more comprehensive in its grasp, and more profound in its investigation. Hence the Puritans, who originally were Catholics, and merely advocated a simpler form of worship; the Presbyterians and the Independents, who at first questioned only the temporal power of the pope, yet driven from those whom they had venerated by the hate which persecution engenders, and disenthralled from the shackles with which custom and superstition enslaves the mind, began fearlessly and candidly to investigate the fundamental principles of faith and practice, and to elaborate theological creeds totally different from those of Catholicism, and vastly superior to them. While the people were rapidly advancing in liberal views of religion and government, the heir of the throne was too much absorbed in magnifying his visionary prerogatives to share in the progress of the age, or to study the character of the people over whom he was destined to reign. When in 1625 he ascended the English throne, under the title of Charles I., the new order of popular sentiment had become an impetuous torrent. Common sagacity might have perceived the inevitable destruction that would await him if he should attempt to stem the popular tide of thought; and prudence would have dictated a practicable compromise of differences rather than the certain alternative of civil war. But Archbishop Laud, a Catholic under the disguise of Protestantism, and who was the medium of the pope's influence, exercised a despotism over the king's mind too absolute to allow his reason to instruct, or his conscience to admonish him. The religious views and secret designs of this professed Protestant bishop cannot be misunderstood. He maintained that the papal authority had always been visible in the realm. He furnished the king with a significant list of the names of all his Catholic and Protestant subjects. He was also the principal actor in the Star Chamber, and Court of High Commission. So well was the pope satisfied with the orthodoxy of this sacerdotal miscreant that he sent him a cardinal's hat, which he declined for the ambiguous reason that the "Church of Rome was no other than it was!" The king, controlled and ill-advised by such a counsellor, blinded by his own bigotry, and elated with self-conceit, was led to scorn the rising spirit of the nation, and to adopt measures for its suppression. But parliament with prudent foresight, and patriotic boldness, taught him that the Commons were the constitutional dispensers and guardians of the public treasury. He next resolved to oblige Scotland to conform to the ritual prescribed by the Church of England; and as parliament had refused to allow him the use of the public funds for that and other purposes, he attempted to raise means for their accomplishment by unconstitutional methods. By this impolitic course he aroused a lion from its den, with whose strength and fury he could not well cope. The Scotch formed a league of Covenanters, composed of all classes and factions, for the defence of their religious liberty; and as the king viewed their enthusiastic and formidable array, and compared it with the suspicious material of his own army, he prudently concluded terms of pacification.

Having frequently called the Commons together in parliament, and finding them more disposed to dictate than to obey, and inflexible in their refusal to furnish him with the pecuniary aid necessary to the accomplishment of his design, he finally determined to rule without a parliament, and by a liberal construction of his prerogatives to arrogate monarchial power. An object so consistent with the dogmas of Catholicism, and so flattering to the vanity of the Episcopal royalists, equally betrayed them into acquiescence. To aid the king in his despotic design the royalists extolled his prerogatives, asserted their divine origin, declared it impious to prescribe any limits to them, and inculcated passive obedience as a Christian virtue and imperative duty. The terror of the Star Chamber, and of the Court of High Commission, was also called into requisition. But neither the eloquent encomiums lavished on the king's prerogative, nor the atrocities of the Star Chamber, nor the severity of the Court of High Commission, nor a rebellion excited in Ireland against parliament, nor the arms of the royal troops, produced anything for the king's prerogatives but disgrace and ridicule.

Dreading the liberalism and inflexibility of the Commons, and the uncompromising hostility against his person and measures which his persecution of non-conformists had excited in the majority of them, yet he was obliged, by the critical state of public affairs, to call them together. This parliament proved the memorable "long parliament." As might have been expected, its embittered and exasperated members opened the session with torrents of scorn and contempt poured on the king and his prerogatives. They also adopted every expedient to inflame the public mind, and to make it accessory to their design of reducing the king to unresisting helplessness. They denounced the Episcopalians, and other advocates of the king's prerogatives, in whom Catholicism and monarchy had disguised themselves under the semblance of Protestantism. They attempted to exclude the bishops from the House of Lords. They so intimidated the royalists of the House that many of them absented themselves from their seats. They restricted the king's prerogatives, abolished the Star Chamber, and the Court of High Commission, passed acts against superstitious practices, executed Laud and Stafford, and as the king had set the dangerous precedent of liberal construction of law and prerogatives, they availed themselves of the same means to justify their measures. The impetuous tornado of their zeal and wrath swept away all the king's elaborate schemes for the acquisition of monarchial power, and poured upon his unprotected head a pitiless storm of wrath. Condemned to be the helpless spectator of the destruction of his hopes of absolute power, which art, tyranny, and usurpation had enabled him to build, he became wild with despair and rage, and, in a desperate attempt to retrieve his fortune by asserting in his extremity his empty prerogatives, he brought his precarious condition to an unfortunate close. Entering the House of Commons, he personally attempted to arrest some of its members. The House, consequently, broke up in disorder; the king saw his error, but too late; he fled from his capitol in terror; two armies arose; the one under the king, the other under parliament: after several bloody battles, the king lost his crown, and finally his life.

Parliament now resolved to rule without a king as the king had resolved to rule without a parliament. The spirit of despotism under the form of freedom, still, however, predominated in the national councils. Cromwell, a professed republican, but a secret monarchist; as intolerant as he was religious, and crafty as he was ambitious; who, as interest instigated, favored or persecuted Catholics, Protestants, Puritans, and Republicans, was this despotic spirit which desecrated the form of Freedom, and which induced him while he governed England as a protector, to seek to govern her as a king, and to plot in secret to reestablish her throne. After the termination of his eventful career, and the resignation of his appointed successor, Charles II., son of James I., in 1660 was crowned King of England.

Illiberal in mind, intolerant in disposition, defective in sensibility, and destitute of honor and generosity, he was base as a man, dishonorable as a prince, and a pliable instrument of the papal intrigues. A hypocrite from his birth, he was capable of assuming any guise; and supremely selfish, he tolerated vice and corruption whenever it administered to his interests. By the licentiousness of his court he degraded the moral standing of the British nation in the eyes of the world and of history, and with a despotic and unprincipled set of measures, arrogated power in defiance of constitutional obstructions, and reduced the people to slavery in contempt of their hereditary valor and independence, and the safeguards with which they had protected their liberty.

The pathway to his elevation to the throne having been prepared by General Monk, he was received with frantic acclamations by conflicting civil and religious sects, and without a struggle succeeded to those dangerous prerogatives which had cost the nation so much blood and treasure. The admonition of past occurrences had induced him to disguise under the cloak of a pacific and accommodating policy, his secret and ulterior designs. But the specious mask fell from his brow when he passed the intolerent act of non-conformity, by which the Presbyterians were peremptorily driven from their livings.

Profligacy, which enfeebles the intellectual powers, and destroys the foundation of public respect, has ever been encouraged in princes or people by the artifice of those whose ambition has plotted to make them subservient to their interest, or dependent on their power. The disgracefulness of this policy has never been too abhorrent to the Roman See to cause it to forego the advantages of its adoption. The profligate character of Charles II., and the dissolute manners which he introduced into his court, ably aided the papal machinery in alienating from him the respect and affection of his subjects, and in making him more dependent on the favor of the pope. His extravagance involved him eventually in such pecuniary embarrassments that he became a pensioner on Louis, king of France; and in consequence became doubly ironed with the papal shackles—the king of France forming one set of manacles, the priests of England another—and both were equally bound to the interests of the papal monarchy. That every thought and action might be discovered in its incipiency, he was furnished with a French lady to amuse him in his retirement This accomplished but abandoned female obtained such ascendency over his mind, that she induced him to make her a duchess. Thus watched, debased and controlled, he became the unconscious tool of the designs of others, and was led to alarm the public mind by forming a disgraceful cabal, by which to concert measures for making himself independent of parliament.

To add to the public dissatisfaction the Duke of York, the heir presumptive to the throne, openly espoused the cause of Catholicism. Strong measures were consequently adopted to remove him from his post, as admiral of the navy, and eventually to exclude him from the throne. The violent factions, and fierce criminations and recriminations to which these measures gave rise kept the people in a state of feverish excitement. In the midst of these wild alarms a pretended popish plot was reported to have been discovered, which received universal credence. The design of this plot was said to be to destroy parliament and assassinate the king. A secret Catholic faction was supposed to exist in the nation, the object of which was to restore the authority of the pope; and circumstances lending credibility to the supposition, the most intense excitement seized the public mind. Parliament was terrific in its denunciations, and the people clamorous for vengeance. Lords were arrested, priests hung, the Duke of York fled from the country in terror, the Earl of Stafford was beheaded, and the king, filled with consternation, yielded to the popular demand the Habeas Corpus act, to avert the storm that was muttering destruction over his head. Fortified with this new safeguard to public freedom, the people became tranquil once more; but the king perceiving the formidable obstacle which parliament obtruded in the way of his acquisition of despotic power, resolved to get rid of it by making it the instrument of its own destruction. After having assembled it severel times for this purpose, and finding it inflexibly opposed to his measures, he determined to dispense with it altogether, and to substitute his prerogatives in the place of its authority. In order to reduce the corporations to an absolute dependence on his will, he employed with as much baseness as tyranny, intimidations to induce them to surrender their charters, so that they might be remodelled in accordance with the claims of the absolute power of his prerogatives. In order to deplete the ranks of non-Catholics, he had recourse to gross and unfounded charges of plots and conspiracies. Lord Shaftsbury, the author of the Habeas Corpus act, was arrested, imprisoned in the Tower and tried for high treason; but acquitted. Dungeons were overcrowded with subjects against whom no allegation laid, except that of love of liberty and opposition to tyranny. But while he was wading through the innocent blood of his subjects to a crown of unlimited monarchy, some desperate spirits were secretly concocting a plot to arrest his atrocious career by the deplorable means of the assassin's dagger. This unsuccessful conspiracy, known as the Rhyhouse plot, which could not escape the omniscient eye of the Catholic machinery, was, of course, discovered before it had matured its plans, and only gave the king a plausible pretence for gratifying his malignancy against the ablest advocates of constitutional liberty. William Russell, who had with undaunted firmness maintained the fundamental principle of free government, was the first victim through this unfortunate affair, to the eagerness of the king's bloodthirsty revenge. Foredoomed, he was tried by a packed jury, and condemned against conclusive proof of his innocence. Alerngon Sidney, another apostle of liberty, was unjustly charged with high treason. The law requiring two witnesses to substantiate allegations of this nature, and but one having appeared, and he as unreliable as he was promptly received, the infamous Jeffrey summoned into court a manuscript which had been found in the closet of the defendent. In this manuscript the author expressed a preference for a free to an arbitrary government. The judge deciding that the document was a competent witness in his court, (although he did not swear it), and that it supplied the want of the other witness required by the law of treason, proceeded to pass sentence of death on the accused.

By means of similar unwarrantable proceedings, and the co-operation of the papal machinery, the king succeeded in dragooning Scotland into conformity, in suppressing the bold Covenanters, and in amassing almost sufficient power for the accomplishment of any purpose. After he had, in defiance of parliament and the laws, and by means of tyrannical measures and execrable usurpations, rendered himself as absolute in power as any despot in Europe, death interposed in the midst of his success, and removed him from a throne which he had disgraced, and a people whom he had oppressed. Had his conduct during his life left a doubt of his genuine Catholicism, and hypocritical profession of Protestantism, the last moments of his existence were sufficient to dispel them. Just before his death he received the sacrament according to the rites of the Catholic church, and having no further need of deception, openly professed himself a Catholic.

James II., brother of Charles II., in 1685 succeeded to the throne of England and Scotland. Educated like his brother, he had imbibed similar religious and political sentiments. While Duke of York he at first secretly, but afterwards openly, professed the Catholic faith. When, in the course of intrigue and conflict, the royal party had gained the ascendency in Scotland, he retired thither; and manifested his barbarous ferocity by personally assisting at the torturing of the Covenanters. The rapid strides which his brother had made towards the acquisition of absolute power, and the paralyzing dread which cruelty and tyranny had cast over the public mind, enabled James II. to succeed to the British throne without opposition. From the hour he became invested with the royal dignity, he adopted every expedient that craft could devise to convert his royal prerogatives into monarchial authority, and to secure the restoration of Catholicism as the religion of the kingdom. As virtue scorns to be the tool of vice, and as sycophants are the most pliable instruments of despotism, he adopted the policy of investing the most unscrupulous with official authority. Supreme among his base and cringing creatures stood Judge Jeffrey. The chief engineer of the papal machinery—the controlling spirit of the king and his councils; insolent, imperious, arbitrary and oppressive, this man was ready for any work that furnished sufficient blood and plunder. By barbarous and inhuman acts, and by the arbitrary execution of innocent subjects, this monster in human form succeeded in casting a deep gloom over the public mind, and in annihilating all apparent opposition to the tyrannical proceedure of the king. Amid the death-like silence which hung on the lips of the people the king threw off his disguise, entered into negotiation with the pope for the reception of England into the papal church, celebrated mass invested with the royal paraphernalia, assumed the power of parliament, nullified all test oaths, filled the councils and army with Catholics, governed Scotland and Ireland by his creatures, organized ecclesiastical tribunals to try such clergy as were suspected of holding liberal sentiments, committed bishops to the Tower for having remonstrated against the propriety of reading a document concerning a popish indulgence which he had commanded to be read in all the churches, and adopted every possible method to subvert civil and religious liberty, and to bind on his subjects the shackles of papal despotism. Towards the final consummation of his calamitous design he appeared to be making rapid strides; but, though the papal machinery was formidable, yet there was another power more formidable still; as wily and as secret: which was quietly maturing its strength for the hour of retribution. The oppressive measures of the king and the failure of every attempt at compromise and conciliation, had created a stern opposition in the mind of the people, of the gentry, and of some lords. Silent but powerful, though this opposition seemed to slumber, yet it was but calmly waiting the destined hour, when it would arise and annihilate dynasties and prerogatives. While the king, deceived by the treacherous calm, was trampling in insolent contempt on the people's rights; while sycophantic priests were chaunting his song of triumph; and while the pope was congratulating him on his success, and stretching forth his hand to receive the kingdom, William of Orange suddenly appeared on the coast of England with a formidable navy and army, and, as with the stroke of an enchanter's wand, changed the calm and brilliant prospects of the king into storms and sights of horror, and the peans of his sycophants into howling and lamentations. Terrified at the sight, the king repealed his unpopular acts, and proffered to his subjects all the rights which they had in vain plead for before. Conscious of their strength, and irreconcilable in the memory of their wrongs, they rejected with scorn and indignation all his generous overtures. As he had ruled as a tyrant, he now absconded as a coward. The throne was declared abdicated, and William and Mary proclaimed sovereigns of England and Scotland. After some fruitless attempts to regain his kingdom, James II. turned Jesuist, and passed the remainder of his life in doing penance.

Edward, the Pretender, grandson of James I., educated at Rome, was another instrument which the pope adopted to establish his authority over the crown of England. This treasonable plot was unanimously supported by the tory party. This faction had ever been a prominent branch of the papal machinery. Under the disguise of Protestantism, in 1680, the tories made vigorous efforts for the subjugation of England to the papal dominion. They were the most strenuous supporters of Charles II. In every scheme of oppression and violence—in the persecution of dissenters, in the banishment of patriots, in the murder of the advocates of popular freedom—in every project of the king to grasp monarchial power, in the abrogation of the free charters, in the assumption of despotic prerogatives, in the efforts to abolish parliament, they were the bold and unequivocal supporters. It was, therefore, consistent with their historic tradition that they should welcome as allies of the pope the invasion of Edward, and be ready to repeat their former atrocities in his cause. England's vigilance, however, defeated Edward's first attempt, in 1742, but he made another in 1745 which was more successful. Landing secretly in Scotland with but seven trusty officers, yet such was the efficiency of the papal machinery, that it soon enabled him to command an army which made England tremble. But the contest was short and decisive. Although he gained some important advantages, yet the signal victory over his forces at Culloden, in 1746, effectually checked his career. Despairing of success, he fled to France, where, through the intercession of the king's mistress, he received a pension. He finally returned to Rome, where he died of diseases engendered by habits of intemperance.

We have now alluded, in this chapter to some of those popish intermeddlings in the political concerns of England, so grossly in violation of international law, and which have been so prolific of treason, of popular insurrection, of civil war, and of all that can empoverish a nation and impede its progress; but we have mentioned but few of them. The limits we have prescribed to this work will not allow us to trace the wily and deadly serpent of papal intrigue in all its secret windings, nor dwell upon the important admonitory lessons its history furnishes to patriots, to rulers, and to mankind: these we must leave to the reflection of the reader.

CHAPTER XIII.

PAPAL POLITICAL INTRIGUES IN FRANCE.

Papal Intrigues in France during the Reign of Clovis—of Childeric III.—of Pepin—of Charlemagne—of Hugh Capet—of Philip IV.—of Louis XII.—of Francis I.—of Francis II.—of Charles IX.—of Henry IV.—of Louis XIII.—of Louis XIV.

THE subtile poison of Catholicism was instilled into the French government under the reign of Clovis, the Great, who succeeded his father Childeric, King of the Franks, in 481. Aspiring to extend the territory of his kingdom, which was confined within the sea and the Scheldt, he made war upon Syagrius, the Roman governor at Soissons; captured and put him to death; subjugated Paris, and the cities of Belgia Secunda; and to obtain assistance in conquering the Allemanni; espoused Clotilda, neice of Gundebald, King of Burgundy. Clotilda, who had been educated by the Catholic priests, became in their hands an instrument for the conversion of her royal husband. Conceiving that the God and religion of Catholicism were better able to aid him in completing his intended conquests than were the God and religious contrivances of Paganism, Clovis submitted to be baptized by St. Remigius, and anointed with some holy oil which the bishop affirmed had been brought by a dove from heaven. The crimes and devotion of the king, in the cause of the church, were rewarded with numberless miracles and instances of divine interposition. A white hart of singular statue and brilliancy became the conductor of his army through secret passes, a dazzling meteor blazed forth as his forces approached the cathedral at Poitiers, and the walls of Angouléme fell down at the blast of his warlike bugle. Imbibing the orthodoxy of the bishops, he imbibed also their hatred to the heretics. "It grieves me," said he to a company of princes and warriors assembled at Paris, "to see the Arians still possess the fairest portions of Gaul. Let us march against them with the aid of God; and, having vanquished the heretics we will possess and divide their fertile provinces." His savage piety led him to declare that had he been at the trial of Christ he would have prevented his crucifixion. He summoned and dismissed a council of Gaulic bishops; and then deliberately assassinated all the princes belonging to his family. After having removed, by violence or treachery, the princes of the different Frankish tribes, incorporated their government into his own, stained the soil with the blood of its proprietors and defenders, bowed in abject reverence before the clergy, and committed the most fiendish and heartrending atrocities, the pope of Rome, in consideration of his piety and usefulness, bestowed upon him the title of "The most Christian King and Eldest Son of the Church."

While the pope professed to be the humble successor of St. Peter, the fisherman, he was secretly laboring to become the successor of the Cæsars, the masters of the world. With this end in view he had scattered his monks throughout Europe to preach the doctrines of humility, of passive obedience, of reverence for the clergy, and of absolute submission to himself. The support which these doctrines gave to despotism rendered them acceptable to kings, and the conveniency with which they supplied the want of morality made them popular with the multitude. The arts and miracles of the holy brotherhood excited the wonder, and commanded the reverence of the crowd; and their tact and sycophancy enabled them to become the companions of kings, the instructors of princes, the confessors of all classes, and the spies upon the most secret recesses of their thoughts. The avaricious character of their religious principles enabled them to accept without scruple the spoils of plundering expeditions, and to augment the stores of their wealth by artful tricks and pious frauds. The success of their missionary rapacity enabled them to build spacious convents, sufficiently sumptuous for the accommodation of pious kings who wished to abdicate their thrones. The dungeons of these sanctuaries sometimes contained a monarch, an heir to a throne, or some distinguished personage whom usurpation, jealousy, ambition or tyranny had there confined; and sometimes their halls afforded a hospitable asylum for the sick, the indigent, or the refugee from oppression.

 The popes having, with their usual skill and prudence, established the various parts of their political machinery in different sections of Europe, and sanctified them in the eyes of princes and people, eagerly watched every opportunity to set them in motion in favor of their cherished design. The Saracens, however, entered Europe, and threatened to subjugate it to the authority of the religion of Mahomet; but the hammer of Charles Martel, Mayor of France, which alone crushed 375,000 of the invaders, checked the career of their triumphant arms. But as the warrior had applied the riches of the church to the necessities of the state and the relief of his soldiers, a synod of Catholic bishops declared that the man who had saved the Catholic church from extinction, was doomed to the flames of hell on account of his sacrilege. The inspired synod, in arriving at this orthodox conclusion was assisted by the reported facts, that a saint while dreaming had seen the soul of the savior of Europe, and of Christianity, burning in hell, and that upon opening his coffin a strong odor of fire and brimstone had been perceived. The pope entertained a better opinion of his son Carloman, whose superstition strikingly resembled the malady of insanity. This Mayor of France, while exercising the regal authority of his office, was induced by his spiritual advisers to resign his dignity; to consecrate the remainder of his life to God by shutting himself up in a convent; and to give all his private possessions and valuables to the church. The design which prompted this intrigue seems to have been, to prepare the way for the usurpation of the crown of the Franks, by Pepin, the Short. The pope well knew Pepin was ambitious of the diadem, and had only been deterred from supplanting Childeric III., the King of France, —who was but a youth—by fear of Carloman. This obstacle being removed by the retirement of the devout warrior, Pepin consulted Pope Zachary about his intentions, who replied: "He only ought to be king who exercised the royal power." Encouraged by this papal sanction of prospective treason and usurpation, he had the office of *Mais du Palais* abolished, himself proclaimed King of France, and Childeric imprisoned in a monastic dungeon, in which he was obliged to pass the remainder of his life.

The interests of the pope and Pepin, by these artful machinations, became deeply interwoven. The critical state of the Holy See soon developed the sagacity and good policy of the pope. The Lombards entered Italy, conquered the Exarchate, and threatened the reduction of Rome. Oppressed with these misfortunes, the holy father appeared in the camp of Pepin, dressed in mourning and covered with ashes, soliciting the assistance of his arms in the defence of the church, and of the Consulate government of Rome. But Pepin was more ready to speculate on the misfortunes of the pope than to assist him in his distress. The cruelties which stained the usurper's crown made him apprehensive of insecurity. He therefore signified to the supplicant a willingness to comply with his wishes, if he would officially sanction all the acts of usurpation of which he had been guilty, crown his two sons, and anoint them with the holy oil which the dove had brought from heaven. Terms being satisfactorily arranged between the two parties, Pepin drew his sword and reconquered the greater part of Italy.

The tricks, sophistry, and eloquence of the monks having failed to convert the Saxons to the church, the pope was disposed to try the efficacy of the sword. Charlemagne, Pepin's son, having succeeded to the Frankish throne, and papal influence having gained the ascendency in his councils, he was without difficulty tempted to unfurl his banner in the cause of the church. But the Saxons were courageous warriors, full of the love of independence and of liberty ; and when the alternative of extinction or Catholicism was presented to their choice, their proud spirit gave a desperate valor to their arms, in the maintenance of their rights of existence and of religious liberty. Against superior numbers, they defended the integrity of their empire for thirty-three years ; and had not their chief advised to the contrary, would rather have suffered extermination than to have submitted to a religion baptized in blood, founded upon fraud and treachery, and forced upon their acceptance against their reason and conscience, and by a sword reeking with the blood of their fellow countrymen. The arms of Charlemagne, and the religion and policy of the pope triumphed ; but not until the land was depopulated, the country converted into a desert, and the cost of subjugation outbalanced the value of the victory.

The competition between aspiring candidates for the opulent bishopric of Rome had often been productive of turmoil and bloodshed. The favorite and intended successor of Adrian I. having been disappointed by the unexpected election of Leo III., his exasperated adherents attacked the sacred procession on the occasion, assaulted the chosen vicar of Christ, and, as it is alleged, cut out his tongue, dug out his eyes, and left him dead on the ground. But a miracle, it is averred, interposed in his behalf; restored his life, eyes and tongue; and enabled him to escape a repetition of the outrage by gaining the invisible precincts of the Vatican.

After having received this assistance from heaven he invoked the temporal aid of the Duke of Spoleto, and of the friendly interposition of Charlemagne in his favor. By the influence of these secular princes he was enabled to ascend the sacerdotal throne, and to exercise his spiritual authority in banishing his competitors and their adherents.

On a visit of Charlemagne to Rome, after these events, the pope abruptly crowned him with a diadem, invested him with the regalia of the Cæsars, anointed him with the holy oil which the dove had conveyed from Paraadise, and pronounced him the pious Cæsar crowned by God. The emperor who, professing to have been astonished at the pope's singular conduct, nevertheless took an oath to preserve the faith and privileges of the church. Agreeably to this oath he entrusted the clergy with temporal and civil jurisdiction, expended more cost and labor in the construction of cathedrals than on useful undertakings, and as the demons of the air had admonished the payment of tithes he enforced their exaction with extreme rigor. The favor and liberal indulgence of the pope enabled the emperor, consistently with his Catholicism to enjoy the possession of nine wives, to divert his capricious fancy with numberless mistresses, to prolong the celibacy of his daughters that it might extend the period of an illicit commerce, and to become the father of numerous illegitimate children, whom, however, in atonement for his indiscretions, he consecrated to the priesthood.

The barbarity and usurpations of which Charlemagne was guilty, in the enlargement of his vast empire, naturally made him suspicious of the loyalty of his subjects; and the frequent outbursts which disturbed the peace of certain sections excited his most painful fears for the stability of his throne. To prevent the disorganization of a power which he had constructed with so much labor, but endangered with so much crime, he imprudently scorned the wisdom of adopting concessionary measures, and had recourse to the artifices of priestcraft. Dividing the empire between two of his sons, he had them crowned and anointed with the celestial oil, in expectation that these superstitious ceremonies would excite in the minds of his subjects such reverence for the imperial dignity as would secure in its favor their devout allegiance. But this arrangement excluding his eldest son—the issue of a divorced wife—from an equal participation with his brothers in the administration of the government, excited him to rebel against the authority of his father. His attempt to obtain by arms the justice denied by parental authority was, in consequence of the loyalty of the papal political machinery, unsuccessful; and the injured son was obliged to expiate the guilt of his unfilial insubordination by serving the church in the capacity of a monk, and passing the remainder of his days in a monastic dungeon.

This conspiracy was not the only result that was produced by the policy of Charlemagne, in substituting superstition in the place of justice in his efforts to conciliate popular dissatisfaction. While it lent a prop to the governmental structure, it furnished an instrument for undermining its foundation. The division of the monarchy gave occasion, after Charlemagne's death, to fraternal disputes and civil conflicts; and as these dis-

orders favored the pope's ambitious desire to succeed to
the crown and dominion of the Cæsars, they were kept
active by his machinery until the empire was disintegrated.

The last survivor of the Carlovingian dynasty was
Charles, Duke of Lorraine. The subjects of the realm
at that period had become greatly dissatisfied concerning the oppressive privileges which the clergy enjoyed,
as well as with the impoverishing exactions which they
extorted from their industry. With these popular
grievances the temper and disposition of Charles engaged his warmest sympathies. Pope John XVI.,
elected in 986, perceiving that the heir presumptive to
the throne would, when he acceded to power, listen to
the complaints and lessen the burdens of his subjects;
and acting on the historic motive of the Holy See, in
making rulers its tools, and changing dynasties to suit
its purposes, induced the Frankish nobility to proclaim
Hugh Capet King of France. But before this sycophantic papal favorite could be crowned king, and
anointed with the holy oil, he was obliged to swear to
preserve the clergy in all the privileges and immunities which they enjoyed. Against this formidable conspiracy Charles found himself powerless; and after
making some demonstrations against the usurper, retired
to Lyons, which place was capable of withstanding a
vigorous siege. With great skill and energy, but without any flattering success, his adversary assailed the
strong-built fortifications. The success which valor denied was, however, accorded by treachery. The bishop
of the city having entered into secret negotiations with
Capet, the gates were thrown open at midnight; and

the usurper entering the precincts amid the stillness of the hour captured the royal family, surprised Charles in bed and threw him into prison, from which he was never liberated. The Capitian dynasty, thus founded in fraud, violence and usurpation, and unsupported by a shadow of legal right, stands forth in history as the grand champion of the legitimacy of kings, or their divine right to rule by virtue of their descent, independent of the consent of the governed.

The dynasties of empires and the political events of nations are so intimately connected with the domestic affairs of royal families, that in order to control the one, papal intrigue has constantly intermeddled with the other. Robert II., who became king of France in 997, married Bertha, his cousin, a lady of inestimable qualities. The royal pair were a model of connubial loveliness and felicity; but when an heir had completed the perfection of their happiness the pope interfered, and by the exercise of his sacred authority, embittered the remainder of their existence. Robert not having purchased of the church an indulgence for marrying a cousin, Pope Sylvester II. pronounced the conjugal union illegal, and commanded the king to abandon his wife. To be guilty of an offence of such a henious character against the most amiable of women; to act in violation of all his matrimonial vows and obligations; to spurn his lawful wife as a prostitute, and to declare his children bastards, was a complication of iniquity which Robert declared to the pope that he would rather die than commit. But the obdurate and savage-hearted holy father, whom the view of no misfortune could move, in order to reduce the king to obedience proceeded to pronounce a sentence of excommunication against him. This act was designed to call into requisition all the appliances of the pope's machinery in blasting the happiness of two persons, whose worth was unequaled in the kingdom, and perhaps unsurpassed in the records of history. Accordingly the churches were draped in mourning; the picures of the images of the saints shrouded in black; the bells were tolled night and day; religious worship was suspended in the kingdom; and no funeral ceremony allowed to be performed. The immaculate Bertha was declared polluted; stories were circulated that she had given birth to a monster, which had the head of a savage and the tail of a serpent; the poor, on whom she had been accustomed to bestow charity, now fled at her approach; her domestics broke the costly vases which adorned the palace, and taking the viands from the royal table dashed them into the fire. Consternation seized the populace; and priests, courtiers and people fled alike from the sight of the amiable couple, as if they were destructive monsters. At length, through the repeated requests of Bertha, Robert agreed to a separation, and allowed her to retire to a convent. This act, by which he placed his wife at the mercy of licentious priests, conciliated the vengeance of the sacerdotal monster.

During the reign of Philip II., who became king of France in 1180, the province of Languedoc enjoyed an eminent degree of liberty and prosperity. The charters which the subjects had obtained from their princes secured them in the enjoyment of many important civil rights, fortified by such jealous guards as effectually protected them against the encroachments of executive power. This liberality in their political constitution encouraged liberality in religious inquiry, which consequently led to doubts of the pope's right to temporal power. At the flourishing city of Albi these progressive ideas assumed a definite shape in an organization of the people, which received the appellation of the Albigenses. The pope finding this sectary increasing in numbers and popularity, in spite of the vigorous counteracting efforts of his appliances of bishops, priests and monks, ordered Raymond VI., Count of Toulouse, to compel the Albigenses, by force of arms, to change their religious views. As Raymond of Rogers, Count of Béziers, nephew of Raymond VI., had declared in favor of the reformer, the Count of Toulouse refuse to oblige the pope by taking up arms against the Count of Béziers. On account of this determination, dictated by a high and delicate sense of duty and honor, the pope pronounced sentence of excommunication against him. In addition to this insulting manifesto, he commissioned his legate to raise an army of the cross, for the purpose of exterminating the reformers and their allies. This authorized desperado, through the energetic co-operation of the pope's political machinery, soon collected a numerous army of crusaders; and imposing on them a horrible oath that they would exterminate the Albigenses without pity for the cries or tears of their wives or children, immediately commenced the work of blood and devastation. As this army of murderers approached the city of Carcassonne, an order was given not to leave one stone upon another, and to put to death every man, woman, youth and infant. The butchery was frightful, and mixed with the most fiendish acts. To arrest the horrible work Raymond of Rogers offered to resign his authority. With execrable treachery the legate pretended to be willing to negotiate; but no sooner had he betrayed the Count into his power than he incarcerated him in a dungeon, where he died after experiencing years of suffering. After the removal of Raymond by this base treachery, Carossonne fell; and thirty thousand men, women and children were butchered in one day. Tired of the terrible carnage, or disgusted at its atrociousness, the chiefs of the army of the cross declared to the legate, that among the crowd they could not distinguish the heretic from the Catholic. "Kill on," replied the holy legate, "God will know those which are his." The murderous army moved on; blood flowed at every step; at Béziers sixty thousand were put to death; nor did the carnage cease until the inhabitants of almost every town in Languedoc, without distinction of age, sex or creed, were weltering in their gore. As an express reward to Simon de Monfort for having surpassed all others in hardihood and cruelty on those days of blood, the pope bestowed upon him the devastated domains as a fief of the church. But the soil sown with the bones of heroes, and enriched with the blood of patriots, was prolific of formidable avengers; who constantly shook the throne, and rendered it a calamity to its blood-stained occupant. His son succeeded him; but not being able to defend it against the uprising of the people, it was incorporated into the French empire; but still the war raged, until 1226, when a peace was concluded with Raymond IV., upon condition of his purchasing absolution at an enormous price, and ceding the greater portion of his domains to France.

In 1285, when Philip IV. ascended the throne of France, the despotism of Rome had perpetually encroached on the rights of the sovereignty of the government, and by an insidious policy subjected it more and more to its influence. Among the privileges which the popes arrogated was the right to arbitrate the controversies which arose between independent sovereignties. A dispute having sprung up between Philip IV., of France, and Edward I., of England, Pope Boniface VIII., wishing to enjoy the advantage of dictating the terms of adjustment, arbitrarily attempted to interfere in the controversy. This officious intermeddling in the affairs of a sovereign state was resisted by Philip with patriotic firmness. The irascible pope, transported with rage at the irreverence and independence of Philip, and at the recollection of his liberal governmental views and measures, interdicted all religious worship in his dominions, and suspended the dispensation of the means of grace. But the policy of Philip, in introducing the "third estates," or deputies of the people, which had been instituted by Charlemagne, but discontinued by Hugh Capet, and in his extending the jurisdiction of parliament over the crowned heads, had fortified him in the affections of his subjects, while the papal establishments, in extracting the life-blood from the industrial classes, had weakened popular attachment to the Holy See. The liberality of the king nullified the virtue of the Vatican thunder; and the generous support which he commanded from the people, and from a faction of the priests, enabled him to resist the intermeddling of the pope with the rights of the crown; nay more, as the tyranny of the holy father had rendered him unpopular in Italy, it placed him at the mercy of a prince whom he had insulted and exasperated, and who was capable of taking revenge. Accordingly, emissaries were sent to Rome who, seizing the holy father while he was defiantly seated in the apostolic chair, dragged him from his despotic throne, and cast him into prison. From this ignominious predicament he was, however, shortly afterwards released; but as his character was black with crime, it was determined to summon a council for his deposition. Depressed with the expectation of certain degradation, chagrined and mortified at the loss of his dignity and the insults to his holiness, and having refused all sustenance in confinement for fear of being poisoned, his constitution broke down, and he died in a paroxysm of rage and fear before arrangements could be completed for his trial. According to Catholic authority, "he entered like a fox, reigned like a tiger, and died like a dog." His condition after his death may be variously conjectured by theologians according to their different creeds; but Dante, who was a Catholic, places him in hell between Pope Nicholas III. and Pope Clement V.

During the reign of Louis XII., who became King of France in 1498, the duplicity and treachery which has in general characterized the history of the papal intrigues obtained an illustration in the conduct of the popes, which would have disgraced the chiefs of barbaric nations. Louis, upon receiving the royal diadem, pardoned the wrongs which had been done to him while he was duke, relieved the industry of his subjects by reducing the burden of their taxation, elevated the literary standard of the nation by the introduction of scientific collections, and displayed a nobleness of disposition, and a capacity for the exercise of the governmental functions prophetic of the highest degree of national prosperity and greatness. Pope Julius II. before his election, had professed the warmest friendship for Louis, and secured his influence in gaining the sacerdotal crown. Having succeeded in this strategic measure, his ambition led him to grasp at another object which he conceived Louis's friendship might be made accessory in realizing. That object was the obliteration of the Venitian republic. He accordingly formed a holy league, called the "League of Cambray," with France, Spain and Germany, for the accomplishment of his object. Faithful to his obligations, Louis fought with distinguished bravery in the pope's cause. His heroism won encomiums from all but from the holy father, who was too jealous not to hate superiority, too selfish for sincere friendship, and too sagacious not to perceive that in the further developments of his aggressive designs he was bound to encounter in the heroism and honor of Louis a powerful antagonist. The formidable valor of the Venitian republicans in the defence of their government, the mutual distrust among the allies, which they managed to excite, and the conflicting interpretations of the terms of the compact eventually dissolved the holy league. But the finesse of the pope, and the adroitness with which he engineered his machinery, gave him the ability to conciliate his difficulties with the republicans, and of inducing that republic to unite with him in a league with Spain, England and Switzerland, against France. Germany and France then called a council at Pisa, for reformation in the head and body of the church; at the bar of which they summoned the pope, to explain his conduct. But scorning the mandate of the synod, he convened a council at the Lateran; and causing a decree to be passed declaring Louis to have forfeited his crown, excommunicated him, and interdicted the celebration of religious worship in his kingdom. Louis was now assaulted by the English at Guingate, by the Spanish at Navarre, by the Swiss at Dijon, while his kingdom was internally convulsed by treacherous priests, crafty spies, false friends, and unpatriotic Catholics. Unable to contend against these formidable antagonists, he had to surrendered all his possessions beyond the Alps and the Pyrenees.

Pope Leo X., who succeeded Julius II., governed by motives of nepotism and ambition, concocted a scheme for obtaining for his family the kingdom of Naples and the duchies of Ferrara and Urbino. At the same time Louis entertained a design of reconquering Milan, which he inherited from his grandmother, Valentina Visconti. The success of these schemes depended on the mutual friendship of the projectors. The pope, in order to secure the confidence of Louis, entered into a secret alliance with him, and pretended to favor all his plans. But while he was flattering his hopes, he was preparing to ruin his cause. To weaken his resources he secretly sent Bambo, his legate, to Venice to detach its alliance from France; and though this treacherous mission was unsuccessful, yet when the French appeared on the confines of Italy, he increased his power by the purchase of Modena, and finally reduced Louis to a formal submission.

In 1515 Francis I, ascended the throne, and immediately commenced preparations for the re-conquest of Milan. Pope Leo X., to defeat this enterprise formed an alliance with Milan, Florence, Artois, Germany and Switzerland. A bloody battle ensued in which tigers and giants seemed to struggle with each other, and which was protracted without intermission for two days and nights. France recovered Milan; the pope was reduced to the last extremity; yet the prudence or superstition of Francis concluded a concordat with him, upon such liberal terms as excited the dissatisfaction of France, and the surprise of the world.

After this signal and generous triumph the belligerant powers became reconciled. This event was hailed by the friends of humanity with united acclamations. But the Holy See, whose policy has ever been to foster wars and controversies between governments, that it might improve the consequent confusion and disorder in aggrandizing its power, received the news of pacification with chagrin and disappointment.

But Milan, which had cost France so much to win, was soon lost by the conquest of Charles V., Emperor of Germany and King of Spain. This prince having formed a league with Pope Leo X. against Francis I., —which league was afterwards joined by Henry VIII., of England—active hostilities were soon commenced. After a war of four disastrous years, the emperor captured Francis, obliged him to relinquish his claims to Naples, Milan, Genoa, Asti, Flanders and Artois; to dismember his kingdom by surrendering Burgundy; and to ransom himself by the payment of 2,000,000 crowns. The popularity and victorious march of the German emperor now alarmed the jealous fears of the holy father, Pope Clement VII., who, apprehending in them his own subjugation, united in an alliance with Francis I., the former antagonist of the Roman See, and with all the Italian powers, to arrest the dangerous triumphs of his new rival. The allies succeeded in humbling the pride of Charles; but in the midst of their victories a plague, more fearful than their foes, broke out in the French army, and thinned its ranks with fearful mortality. This circumstance led to the peace of Cambray. But the ambition of Francis, and his indomitable thirst for the reconquest of Milan, soon led him to violate the terms of this covenant. Confederating with Solyman II., Sultan of the Ottoman empire, he drove Charles before his forces. The interest of the Holy See being threatened by the successes of the allied army, and perhaps in the event of the triumph of Charles not perfectly secure, Pope Paul III. interposed his friendly mediation, and induced the belligerents to conclude a truce of ten years.

In 1559 Francis II., son of Francis I., succeeded to the crown of France. Amid the flattering successes of the papal intrigues, the rapid progress of Protestantism in Europe, and the fearless boldness of its advocates, occasioned great uneasiness to the Holy See. Scorning the mild but able services of reason and conciliation, it counselled the most sanguinary measures. The records of the times are consequently filled with accounts of disorders, assassinations, massacres, and the most deplorable conflicts. The French nation was divided into two great factions; the one in favor of Catholicism, the other in favor of Protestantism. By means of the papal machinery of bishops, abbots, priests, monks and spies, the Catholics were made to believe that the religious disorders which had convulsed the empire were but a prelude to an intended extermination of all Romanists. To narrow-minded bigots, who absurdly believed that their church afforded the only possible method of escaping the pangs of purgatory, and of obtaining eternal happiness, all the zeal which their hopes and fears of eternity could inspire was awakened in the defence of their religion. While the Protestants who, on the other hand, believed that Catholicism was idolatry, subversive of Christianity, demoralizing in its tendency, and destructive of the rights of conscience, reason and religious liberty, became equally heated in the defence of their faith. Both factions had been educated in intolerent principles; in the belief that error of opinion was perilous to the soul; that it rendered a person a proper object of aversion and denunciation; and, that a difference of opinion was a sufficient justification of hatred and persecution. Both factions being educated in the principles of bigotry and intolerance, nursed amid convulsions and barbarity, embittered against each other by mutual provocations and injury, were incapable of pacification by just and reasonable concession. The Catholics, having the power, were enabled to inflict on the Protestants the deeper injuries; and, to the credit of the Protestants it will ever be remembered, that they sought not to exterminate their foes, but to obtain equal rights with them.

The Cardinal of Lorraine, who had supervision of the clergy, and Henry, Duke of Guise, the uncle of the king, who directed the military affairs, were both uncompromising in their hostility to the Protestants. Antony of Bourbon, King of Navarre, and his brother Louis, Prince of Condé, being excluded from the governmental administration, united with the Calvinists for the overthrow of the regime, under pretext of religious zeal. Catherine de Medici, mother of the king, and niece of Pope Clement VII., jealous of a power in which she could not participate, favored the designs of Louis, and employed her art in stimulating the opposition of the reformers to the administration of the Duke of Guise. Under these circumstances a conspiracy against the duke was formed at Amboise, which led to a murderous onslaught, and inaugurated civil war. Louis was captured and condemned to death.

In the midst of the distraction of conflicting parties Francis I. died, and Charles IX., in 1560, succeeded to the throne at the age of ten years. Catherine de Medici, his mother, with the acquiesence of parliament, administered the affairs of government. Although a bigoted Catholic, yet having no principle but the love of sway, she was ready to support any faction or creed that administered to her power, or removed an obstacle to her ambition. Without profound views of policy, she was incapable of either originating a great national object, or of supporting it by adequate measures. So indomitable was her passion for dominion, that it as much obdurated her maternal feelings as it disqualified her for a judicious regent. She even studied to incapacitate her sons for the exercise of the governmental functions, and to divert their attention from the state of national affairs. With this end in view she involved them in the grossest dissipation, and strove to keep them in a perpetual whirl of voluptuous intoxication. Perfect in the art of dissimulation, she cajoled Catholics and Protestants. Anxious to obtain the support of all parties, she alternately favored the one and the other. To embarrass the Duke of Guise she threw everything into confusion; but to conciliate the Protestants she had to redeem her pledges; and in spite of the opposition of the court, to issue an act of toleration in their favor.

The lines of party became now distinctly drawn. The Protestant faction, headed by the Prince of Condé, and Coligny, admiral of France, was assisted by the English; and the Catholic faction, headed by Francis, Duke of Guise, was assisted by Spain. At a season of intense public excitement the Duke of Guise, with a band of adherents, was passing a barn in which some Calvinists were singing psalms. Irritating taunts were mutually exchanged between the two parties. This exasperating conduct brought on a collision, in which sixty Calvinists were killed, the flames of civil war ignited, and the empire divided and distracted by the hostile conflicts of the two religious parties. The duke, at the head of his forces, pursued the Protestants with pitiless revenge, and the Protestants retaliated his cruelties with fearful retribution. Desperate conflicts perpetually took place, and the land was drenched with blood. The bigotry of both factions stained their cause with deplorable excesses. At the battle of Dreux the belligerents came to a decisive engagement. The Protestants were defeated, and Condé captured. The Duke of Guise designing to crush Protestantism by striking a blow at Orleans, its centre, commenced active preparations for the enterprise; but while he was engaged in them he was shot by Poltrot de Mercy, a Huguenot nobleman. Advising peace in his last moments, terms of conciliation were accordingly offered the Protestants, which being accepted, tranquillity was restored to the empire.

The arts of Catherine, the intolerance of Catholicism, and the suspicion and fervor of Protestantism, soon convulsed the nation again with the disorders of civil war. Aspiring to rule with more absolute power than she had hitherto been able, Catherine conceived the idea of having the king, whom she held helplessly under her control, declared to be of competent age for the exercise of the royal functions. This accomplished, she made a tour through the empire in company with him. At Bayonne the young king had an interview with his sister, wife of Philip II., King of Spain. The suspicions of the Calvinists were immediately excited; they precipitately armed themselves for defence, and formed a conspiracy to assassinate the king. Civil war consequently broke out. A severe and bloody engagement took place at St. Dennis. The losses were heavy on both sides; but Montmorency, a prominent Catholic leader being killed, another treaty of peace was concluded. But the artifice and dissimulation of Catherine only made treaties which contained the elements of future wars. They satisfied neither the Catholics nor the Protestants; and were evaded by both. Contrary to the stipulations of the treaty of St. Dennis, the Calvinists still continued to hold places which they had contracted to surrender, and to continue correspondence with England and Holland, which they had agreed to break off. The inflammable material of religious bigotry, together with these circumstances, provoked another intestine war. The Duke of Anjou, afterwards Henry III., commanded the Catholic faction; and Condé, and Admiral Coligny headed the Protestant faction. At the battle of Jarnac, Condé was captured and shot; and at the battle of Montcontour Coligny was defeated. Amid these discomfitures of the Protestants a peace was offered them on terms of such extraordinary generosity by the Catholics, that they were unconditionally accepted.

Henry of Navarre, Condé's son, subsequently Henry IV., on hearing of his father's death swore to revenge his murder; but the peace which had just been concluded rendered him destitute of means and arms. His mother, Queen Jeanne d'Albret, after the death of her husband, Condé, King of Navarre, had, in order to avoid the intrigues of Catherine, retired from the French court to Bearn, her hereditary possessions. In this retreat she declared herself in favor of the Huguenots. When her son was but eleven years old the Guises, in conjunction with Philip II., King of Spain, devised a plot for depriving the young prince of his hereditary possessions in lower Navarre, and of placing him in the hands of the latter tyrant. The sagacity of Elizabeth, Queen of England, however, detected this conspiracy in time to frustrate it. In consequence of this base machination, Queen Jeanne d'Albert placed her son Henry, when he was but sixteen years old, at the head of a Protestant army, and caused him to take an oath to shed the last drop of his blood in the defence of his kingdom and religion.

Henry Guise, son of Francis Guise, Duke of Lorraine, became the commander of the royal army. The bloody Catherine, in collusion with this ambitious and bigoted duke, concocted a plot for the total extermination of all the Protestants in the French empire. The peace which had been concluded with the Protestants at Jarnac and Montcontour was but the preliminary measure in the accomplishment of this horrible project. The terms it accorded were so surprisingly advantageous to the conquered forces, that the more cautious Protestants regarded it with suspicion. The next device in this insidious plot, was a specious pretence of uniting all parties in interest and harmony by the bonds of two marriages, the one between the king, Charles IX., and Elizabeth, daughter of Maximilian II., Emperor of Germany, and the other between Margaret, the queen's sister, and Henry, Prince of Navarre. All the distinguished Protestant leaders were earnestly invited to be present at the celebration of the royal nuptials. Fearing treachery many of them, however, declined the honor. Amid the magnificence and festivity of the occasion Queen Jeanne d'Albert was poisoned. Shortly after Coligny was wounded by a shot from a window. The king swore to punish the villain who had attempted the assassination. His mother assured him Coligny had the same designs on his life. Bursting into rage he exclaimed: "Kill every Protestant—kill Coligny." Catherine then held her council of blood. All having been concerted for a general massacre, on Bartholomew's eve, at midnight of the day fixed, the church bells announced the signal for commencing the horrible butchery. Wild shrieks and murderous clamor immediately shook the air. "Spare none; it is God's, it is Catherine's it is the king's order." shouted the Catholic leaders as they led on their gangs of remorseless bigots. In the red glare of terrifying flambeaux, were seen daggers dripping with the blood of men, women, and even babes. The people without means of defence or flight saw they were doomed to perish without mercy or revenge. Coligny awakened from his sleep by the terrific yells and screams that filled the air, arose from his bed and opened the door of his mansion. Meeting the assassins, he courteously invited them into his chamber. "Companions," said he, "finish your work. Take the blood sixty years of war have respected: Coligny will forgive you. My life is of little consequence, and though I would rather lose it in defending you, yet take it." Touched at these words, and his calm, majestic countenance, the ruffians fell upon their knees; one of them threw away his dagger; another embraced the knees of his intended victim, and the courage of all dissolved into tears. Besme, the commander of the gang, who had waited in the court for Coligny's head, becoming impatient entered the chamber, and seeing the assassins overcome by humanity denounced them as traitors to Catherine. At this denunciation one of them averting his head, drew his sword and plunged it into Coligny's breast. For thirty days in every part of the kingdom the most atrocious acts were perpetrated. Doors were burst open; men and women assassinated night and day; babes torn from their mother's arms were murdered before their parents' eyes. Over this dreadful calamity the friends and foes of France might have together wept; but Rome was illuminated, cannons were fired in its honor, churches were shaken with the peals of thanksgiving, priests formed themselves into holy processions to testify their joy, jubilees were proclaimed, and the pope, jealous of the authorship of atrocities that shook the world with horror, had medals prepared to immortalize his right to the honor of having originated the most horrible massacre on record. When we consider the atrociousness of the massacre, and the exultations of the holy father, we are at a loss which most to pity, the victims of the catastrophe, or the fiend that rejoiced over it. After the incidents of that day Henry of Navarre and the Prince of Condé had to profess Catholicism in order to save their lives. This device defeating the designs of Catherine on the life of Henry, she next added to the ignominy of her character by attempting to dissolve the marriage which, through her influence, had just been consummated. Foiled in this scheme, she then sought to poison the happiness of the royal pair. To hold Henry spell-bound in the power of her fascinations, she spread around him all the voluptuous allurements of sensual pleasure. But the native magnanimity of his spirit broke the thralls of her enchantment; and secretly escaping from a corrupt and besotted court, he recanted his Catholicism, and placed himself at the head of the Protestant League as King of Navarre; a title which he had rightfully assumed since his mother's death. The revenge which was now rife on the lips of thousands, for slaughtered relatives and citizens, and the portentous disasters which overhung the empire, convinced Catherine of her error; and Charles, tracing the calamities of the nation to her ambition, resolved to atone for his past neglect by governing the empire himself: but death too soon deprived him of an opportunity to make this atonement.

On the death of Charles IX., Henry III., his brother, succeeded to the throne. But being then King of Poland, Catherine, his mother, was permitted to govern in his name until he should be able to assume the administration himself. Catherine immediately concluded a peace with the Huguenots, which granted them religious liberty But this liberal concession exasperated the Catholics, and afforded Henry Guise a pretext for perfecting a league which had been projected by Cardinal Lorraine. The professed object of this league was to defend Catholicism, and extirpate religious liberty; but it had also a secret object, which was to usurp the throne. After Henry III. had returned to his domains, his profligate disposition, and his want of decision and firmness made him the dupe of his mother's intrigues. By her machinations he was kept imprisoned in the royal palace, occupied with frivolous intrigues and stupefied with debauch, even while dissension was shaking his government, and treason plotting his downfall. Besides the unpopularity which his neglect of national affairs engendered in the minds of his subjects, his marriage with the Countess of Lorraine, giving the Guises increased influence in the government, added suspicion to the popular discontent.

By the support of the papal machinery, Henry Guise became sufficiently powerful to dictate laws to the king. He obliged him to annul all provisions in favor of the reformers, and carried his insolence so far that the king forbid him to approach the capitol. It was now discovered that the duke intended to kidnap the king, imprison him in a monastic dungeon, and usurp the imperial authority. Conscious of his power, the duke boldly violated the king's command, that he should not enter Paris. At this defiance the king called on his troops for assistance; but so effectively had the pope's machinery operated, that the people attacked the royal troops, drove them away, and thirty thousand papists sprung to arms in the defence of the duke. Such was the helplessness of the king that he had to fly for safety to Chartres, and to conclude a treaty with his enemy. Upon the assembling of the Estates of Blois, they decided that the duke was too powerful to be brought to trial, but that his open treason would justify the king in having him assassinated. Appearing to be reconciled to him he then partook of the eucharist in company with him; but while he did so, gave secret orders for his assassination. In a few days after this event the duke was stabbed as he entered the royal palace, and Cardinal Lorraine met the same fate in a dungeon.

The severe disappointments which these melancholy events occasioned to the hopes of the Papal See, gave rise to a holy league against Henry III., headed by the Duke of Mayenne, brother of the Duke of Guise, which league was supported by all the resources of Rome. Every department of the papal machinery was now set in the most vigorous action. Paris and the principal cities of France were incited to declare against the king. The Serbonne, the highest Catholic university in the empire, absolved the subjects from their allegiance to him; the pope threatened him with excommunication; and his assassination was publicly preached in the churches. But by a fortunate coalition with Henry of Navarre the king defeated the pope and his league, re-captured Paris, and established again his authority in the empire. Yet the Catholic church, which never forgives an offence, and scruples at no means to remove an obstacle, found a Dominican monk who executed her vengeance by the assassination of the king.

Henry III. left no male heirs; consequently Henry of Navarre became the legitimate inheritor of the throne of France. The papal machinery which in vain had been called into requisition to destroy him, was now set in vigorous operation to prevent him from establishing a legal right to his heritage. The Duke of Mayenne, at the head of the Catholics, declared against him; Philip II., king of Spain, claimed the crown; and several unsuccessful attempts were made to assassinate him. But the valor and sagacity of Henry defeated his enemies, and triumphed over all difficulties. The papal machinery was, however, still formidable; and Henry IV., convinced that the blood of his subjects must continue to flow as long as they were governed by a Protestant sovereign, decided to profess the Catholic faith, which of all others he must have sincerely detested. By this politic act of humiliation he acquired for his subjects political security and entire religious liberty, and obtained from the pope a concession to his right to the crown. But in sacrificing principle to expediency he did not conciliate papal malice, nor secure tranquillity to his reign. Conspiracies were rife, female intrigue abounded, bigotry and intolerance gave birth to much violence and disorder, and finally, the long-premeditated assassination of Henry IV. was accomplished by Ravaillac, who stabbed him to the heart with a double-edged sword, the papal symbol of spiritual and temporal power.

The papal machinery during the past reigns had demoralized the nation. The national policy was characterized by a system of falsehood, corruption and intrigue. Princes of the blood were excluded from the throne, on account of their liberal proclivities. Innocent men, women and children were imprisoned, murdered and burnt. Female intrigue, the bane of national peace and virtue predominated in political circles; and public robbery and extravagance laid the foundation of a debt which ultimately broke down the government.

Under Louis XIII., who became King of France in 1610, the papal machinery was directed by Cardinal Richelieu, who governed the king; by M. Tellier, his confessor, and Madame Maitenon, his prostitute, who governed the cabinet. Richelieu gave boldness and craft to the national policy, and consummated the governmental absoluteness which had been initiated by Louis XI. Division of power being more friendly to justice and republicanism than consolidation, the papal political machinery has always vigorously, as well as universally, labored to defeat the first and encourage the second. But what is unfriendly to republicanism is destructive to national prosperity; and consequently the papal intrigues and appliances in favor of absoluteness in France destroyed the greatness of the nation.

The political security and religious liberty which Henry IV. had secured to the subjects were annulled by the repeal of the Edict of Nantes, and Catholic intolerance again domineered over the lives and fortunes of Protestants. Kings had been taught by their teachers and spiritual guides that "to dissemble was to reign," and that "to become a great man it was necessary to become a great villain." The consequence was national weakness and demoralization. Mock treaties were made to conceal real ones, and kings, to disguise their intentions, acted differently from what they thought. A succession of weak, bigoted, tyrannical, and criminal rulers had oppressed the industry of the country, and drove thousands of subjects to seek a livelihood under less oppressive government. Despotic ministers, rapacious favorites, intriguing prostitutes, foolish enterprises absurd laws, professed rakes in the garb of priests and cardinals, prodigality, corruption and tyranny withering the vitality of the nation, and accumulating on the heads of the people an insupportable load of taxation and misery, were the deplorable results of the operation of the pope and his political engine. But while such were the calamities which Catholicism was maturing, the eloquent writings of Voltaire, of Rosseau, and other liberal authors were awakening a spirit of inquiry in the public mind, and preparing the way for political regeneration. The smouldering fires of freedom which burned in the breast of the nation, rendered the conflict between monarchy and republicanism inevitable. It finally took place; the majesty of the people was vindicated; and, a national assembly convened consisting of three hundred and seventeen clergymen, three hundred and seventeen nobles, and six hundred and seventeen deputies of the people; all of whom took an oath never to separate until they had given France a free constitution. From the ruins of the monarchy a republic arose in majesty and power. The feudal estates were abolished without indemnification. The invidious game laws, the feudal tribunals, the church tithes, the ecclesiastical revenues, the hereditary descent of officers, the exemption of church dignities from military taxation, the laws excluding Protestants from offices of trust or profit, and denying them the right of inheriting, acquiring or bequeathing property, and all that the toil of the papal machinery had accumulated on the heads of the people, were swept away by the spirit of liberal government. To obtain this freedom the nation had poured out its blood. But the nation had been educated in Catholic bigotry and intolerance; and now it visited on the heads of its tutors the lessons which they had taught. The people swept away the despotism of the throne, but left it remaining in the national councils; and, while they made a wreck of oppression, they preserved its elements to be reconstructed in another form. It is not, then, surprising, that hard as their freedom was won, it was so easily betrayed by the genius of Napoleon Bonaparte, once its advocate, but always its foe; who hated republicanism as much as he hated papacy, for they both were in conflict with his designs; and who loved nothing but himself and supreme dominion. But the boon he sought his ambition defeated. While he stood at the height of his fortune, with the conquest of Europe in his grasp, the mask fell from his brow. The confidence of freemen forsook him; and his glory, which else might have outrivalled the splendor of the greatest, flickered, grew dim, and soon vanished away; leaving the world as much astonished at the obscurity it left as it had been at the effulgence it had emitted.

CHAPTER XIV.

PAPAL POLITICAL INTRIGUES IN GERMANY.

Papal Intrigues in Germany under the reigns of Otho I.—of Henry IV.—of Henry V.—of Frederic I.—of Frederic II.—of Conrad IV.—of Albert I.—of Henry VII.—of Louis of Bavaria—of Charles IV.—of Sigismund—of Charles V.—of Ferdinand II.—Papal Intrigues in Austria—in Prussia—and in the Netherlands.

WITTIKIND the Great, King of Saxony, after a vigorous resistance for thirty-three years against the arms of Charlemagne, the confederate of the pope, submitted to be baptized to spare the further effusion of the blood of his subjects. But in the events of one hundred years, the conquered became the emperors, and the Franks were supplanted on the throne by the Saxons. From the time that the Carlovingian dynasty was established until the dissolution of the empire in 1806, the secular power had to continually struggle against the intrigues and usurpations of the Papal See.

The pope's claim of being the disposer of crowns, and the source of secular power, acheived something of a triumph in 962, when through a crafty policy the pontiff bestowed the diadem on Otho. From motives of policy the emperor conceded the spiritual claims of the pope, but prudently nullified them by placing him under his authority. While Otho acknowledged that he was emperor by the grace of God and the pope, he required the latter, who was John XII., to swear allegiance to him, and the Roman See to enter into a solemn agreement with him that henceforth no pope should be chosen except in the presence of a Germanic imperial commission. This judicious check on the intriguing policy of the Papal See, was too unpleasant to be tolerated longer than weakness made it unavoidable. Presumptuous as false, Pope John XII. was led to violate his oath of allegiance, and to take up arms to acquire inependence of secular authority. For this act of perjury, treason, and violation of a solemn treaty—which in a layman would have been a capital offence, but in a priest was aggravated by the additional crime of hypocrisy—the emperor could not do less than depose him.

In the papal monarchy virtue and ability were seldom conspicuous, and generally when either appeared in its administration, it was less the offspring of Catholicism than of the Germanic authority. The emperors of Germany were far better men than the popes of Rome. While the first labored to reform the church, the latter did little else than corrupt it. Virtue, the foundation of public order and concord, could not but be encouraged in the subjects by a sagacious monarch; and vice, the indulgent mother of fraud and imposition, could not but be cultivated by a crafty and ambitious priest. In the progress of the conduct of the papal and the imperial policy, so mutually antagonistical, Henry III., who became Emperor of Germany in 1046, had to depose three popes, and to fill the papal chair during his life with men of his own choice. He also held the papal monarchy under strict surveilance, and forbade the bestowal of any spiritual dignity, or the appropriation of any church property without his sanction. The wholesome effects of his severity won commendations even from those upon whom they were most rigorously enforced; in proof of which it may be stated that the clergy spontaneously bestowed on him the title of "The Pious," which he condescended to accept.

In 1056 Henry IV. ascended the throne of Germany. The Papal See, bitterly groaning under the jealous restraint which had been imposed on it by the secular authority, eagerly watched, and artfully intrigued for an opportunity to remove them. The impolitic and tyrannical conduct of Henry IV. appeared, perhaps in its eye, as a providential circumstance designed to aid the success of its long cherished design. The emperor, governed by the advice of Archbishop Adelbert, attempted, by building castles, and committing brutal and violent acts, to rule his people through the terror of his authority. Neglecting to guard popular interests, which alone can secure popular attachment, his efforts to overawe his subjects produced only dissatisfaction and insurrection. In an outburst of popular violence provoked by his imprudence, considerable damage was done to some churches in Saxony and Thuringia. These disorders gave Henry the opportunity of gratifying his revengeful feelings in accusing the inhabitants before the pope of sacrilege, and of entering their territory and perpetrating the most barbarous cruelty. The consequences of this proceeding eventuated in such a favorable crisis to the papal designs, that, had the ablest pope projected and engineered them they could not have culminated more propitiously. The injured and exasperated inhabitants appealed to the pope. Pope Gregory VII., having ascended the papal throne without the consent of the German court, eagerly embraced a cause which enabled him to assert his claim claim to independent sovereignty, and supremacy over all secular authority. Fully aware that the tyranny of Henry had deprived him of the affections and support of his subjects, he commanded the unpopular monarch to appear before him, under pain of excommunication. In punishment for this ferocious warrant the emperor summoned a council of bishops at Worms, and obliged them to renounce their allegiance to Gregory. This daring act so irritated the pope that he began to lavish, with unsparing liberality, anathemas on the head of the monarch. Henry at first treated this display of arrogated divinity with scornful indifference, but his vices had too much disembarrassed the action of the papal machinery not to allow it to disable his power and revenge. His subjects disowned their allegiance to him; his friends deserted him; his soldiers disobeyed his orders; and he found himself helplessly at the mercy of a revengeful and irritated priest. With a refinement of malice that seems to do credit to papal ingenuity, at least, the emperor was required to dress in penitential robes, formally to solicit for three days an interview with the sacerdotal despot, and then to promise unconditional obedience to him in all things. But the acts of tyranny carry with them the seeds of retribution. The tyrant who could impose such conditions on a fallen foe, could also have been guilty, in the exercise of his power, of inflicting injuries on his subjects which would be calculated to excite a disposition to revolt and retaliation. This was precisely the case with Pope Gregory VII. He had oppressed the Italian provinces to such a degree that the inhabitants longed for an opportunity to depose him; and now the misfortunes of Henry appearing to render him an available agent in the accomplishment of their designs, they proposed a coalition with him. The pope becoming acquainted with this secret machination, set about to counteract it. By the operation of his skilful machinery he was enabled suddenly to create a conspiracy in the heart of Germany, for the deposition of the emperor; but the vigilance and valor of the latter defeated the revolutionary movement. Having in vain exhausted all resources to subject the incorrigable monarch to his absolute authority, he now sought to beguile the mortification of his defeat by hurling anathemas at his obstinate head. But the temper of Henry not disposing him to indulge the chagrined pope in insolent sports, summoned a council of German and Italian bishops at Brixen, and by proving to their satisfaction that Pope Gregory VII. was a heretic, a sorcerer, and had dealings with the devil, effected his degradation, and placed Clement III. in the papal chair.

The spirit and pretensions of Catholicism are so inimical to secular authority that, to whatever extent they obtain a controlling influence in a government they tend to abridge its sovereignty, and threaten its subversion. This tendency, so clearly indicated by the principles of the papal monarchy, and so fearfully illustrated in its history, is incapable of being restrained by any sense of gratitude, or by any obligation of oaths. A knowledge of this unhappy truth will prevent surprise that the munificent favors which Henry bestowed on Pope Clement III., in elevating him to the papal dignity, should not have caused the repeal of the anathemas and excommunications which had been pronounced against him, nor arrested the papal machinery in its insidious and treacherous operations, in fostering the elements of discord which existed in the empire. Nothing but the surrender of the principles of sovereignty will ever conciliate a pope to the authority of a secular government. The prudence, courage, and talents of the king were hence constantly called into requisition to defeat the secret machinations of his enemies. His eldest son was instigated to rebel against him. After he had subdued him, his second son, whom he had crowned as his successor, obliged him to surrender into his hands the imperial authority. By the implacable revenge of the Papal See, operating through its varied machinery, he was deprived of power, reduced to scorn and neglect, and after it had murdered him by degrees, prohibited the interment of his anathematized corpse in consecrated ground.

After Henry V., in 1106, had wrung from his father's hand the imperial sceptre, he sought to have this atrocious act sanctified in the eyes of his subjects by being crowned at Rome by the pope—Paschal II. This sanction of unfilial conduct the pope was willing to accord; but as it seemed to present an opportunity for making a good speculation, he exacted, as the only condition on which the favor could be granted, a concession to the Holy See of all the rights and privileges which had been claimed for it by Pope Gregory VII.

This proposition startled Henry; he saw the ambitious designs of the pope, and he felt the importance of checking them. Boldly denying the papal pretensions, and rejecting with indignant contempt the proposition of Paschal, he marched his army on Rome, dragged the pope from the altar while he was celebrating mass, and casting him into prison, determined that he should there remain until he consented to crown him without any condition. To be restored to liberty and luxury the pope acceded to all the terms dictated to him by the emperor, but with a secret disposition to render them nugatory at the first opportunity. Disturbances occurring in Germany, the pope was agreeably relieved of the embarrassing restraints of the emperor's presence. To suppress the Germanic revolution the skill and valor of Henry was occupied for two years. In the meantime the pope, in order to nullify the concessions which he had made, organized an Italian conspiracy against the emperor. Soon as Henry had quelled the insubordination in Germany, he therefore returned to Italy to punish the author of the calamities of his reign. But Pope Paschal evaded the designed chastisement by absconding to Apulea, where he shortly afterwards died.

Pope Galatius II., an enemy of Henry, having obtained the papal dignity, the latter deposed him, and caused Bourden, under the name of Gregory VIII., to be substituted in his place. The deposed pope and his cardinals, having the control of the papal machinery, were enabled to oppose, with great success, the policy of Henry in every part of his dominion. Galatius assembled a council of bishops at Vienna and excommunicated him; Calaxtus II. convened one at Rheims, and repeated the sentence; the nobles broke out in frequent rebellion; and finally such insubordination prevailed in the empire, and such violent outbursts so frequently disturbed the public peace, that in order to restore tranquillity Henry was compelled to subscribe to a concordat at Worms, in which he renounced the right of investiture, and to any interference in the consecration of bishops.

Frederic I. succeeded to the imperial throne in 1152. The increasing opulence and power of the Italian and Lombardine cities owing allegience to Germanic authority, the ambitious aspirations of the Papal See for illimitable dominion, and the insidious operations of its machinery in producing public taste and opinion in harmony with its desires, had, at the beginning of the reign of Frederic I., produced revolts and usurpations in Lombardy and Italy, which obliged the emperor to visit and chastise the insurrectionary districts. Pope Alexander III., the chief source of the public discord, fled on the approach of Frederic to France, and excommunicated him. A league was then formed between the pope, Venice, and the Greek empire against Frederic; and for twenty years the calamities of war were protracted. The cruelty which the emperor had exercised towards the rebellious cities created a desperate opposition to his authority, and exercised an important influence in stimulating the valor and energy of the people, by which their freedom was finally achieved in the treaty of Venice in 1177.

The spiritual and temporal crown of the world which the Roman See attempted to manufacture out of the fishhooks of St. Peter, however visionary it might originally have appeared, assumed in the progress of the papal political intrigues, the appearance of a stubborn, formidable and frightful reality. With the profound policy which it elaborated, and the systematic course of measures which it adopted, accommodated to all exigencies and pursued through all periods, and at all places; with its machinery ramifying the political, social, and literary institutions of Christendom; with its confessors transmitting to Rome every important fact; with its inquisition extorting from victims an admission of every false charge of which ecclesiastical interests required the establishment; with its preachers and spiritual guides manufacturing, private and public opinion suitable to its demands by perverted facts and false statements; and with its army of monks, knights, sycophant princes, servile kings, and deluded devotees; it had at the period of Pope Innocent III. subjugated Christendom under its despotic authority. During the progress of its aggressive course the voice of reason and patriotism had often lifted up remonstrances against its advancement; but the eloquent tones died away unheeded amid the clamorous chaunts of superstitious rites. But now, after supineness had allowed it to amass supreme and despotic power, and fortify itself by every means of defence, the antagonism of the people began to be energetically manifested. It is the fate of despotism of every form, when it has developed the full strength of its all-blasting power, to awaken another power destined to trample it in the dust. That power is the strength which slumbers in the popular arm. When the papal despotism was no more a pretension, but a fact, when it stood distinctly before the world clotted with the blood of generations, surrounded by broken sceptres and crushed thrones, with its feet on the neck of kings and people, and its usurping hand grasping at the crowns of earth, heaven and hell, a murmur of horror broke from the lips of the world. Then learning began to scoff at its claims, research to expose its frauds, wit to ridicule its pretensions; and then religious liberty, through the Albigenses and Waldenses uttered that memorable peal, which is destined to reverberate as an undying tone through all future ages. Then arose the free cities from their long degradation, and began to perfect their internal organizations by the establishment of corporations; then appeared the first universities, arousing the dormant spirit of free inquiry and investigation; then the abrogation of the system of violence began to restore public security; and then the separate members of the empire began to be assembled and deliberate on public affairs, originating the principle of the provincial diets.

Frederic II., son of the emperor Henry VI., was born at this illustrious period of German history. Philip, Duke of Suabia, was nominated regent during Frederic's minority, but the pope, wishing a more pliant instrument, substituted Berthold. Finding this scheme impracticable he recommended Otho, and Philip being murdered, the papal policy succeeded. But the pope soon found that his intrigue had vested with power a mortal foe to the Papal See. For Otho clearly manifested a design of not only wresting Sicily from Frederic, which the latter inherited from his mother, princess of Constance, but of establishing the authority of Germany over certain possessions of Italy which it claimed as an inheritance. To counteract the mistake of his policy the pope took Frederic under his protectson, and called into requisition all the power of his machinery. At the age of twenty-one years he crowned his protege Emperor of Germany; but in order to bind him to his interests he exacted a coronation oath that he would undertake a crusade in behalf of the church. Frederic, enjoying the favor and influence of the pope, and the advantageous co-operation of his machinery, soon defeated Otho, and became sole sovereign of the empire.

With a grasp of intellect, and versatility of talent that rarely have sprung from a royal cradle, Frederic II. elaborated projects which, although they transcended the liberality and enlightenment of his age, yet laid the foundation for their development in a future period. The possession of the German and Sicilian crowns led him to hope that he would be able to repress the powerful hierarchy of Rome, and reduce the pope to the dignity of a bishop. Impressed with the importance of this object, and the difficulty of its accomplishment, he slowly and cautiously removed obstacle after obstacle, and selected the elements for his great enterprise. As a preliminary measute he caused his son to be crowned King of Rome. This act alarmed the jealousy of Pope Honorious III., who desired to be acquainted with the motive of it. The emperor replied that his coronation oath required him to undertake a crusade, and the fulfilment of it rendered it necessary to invest his son with regal authority. However ungratifying this reasoning was to the pope, he could not refute it, and as the emperor promised to deal severely with the heretics, and to exclude them from offices of trust or profit, he became greatly pacified. In maturing his measures for the restoration of the Italian empire, the emperor procrastinated for twelve years the fulfilment of his undertaking, a crusade; and though the pope frequently reminded him of the solemnity of his obligation, yet his apologies were so plausible that they seemed fully to justify the delay. The inexplicable mystery of Frederic's conduct, however, excited the apprehensions of Pope Gregory IX.—and to get rid of his presence in Europe he peremptorily demanded that he should undertake the promised crusade. With a show of obedience to the pope's injunction, he commenced preparing for the enterprise, but upon such an extensive scale, and so interruptedly and slowly that it damped the fire, consumed the provisions, and thinned the ranks of the pilgrims. At length he set sail with his fleet, but becoming indisposed after three days' voyage returned home. The return of his formidable army alarmed the fears of the pope, who appears to have equally dreaded the success of his arms abroad and of his presence at home. Adopting the customary policy of the popes in their emergency, he endeavored to embarrass the designs of Frederic by pronouncing sentence of excommunication on him, and suspending all religious services in his dominions. The justice of this sentence being attempted to be supported by the failure of the emperor to fulfil his coronation oath, Frederic endeavored to nullify it, if not in the eyes of the pope, yet in those of the people, by undertaking a vigorous crusade. But the infallible pope who had excommunicated him for not becoming a crusader, now excommunicated him for becoming one. During the emperor's absence the pope preached a crusade against him in his own dominions, organized a conspiracy against him, and devastated his empire with his own troops. That he might weaken the power and popularity of the emperor abroad, he ordered the bishops and knights of the army of the cross in Palestine to dispute his command and oppose his designs. But the remarkable genius of Frederic, undaunted by difficulties, and unimpressible by discouragement and reverses, made him victorious, as well over the arms of the Turks as over the intrigues of the pope. He entered Jerusalem in triumph; and, not finding a bishop who would incur the papal anathemas by crowning him, he performed the ceremony himself. The success of Frederic filled Christendom with joy, but the pope with indignation. He declared every church into which he entered profaned; interdicted the celebration of divine worship in Jerusalem; and such was his influence with the chivalrous knighthood, that among its members were found persons base enough to secretly inform the Sultan how he might dispose of his victor, by assassination, in his customary visits to the river Jordan. But the magnanimity of the Sultan rejected the proposition with contempt, and communicated the matter to the emperor to place him on his guard.

While Frederic exacted from the pope what justice and self respect demanded, he was so far from being disposed to treat him with unnecessary rigor that, when his vices and tyranny had excited his subjects into a rebellion, he interposed in his behalf and restored tranquillity. An act so generous in the emperor should have awakened in the pope an equal degree of magnanimity, but so far was he incapable of any sense of gratitude, that he instigated the emperor's son to conspire against him, and assured him of the assistance of the Lombards. This conspiracy was detected, and defeated in its bud; and, the emperor regarding his son more as the victim of sacerdotal craft than as a real foe to his authority, pardoned his disloyalty. The sense of gratitude naturally arising from this act of clemency, added to the weight of filial affection, should have been sufficient to form a disposition which would have subjected the son to the most affectionate subordination to the father. But the dispensations and absolutions with which the church pretends to nullify social and civil obligations, unhappily interfered with the natural instincts of the son's mind, and led him to add to the guilt of his treason, the ignominy of attempting to assassinate his father. This atrocious act cancelling every obligation of nature, would have justified the emperor in proceeding to extremes; but his native magnanimity prevailed, and he sentenced his son to perpetual banishment.

The success of the policy of Frederic comprehended a union of the hostile elements of his southern territory, the subjugation of the Germanic aristocracy, and of the Italian cities in alliance with the pope. Preparatory to the execution of this policy he made some conquests in Lombardy These successes excited the revenge of the pope, who accordingly visited on his head another excommunication. But the Vatican thunder was allowed to roll on, as amid its music the emperor marched on from victory to victory. At length, in the development of the policy of Frederic, the time arrived for striking a decisive blow at the heart of the public disorder. By a sudden movement he entered the papal dominions. The pope trembled on his throne. He saw his monarchy at the mercy of an emperor, whom he had anathematized, whose son he had taught to rebel, whose subjects he had corrupted, and whose downfall he had labored to effect. The consummation of the policy of Frederic was in his grasp; but the magnificent prospect which skill and valor had obtained, superstition blasted. Having some reverence for the office, though none for the character of the pope, and conscious of the powerful influence it wielded over the superstitious, he ventured to listen to the papal monarch, who professed a willingness to concede all his demands, but proposed that they should first be sanctioned by a council of the bishops of the church. The emperor soon perceived, but too late, that this specious proposition was but a popish device. The preliminaries for holding the proposed council established the fact, that the pope intended to have it chiefly composed of the most inveterate enemies of the emperor; in fact none but such were invited to participate in its proceedings. Frederic felt justified, therefore, in forbidding the convention to assemble. As his prohibition was disregarded, he intercepted a Genoese fleet of one hundred bishops, and brought them captive to Naples. This manœuvre broke up the council, and perhaps broke the pope's heart, as he shortly afterwards died.

Cardinal Fiesco, a warm friend of the emperor, became Pope Innocent IV.; but the dignity of pope making him regard the emperor as hostile to his monarchial pretensions, converted his former friendship into bitter annimosity. Returning to Lyons, he confirmed all the aathemas that had been pronounced against Frederic, and summoned him to appear at the bar of a grand council to be convened at that place. In the proceedings of this council the most ridiculous and groundless charges were preferred against Frederic, and though completely refuted by his deputies, yet as the proceedure was merely the semblance of a judicial trial, to sanction preconcerted malice and revenge by forms of lagality, the council did not hesitate to declare him guilty, any proof of innocence to the contrary, It seems to have concentrated its ingenuity in devising new and unheardof methods to give terrific importance to the ventilation of its hate. An anathema was pronounced on the body and soul of the emperor, and on all his interests, friends and allies. While pronouncing these religious curses, the priests, like fiends administering at some infernal ceremonies, held in their hands lighted torches, and upon its conclusion suddenly extinguished them; and by the theatrical trick of uttering discordant shrieks and howls, seemed in the darkness of the cathedral to have converted the holy place into the lower regions, peopled with the arch-fiend and his agents. Though these artistical elaborations were not without some effect, yet the vigor of the emperor's genius, the magnanimity which he constantly displayed, his vast popularity, and the triumph of his arms—which continued to his death—demonstrated to the intelligent that there was no real curse in the papal anathemas.

Conrad IV., son of Frederic II., became emperor of Germany in 1250. Innocent IV., whose policy it was to profess any friendship, and violate any obligation that contributed to his interests, determined to complete on the son the vengeance he had commenced on the father. Presumptuous as vindictive he declared that inasmuch as Frederic II. had been excommunicated, his son could not inherit the throne. On the ground of this ridiculous pretext, he pronounced him dispossessed of all his inheritance; laid on him an interdict; and persecuted him by all the means which his power and influence afforded. But notwithstanding a revengeful pope, whose malice through his machinery operated everywhere, yet, he had more than his equal to contend with. The courage and heroism of Conrad defeated the papal army, kept the pope's allies in check, and was about to enter Lombardy with the fairest prospects of success when his illegitimate brother, by administering poison to him, relieved the pope of a formidable adversary.

Conradin, son of Conrad IV., the last of the noble house of Hohenstaufen, was the heir to the throne. The pope refused to acknowledge his right to succession, because his father had been excommunicated. He declared also that Conradin had forfeited his right of inheritance to the crown of Naples and Sicily, and undertook to bestow it on Charles of Anjou. But Conradin entered Italy and defeated the usurper; but while he was pursuing the flying enemy with too much recklessness, he was captured by the vanquished. The world expected that his youth and valor could not but win compassion even from the iron-hearted pope, but the intense hatred of the papal monarch to the noble house of which this intrepid lad was the last scion, would not permit him to allow an opportunity to escape of extinguishing it forever. Conradin was therefore, though but sixteen years old, publicly executed as a criminal; but his heroism, and the circumstances under which he met death, crowned his memory with immortal honor, while it cast a deeper tinge of ignominy on the already blackened character of the pope.

The usurpation of territory, and interference in political affairs, which are so strongly characteristic of the papal policy, originate from the constitutional principles of the Roman See. In conformity with them Pope Boniface VIII. proclaimed himself King of Rome; and declared that the Roman See was the source whence the Germanic electors derived their rights. Albert I. being chosen emperor by the electors in 1298, was summoned by the pope to appear before him and apologize for having accepted the crown without consulting his pleasure, and to expiate the guilt of his offence by the performance of such penance as should be prescribed. To enforce compliance with this injunction the pope formed an allegiance with the archbishop of Mentz, a powerful military bishop, and a former friend of Albert. To resist the belligerent pope Albert effected an alliance with Philip la Belle, of France. Making a sudden diversion into the electorate of Mentz, Albert obliged the bishop to form a league with him for five years. The pope then suggested peaceful negotiation rather than disastrous war. It was finally agreed between the two contracting parties that the pope should give to Albert the possessions of his ally, and that Albert should acknowledge that the western empire was a grant as a fief from the pope, that the electors derived their right from the Roman See, and that he would defend the papal interests with his arms. The pope then proceeded, by virtue of an excommunication, to invalidate the title of Louis la Belle, of France, to his kingdom, and officially to transfer it to Albert I.

During the reign of Henry VII., who became emperor of Germany in 1308, the tyranny and ambition of the pope were held in decent check, and the Papal See was unusually quiet and respectable. The emperor, whom the pope hated, but whom he dared not anathematize, was finally removed by poison administered in the sacramental wine, by Moltipulcian, a Dominican monk. Soon as this event occurred the pope's vengeance, which had been accumulating in fury for years, but which was too much overawed to utter a murmur, now burst forth with the most impetuous and indecent violence in anathemas on the soul, the corpse, the coffin, and the tomb of the dead emperor; but it is not supposed that they done any damage, except to the character and good sense of the Roman See.

Louis IV., of Bavaria, became emperor of Germany in 1330. To arrest the encroachments of the Papal See on the rights of the sovereignty of the empire, the diet of Rense framed a constitution, in 1338, which provided that the choice of the electors of the union should be final in its decision, and independent of the Pope of Rome. These patriotic proceedings seemed to the pope to be interfering with his rights; and John XXI. accordingly prohibited the performance of divine worship in the empire, until the obnoxious constitution should be annulled. But Louis soon repaired this calamity by the creation of Pope Nicholas V., who, having equal authority with Pope John XXI., nullified all his acts. Pope Clement VII., who succeeded to the papal throne in 1342, excommunicated Louis, and by his intrigues caused five electors to declare in favor of Charles of Luxemburg. This violation of the celebrated constitution of 1338 induced three electors to assemble at Lahstein, and declare the choice of Charles null and void; and as Louis had died, they elected Edward of England, but he declining, they elected Frederic the Severe; he also declining, the crown was finally settled on Gunter of Schwarzburg. But Gunter being removed by poison, the papal policy triumphed in the coronation of Charles of Luxemburg.

Charles IV., in 1346, wishing to be crowned by the pope at Rome, visited Italy to negotiate for that favor. Pope Innocent VI., always inclined to make the vanity and ambition of his subjects administer to his aggrandizement, signified a disposition to accommodate the emperor, but on such disgraceful conditions that, by accepting them he subjected himself to the scorn and derision of the world. This self-degradation was much aggravated by the fact that many distinguished Romans, oppressed by the papal administration, united in requesting Charles to claim the city of Rome as a portion of his empire. Instead of improving this opportunity to extend the limits of his government, he renounced all rights, not only to the city of Rome, but to the States of the Church, to Naples, Sicily, Sardinia, and Corsica. He also consented to impose a tax on the empire for the benefit of the Papal See, equal to one-tenth of the ecclesiastical revenues; and further added to his disgrace by taking an oath never to enter Italy without the pope's sanction. For this base sycophancy he was assailed by princes and people with a storm of indignation. To allay the fury of this tempest he announced an intention of convening a council for the reformation of the clergy, and for making liberal concessions to the popular demands. But this attempt to calm the people aroused the indignation of the Papal See. The pope exhorted the electors to depose him instantly. Assailed on all sides, dangers thickening around him from all quarters, but dreading less the indignation of the empire than the anathema of the Roman See, he yielded to the dictation of the pope, and confirmed the clergy in all their privileges, sanctioned all their abuses, protected them in all their possessions, and made them entirely independent of the secular power.

The papal power, at the period of Frederic II., seemed to tremble on the verge of inevitable destruction; but by a profound and unscrupulous policy, and a system of crafty intrigues, aided by a political machinery whose various parts ramified every portion of the empire, and acted in concert through all ages and dynasties, it had steadily carried its advancements through the blood of millions and the ruins of thrones, until, at the time of Charles, it had regained its supremacy in the empire; and dictated treaties to the emperors, measures to the diets, and laws to the people. A power that could at its option excite or quell a popular outburst, create or destroy a dynasty, might be an object of terror to people and princes, but never an object of reverence. The dread it cast on the mind was always unpleasant, and in proportion as its power became oppressive and disadvantageous, opposition and resistance were inevitably excited. The love of independence, the native individualism of the Germanic character, was always a mortal foe to papal despotism. It might be cowered into silence, but it still grew in vigor, became more impatient as the pope became more despotic, and bolder as it became more conscious of its numerical strength. This spirit, in 1411, when Sigismund became Emperor of Germany, displayed an energy prophetic of stirring events and important consequences. The spirit of Germanic individualism led distinguished men of the nation to deny, with emphatic boldness, the pretensions of the pope; to denounce the profligacy of the clergy; and to demand in the body and head of the church a thorough reformation. Prominent among the apostles of religious freedom, which rose into consequence at that time, was John Huss, and his disciples. The success of these reformers excited and alarmed the pope. Hating any semblance of a right to participate in his authority, or to assume any approach to an equality with him, he was strongly averse to the assembling of a deliberative council; but conscious that his divine attributes and prerogatives were not adequate to the existing emergency, he consented that the Council of Constance should be called, on condition that it should adopt the most energetic means for the extirpation of the heretics. With the secret design of betraying the amiable reformer, John Huss, he was invited to respond in person to a summons of the council. To quiet his apprehensions of danger, the emperor furnished him with a safe conduct, and the pope pledged his honor to protect him from harm. Thus guarded by the honor of the state and the church, he was, notwithstanding, perfidiously betrayed, and condemned to be burnt alive. The perfidy of the infallible pope is justified by the saints and authorities of the Catholic church, on the ground that no pledge, assurance, or oath, can rightfully protect a heretic from punishment. Sigismund attended the horrid ceremonies; and being reminded by a by-stander that the course of the wind might bear an offensive effluvia to the position he occupied, answered: "The odor of a burning heretic can never be offensive to Sigismund."

The death of John Huss was terribly revenged. The stake became the watchword of union. The hitherto mild and submissive reformers became desperate revengers. Churches and convents were burnt; monks and priests slaughtered without mercy. The insurgents met and defeated the imperial forces. The strongest armies of the cross withered before their ferocity. For fifteen years they devastated the Papal dominions, and shook the government with the violence of their retribution. Seeing it impossible to restrain their rage, Sigismund obliged the Council of Basle to negotiate with them for the adjustment of their difficulties. This politic measure so incensed Pope Eugenius IV., whose uncompromising vengeance longed for the extermination of every opponent to papal despotism, that he ordered his legates to dissolve the obnoxious assembly. But the laity had advanced in liberality and knowledge far beyond the possible attainment of a papal despot, and in defiance of his maledictions and intrigues, continued their useful session, and terminated, by peaceful concessions, the war with the Hussites.

The grand struggle between religious freedom and Catholic despotism was visibly approaching when Charles V., King of Spain, in 1519 became Emperor of Germany. His design was to conquer the world, and his policy was to unite all parties in augmenting the national strength. To secure the favor of the pope, and the co-operation of his extensive and effective machinery, he declared himself the defender of the Catholic faith. To conciliate the Protestants he convened a diet at Worms, at which, under a plausible show of toleration he allowed Luther, in his presence, to defend the principles of the reformation. But his ambiguous policy becoming offensive to the Roman See, he issued an edict against the Protestants. A Catholic from interest, he was more disposed to make the pope auxiliary to the success of his designs than to be governed by him. Hence, when Francis I. preferred claims to certain portions of the Germanic empire, he leagued with the pope and accomplished the defeat of the king; but he was equally disposed to defend his interests against the pope. The papal monarch, always apprehensive of the political power of friend or foe, seeing that his confederacy with Charles had vastly augmented the latter's preponderating power, and placed the papal interests at his disposal, formed against him a counter league with the Italian States. This effort to retrieve the errors of his policy only aggravated his misfortune. The forces of the Holy League were defeated by the arms of Charles, Rome taken by storm, the city plundered, the pope imprisoned, and four hundred thousand crowns of gold demanded for his ransom. When Charles heard of the success of his arms,

in evident mockery he dressed himself in mourning for
the pope, ordered masses to be said in all the churches
for his deliverance from prison, and in alleviation of his
misfortune reduced the ransom to 100,000 crowns.
The power of Charles overawing the papal throne,
it prudently refrained from venting in insulting anathemas the ebullitions of its wrath. Pope Clement VII.,
after the peace of Cambray in 1592, crowned Charles
as King of Lombardy and Rome.

On this occasion the emperor dutifully kissed
the feet of the papal monarch. The cause of this
affection and harmony was shortly afterwards manifested in an intolerant edict against the Protestants. This significant menace led the Protestant
princes to form the Smalkalden League for the protection of Protestantism. Two years afterwards a holy
league was formed by the Catholic princes for the protection of Catholicism. After some abortive attempts
at negotiation, the Protestant league raised the standard of war. The emperor by strategetic movements,
and by creating jealousy and divisions among the Protestant confederates, obtained important advantages
over their arms, and finally succeeded in dissolving the
league. But Maurice of Saxony had secretly formed
another league, which was joined by Henry II., King of
France. While Charles was at Innspruck, attending the
Council of Trent, Maurice suddenly appeared at the
head of an army, and the emperor barely escaped
amid the darkness of a stormy night from being captured. The council was consequently dissolved, and
the Protestants dictated the terms of peace at Passau;
which the emperor ratified at Augsburg. By the terms

of this treaty it was agreed that no one should be attacked on account of his religious belief; that no one should be molested in the enjoyment of his property or mode of worship; that religious disputes should be adjusted by pacific means; that persons for religious reasons should be allowed to change their residences; that bishops on becoming Protestants should forfeit their office and salary; and that every Protestant should enjoy his faith until a religious compromise should be established.

Charles, broken down in health and constitution, enfeebled in mind, and conceiving that he was haunted by some invisible power which blasted all his prospects, abdicated the throne and retired to a monastery, where he passed the remainder of his life in making wooden clocks, and in performing his funeral ceremonies.

Ferdinand II., King of Spain, succeeded to the crown of Germany in 1619. He was by nature of a morose and revengeful disposition, and the bigotry and prejudice which had been instilled into his mind by Catholic preceptors made him an accomplished instrument in the hands of the church, in executing its exterminating vengeance on the heretics. During the course of his tutelage he made a pilgrimage to Rome, where an oath was administered to him by the pope, that if he should ever become emperor he would exterminate heresy in his dominions. When he ascended the throne Germany was divided into two factions. The one was known as the "Catholic League," and the other as the "Evangelical Union." The Catholic League was headed by Maximilian, elector of Bavaria, and comprised the bishops and princes attached to the house of Austria.

The Evangelical Union was headed by the Duke of Wittenberg, the elector of Saxony and Brandenburg, and composed of Lutheran and Calvinistic princes and knights. A number of the princes of Bavaria assembled at Prague, and declaring that they would not submit to Maximilian, chose for their king Frederic, elector of the Palatina, a member of the Evangelical Union. This revolt benefited the Evangelical Union by a powerful accession. A desperate and bloody struggle was imminent between these two parties. Notwithstanding the Protestant influence in Bavaria, Ferdinand succeeded in having himself elected king.

After this event he tore up in a violent rage the charter which Rudolph II. had granted the Bohemians, because it allowed them to build churches and schoolhouses. He then showed his remembrance of his popish oath by persecuting the Protestants, banishing their preachers, and depopulating the kingdom by an intolerance which caused emigrations of whole sections from his dominions. The victory of his troops near Prague enabling him to dictate a treaty which crushed the Protestant cause, and dissolved the Evangelical Union, he proceeded to restore the ecclesiastical institutions which had been abolished by the Protestants, to exclude Calvinists from the benefits of the religious peace of Augsburg, and to require Protestants living under Catholic princes to believe in Catholicism. Besides these decrees, enforced by the military power, the conquest of the Palatinate of Frederic, the bestowal of that dignity on Maximilian, the emperor's favorite, giving the Catholics the ascendency in the electoral college, the army of Tilly in Lower Saxony, where no existing enemy made it excusable, depriving the Protestants of their churches, committing wanton violence on the Lutherans, and compelling thousands to abandon their homes, property and country, were such gross violations of treaties, and such strong incentives to resistance, that the Protestant princes were impelled to unite in a league with the King of Denmark and the Duke of Holstein, determining to exhaust every resource in the defence of religious liberty. After some successes the confederated forces were defeated, and the Protestants lost all that they had acquired since the peace of Augsburg. At this dark hour in the fortunes of the league, Gustavus Adolphus, with an army of thirty thousand veterans, espoused its cause. His heroism, strategetic skill, and indomitable valor soon annihilated Tilly's army, reduced the imperial allies to extreme distress, conquered Lower Saxony and Bavaria, and delivered the Protestants from their perilous situation. Tilly having died, Wallenstein assumed command. Having raised an immense and formidable army, the new general was enabled to attack Adolphus with such overwhelming force that he compelled him to retire from Bavaria. In 1642, at Lutzen, the two powerful armies came to a general and decisive engagement; the genius of Adolphus crowned his arms with victory, but his intrepidity cost him his life. Through a wise policy the Swedes still continued a triumphant career, victoriously marching through the empire with incredible rapidity, and finally, after the battle of Prague, dictating the peace of Westphalia.

By the terms of the peace of Westphalia Calvinists acquired the same rights with Lutherans; princes were bound not to persecute subjects on account of religious differences; all acquisitions of Protestants since the peace of Augsburg were confirmed; entire equality of sect, liberty of conscience, and the exercise of all modes of religion were guaranteed, and the independence of Switzerland and of the Netherlands acknowledged.

Pope Innocent X. strenuously protested against this peace, complaining in bitter terms of the deep injury it inflicted on the church. Though the consequences of the treaty have been of the most benignant nature to Europe, still the Papal See has, through all periods maintained, with unabated animosity, its original opposition to the invaluable treaty.

The papal intrigues, so prolific of disastrous wars, were no less pernicious to Austria than they had been to other powers. Upon the death of Duke Frederic, its ruler, Frederic II., of Germany, declared the duchy a vacant fief of his empire, and appointed over it a governor. Pope Innocent V. persuaded Margaret, the sister of the deceased duke, and Gertrude, his neice, to claim the duchy as their inheritance. The Margrave Hermann, by the aid of the pope and his machinery, was enabled to command a strong party in support of the project. After a war of thirty-six years the dispute was settled by the interference of the emperor Rodolph, who gave it to his two sons, Albert and Rodolph.

On the death of Maria Theresa, Joseph, her son, succeeded to the throne of Austria. Maria Theresa was a very devout and superstitious princess, a circumstance which enabled the sacerdotal fraternity to gain and betray her confidence. But in making her an object of their craft they made her son their enemy. Their duplicity having excited in the mind of Joseph a strong aversion to the intermeddling and intriguing profession, he no sooner ascended the throne than he manifested a disposition to adopt a policy more in accordance with the enlightenment of the age than was agreeable to the pope and the clergy. The world with pleasure, but the church with consternation, beheld him enlarging the liberty of the press, tolerating the Protestants, treating the Jews with moderation, annulling ecclesiastical sinecures, and abolishing such monasteries and nunneries as were not useful as schools or hospitals. Uneasy at these useful reforms, yet not daring to mutter his Vatican thunder, and finding his machinery unable to stop their progress, Pope Pius IV. sought a personal interview with the liberal minded emperor, to dissuade him from the further prosecution of his beneficent intentions. But notwithstanding the earnest remonstrances of the vicar of Christ, the emperor still continued to reduce the number of the monasteries, and to effect reforms in the churches, and in the various departments of the government. This wise and sagacious policy, which relieved the people of the oppression of spiritual despotism, and renewed the vigor of national energy, was not appreciated by the masses through the ignorance and superstition of the age. The emperor not only had to contend with opposition from those for whose moral advancement he was laboring, but also with the disguised hostility of the pope, and the subtle operation of his treacherous machinery. But still, amid wars, seditions and rebellions, he pursued his magnanimous policy; and if he did not effect all the reforms in the church, and in his government, that he had contemplated, it was more through the intrigues of the pope than through any want of disposition, skill and energy on his part.

The various orders of knights, whose avocation it was to enforce conformity to the demands of Catholicism by the vengeance of the sword, was an important part of the papal machinery. All who yielded not to this argument were threatened with extermination ; all who did, became the slaves of spiritual despotism. Under pretext of protecting Poland from the ravages of Prussian heathen, the Teutonic Knights, in 1226, won from Conrad of Masovia a small strip of land on the Vistula. For fifty-three years they carried on a war against the Persian tribes, and finally obliged them to embrace Catholicism. This war, suggested by papal craft, continued by incredible barbarity, culminated in the grossest perfidy. In their protection of Poland they inflicted deeper injuries on her than the savages of Prussia had ever contemplated, or in fact had the ability to inflict. They subjugated the Baltic seaboard, from the Oder to the Gulf of Finland, and wrung from her her maritime commerce, and her northern line of defence. Poland and Prussia having both been plundered and oppressed by the knights, united in a bond of union against their common enemy, and a ferocious war was inaugurated, during which the knights lost a great portion of their territory, and finally their power was broken. In the various vicissitudes of the succeeding fifty years the knights became abolished in Prussia, and their possessions converted into a hereditary duchy, under the male line of Prince Albert, which, under Francis III. became the kingdom of Prussia.

The papal intrigues with regard to the Netherlands, were fruitful of sanguinary and deplorable consequences. Under the reign of Charles V. one hundred thousand Protestants fell a sacrifice to the papal intolerance. Philip, his son and successor, narrow in his views, irritable in his temper, and implacable in his hate, transcended even Charles in the inhumanity of his measures towards his Protestant subjects. Cardinal Granvella having introduced into the Netherlands the inquisition, for the extirpation of religious freedom, the Prince of Orange, in conjunction with other distinguished personages, remonstrated against the measure. This remonstrance was regarded by the government as an act of treason. The haughtiness of the cardinal, and the severe measures he introduced to intimidate the people, produced great disorder and alarm. The nobles conspired to defend their rights; the Protestants boldly celebrated their religious ceremonies, and the people fled in crowds to England and Saxony. In spite of intolerant edicts and excruciating torture, a bold spirit of resistance was excited in the provinces. Philip recalled Cardinal Granvella, but appointed in his place Alva, a more cruel and implacable tyrant. Proud, fierce and imperious, this man knew of nothing but to command in a despotic tone, and expect his subjects to tremble and obey. Sixty years of warfare always successful, had familiarized him to deeds of blood, without humbling him by the salutary lessons of misfortune. Death, the usual penalty of disobedience to his commands, gave his mandate a terrific importance. As soon as he had assumed the direction of the Netherland provinces, he established a council of blood by means of which he condemned all whom he suspected of heresy, or whose fortunes excited a prospect of increasing his own. The noblest of the nation fell under the axe of his executioner; and as avarice had always been a prominent trait of his character, he now illustrated the obduracy with which it is capable of debasing humanity, by confiscating the property, not only of the present but of the absent; not only of the living but of the dead. Having cited the Prince of Orange to appear before his council, and that prince having refused on the ground of his exemption by privilege, law and usage, he declared him dispossessed of all property, and seizing on his son, sent him to Spain as a hostage. The prince, heretofore a liberal-minded Catholic, now declared himself a Protestant, and drew his sword in favor of religious freedom. By a perseverance which no difficulties could prostrate, a sagacity which no subterfuge could deceive, a heroism which no danger could appall, and a magnanimity which commanded the admiration of the world, he struggled through discouragement, vexation and defeat until he had laid a solid foundation for the freedom of the provinces, by reconstructing them in a judicious confederacy, under the name of the United Provinces of the Netherlands, and inducing them to renounce allegiance to Spain. Philip hence declared the prince an outlaw, and offered a reward of two hundred and fifty thousand dollars for either his apprehension or his assassination. In 1584 the noble prince was shot dead by Balthazar Gerard, who confessed that he had been instigated to the deed by a Franciscan monk and a

Jesuist priest. But though the founder of the republic fell a victim to Romish treachery, its defence was continued with insuperable skill and valor. Army after army sent against the republic was annihilated by the indomitable bravery of its troops, until its soil became the cemetery of the military strength of Spain. Its tolerance gave it population; its freedom, energy; its maritime contests, a knowledge of navigation; and its enterprise, commerce trade and prosperity. After a war of thirty years, replete with heroism and magnanimity, it wrung from Spain, in the Westphalia treaty, a full recognition of independence.

CHAPTER XV.

PAPAL POLITICAL INTRIGUES IN PORTUGAL AND SPAIN.

In Portugal, under the reign of *Alphonso I.—Sancho II.—Dionysus—John II.—Emanuel—John III.—Sebastian—Philip II.—Joseph I.—Maria Francesca Isabella—John VI.—Pedro VI.—and Dona Maria.*

In Spain, under the reign of *Reccarred I.—Charles V.—Philip II.—Philip III.—Charles II.—Charles III. Charles IV.—and Ferdinand VII.*

ALPHONSO, in 1139, in the cause of the church and of national independence, subjugated the Moors of Portugal. The victor was saluted on the field by his army as king of the conquered dominion; the Cortes Lamego invested him with regal authority; and Pope Alexander III. acknowledged his legitimacy, the independence of the nation, and the laws and constitution which were prescribed. By a provision of the constitution, which probably sprung from the religious tolerance of the Moorish régime, the king was prohibited under forfeiture of the crown, from becoming tributary to any foreign power. But notwithstanding this proud interdiction, Alphonso in the course of severe conflicts which afterwards took place between him and the kings of Castile and Leon, made his kingdom, in violation of his own constitution, a fief of Rome, in order to secure the papal support.

In consequence of this concession to papal supremacy, Sancho II., in 1245, became involved in a dispute with the clergy; and upon appealing to Pope Innocent IV., had the misfortune to lose his crown.

Alphonso III. succeeded to the regal dignity. Jealous of the rights of sovereignty, and determined to transmit them unimpaired to his successor, his reign was, in consequence, a perpetual contest with the intrigues of the clergy. Inflexibly firm and resolute, he defeated their artful attempts to extend their landed estates; to obtain exemption from taxation; to acquire for their persons and possessions an independence of secular jurisdiction; and to subject the temporal to the spiritual authority by an insidious and gradual encroachment on the rights of the crown.

Dionysus, who succeeded Alphonso III., opposed with prudence and firmness the papal intrigues, which had disturbed the peace of the kingdom from its foundation. In order to moderate the selfishness and tyranny of the first and second estates, composed of the clergy and nobility, he erected the cities into a third estate, of equal legislative authority. By elevating the dignity of the commonality, and taking advantage of the commercial resources which the geography of the country afforded, he awakened in the nation a spirit of indomitable enterprise which laid the foundation of its subsequent greatness. This liberal and enlightened policy cost him the friendship of the papal court, but he disarmed its malice by an admirable course of prudence and courtesy.

John II. became King of Portugal in 1450. During his administration Ferdinand and Isabella, of Spain, governed by the spirit of Catholic intolerance, instituted a rigorous prosecution against the Jews, by which thousands of them were deprived of their fortunes, and driven into exile. The Jews had arisen in Spain into considerable political influence; they had become farmers of the revenue; and their characteristic avarice had rendered them obnoxious to the people. Instead of rectifying the evil by adequate measures, the crown and people, influenced by the church, were made instrumental in gratifying its hatred against the Hebrew race, by a persecution as unjust as it was impolitic. John II., with more liberal views of government, improved the injudicious measures of Spain, to the advantage of his own kingdom. Discarding the intolerance of his religion, he invited the persecuted Jews to his dominion; and by affording them a peaceful asylum, added largely to the wealth, population, prosperity and importance of the nation.

Emanuel, son of John II., succeeded to the throne of Portugal in 1495. He married Elenora, sister of Charles V., of Germany. He had imbibed the beneficent toleration of his sire, which had been so advantageous to the nation, but which was too antagonistical to the spirit of Catholicism, to command its support. The craft of priestly policy might conceal its hostility to tolerance from public perception, but machinations for its subversion would be no less incessantly at work. In the pious system of sacerdotal intrigue the amiable qualities of human nature are the most available, as they are the most insidious, and least liable to be suspected. Devoid of the finer sentiments of honor, the priests, in their capacity of spiritual advisers, scruple not to abuse the privileges accorded them, in making the influence which a female may exercise over a husband, lover or parent, subservient to their own purposes. This species of ecclesiastical intrigue is illustrated in the conduct of Queen Elenora. Having acquired a controlling ascendancy over the king's mind, she was induced by her spiritual advisers to extort from him a promise that he would require the Jews to embrace Christianity under pain of being reduced to slavery for life. By whatever considerations, Emanuel was led to promulgate a decree so injurious to the national welfare, and so inconsistent with the tolerant spirit he had manifested, yet he had the humanity or sagacity to procrastinate its execution for twenty years, and thus to ameliorate the horrors with which it was fraught; and to place the development of the catastrophe beyond the period of his administration.

John III., son of Emanuel, was crowned King of Portugal in 1521. A pliant tool in the hand of papal intrigue, he gave a fatal blow to the tolerance and prosperity of his kingdom. The implacable hatred of the church towards the Jews, hoarded for so many years, now relieved of all restraint, exhibited its fiendish barbarism in deeds of exterminating cruelty. To escape the persecution to which they were exposed, the Jews practised the externals of Catholicism, while they secretly observed their ancient rites. The vigilance of the papal machinery, like a monster with a thousand eyes, penetrating all secrets, soon detected this evasion. In order to discover the persons who thus consulted self-preservation and the dictates of consciences, the inquisition was introduced, and a crusade of blood and devastation preached against the whole Hebrew race. Their property was confiscated; their children were torn from them and placed under Catholic control; and they themselve reduced to slavery, or subjected to the tortures of the inquisition.

While John III., during his reign, was the wretched instrument of Catholicism for the accomplishment of its atrocious designs, his grandson, Sebastian, who in 1557, at the age of three years succeeded to the throne, was educated, by the express injunction of his father's will, by the Jesuists, and consequently was moulded to the same purposes, and reduced to the same flexible subserviency. Inclined to extravagance by temper and disposition, and educated by bigotry and craft, his ambition became singularly whimsical; his devotion to the pope absolute; and his thirst indomitable and unquenchable to engage in some enterprise in which he might shed the blood of infidels and heretics. When he arrived at majority, in order to express his devotion to the pope, he assumed the title of "Most Obedient King." At the age of twenty years his restless fanaticism led him to undertake an expedition against the unoffending infidels of Tangiers; and suddenly falling on the astonished inhabitants, gained an easy victory over them. The success of his forces against these defenceless mountaineers led him to imagine that his arms were invincible. Muley Mohammed having conspired against his uncle Muley Moloch, the governor of Moroco, Sebastian conceived that by aiding the conspirators with his personal valor and military forces, he might acquire some distinction for his name, and some advantages for the church. The dictates of prudence and sound policy, the protestations of his ablest counsellors, and the munificent offer of Muley Moloch to purchase his neutrality by the cession of five fortified places on the coast of Africa, were feeble remonstrances to a mind like that of Sebastian's, in which fanaticism had supplanted principle, and despotism humanity. To popularize the hazardous undertaking, the papal machinery began to work industriously in its favor. Collecting an army of twenty-one thousand three hundred men, comprised of Portuguese, Germans, Spaniards, Frenchmen and Italians, and a fleet of one hundred vessels, he sailed for Africa, and landed with safety at the port of Alzira. Although the number and skilful disposition of the Moorish troops left little doubt of their triumph; although Sebastian's provisions were nearly exhausted; although Muley Moloch, more concerned for the safety of the misguided fanatic than from any apprehension of the success of his arms, again attempted to negotiate a peace; although some of the Portuguese commanders advised a retreat, and all of those of the conspirators a retreat to the coast, yet so confident was Sebastian of the interposition of divine providence in aiding him to butcher the infidels, that he even refused to defer the engagement until the afternoon, in order that he might have the darkness of the night to cover a retreat, should such a measure become inevitable. Sebastian fought with distinguished bravery, yet his desperate fanaticism was equalled, if not surpassed, by the heroic courage of those who had been tortured, outraged, and exiled by his intolerance. The martial semicircle of the Moors enclosed his forces in a volume of destructive flame, and their disciplined valor and skilful manœuvres completely annihilated them. The bodies of the vanquished that strewed the battlefield were, in general, too horribly disfigured with wounds to admit of their persons being identified; and Sebastian's corpse being among the number, his actual death became doubtful. This circumstance, twenty years afterwards furnished the papal machinery with a convenient opportunity for manufacturing a bogus Sebastian. But although Joseph Taxera, a Dominican monk, traversed Europe to enlist the imperial courts in its favor, yet the numerous spurious Sebastians that had sprung up, and the eagerness of several crowned heads to seize the kingdom, defeated the object of his mission. The controversy was finally settled by the battle of Alancatura, which, crowning with victory the arms of Philip II., of Spain, one of the claimants, subjugated Portugal to the dominion of Spain.

The religious frenzy and whimsical ambition of Sebastian, the result of his Catholic education, cost Portugal the flower of her nobility, the strength of her army, and her national independence; overloaded her with debt, and degraded her under the dominion of a government distracted by unsuccessful wars, and governed by a rapacious and unprincipled administration. When John III., in 1540, introduced the Jesuists into his kingdom, the doom of Portugal was sealed. From that period, under the intolerant measures of his administration, its power began rapidly to decline, until its disastrous connection with Spain secured its downfall. Guinea, Brazil, the Molluccas, and all the fairest dominions of Portugal were wrung from her grasp. Spain oppressed her with rapacious tyranny;

England and the Jesuists monopolized her trade, and the calamities which had visited her in such frightful succession exhausted her resources.

The capacity of the nation for greatness, notwithstanding the degradation into which she had sunk, still animated the patriotic Portuguese with the hopes of a national redemption. In 1640 a powerful conspiracy was formed against the Spanish regime, and in 1750 the political independence of Portugal was achieved, and Joseph I. elevated to the throne. Duke Pombal, an able statesman, and the prime minister of the government, regarding the Jesuists as the origin of the weakness and disgraces of the government, and believing that their secrecy, dissimulation and treachery, absolved him from any obligation he might assume with regard to them, inconsistent with the public good, became a member of their order that he might acquire a correct knowledge of their principles and mode of operation, and be qualified to counteract their pernicious machinations. With profound dissimulation, he so completely deceived them that they admitted him to an intimate knowledge of all their secrets, plans and designs. After having fully obtained his object he made a public exposition of their secrets. He disclosed the dangerous principles of their constitution, their political objects, the oaths by which they were bound, the baseness of their intrigues, their false professions, their horrible deeds, and their disgraceful rapacity and profligacy. By the exposure which he was enabled to make he succeeded in having them removed from the important position of confessors to the king, and instructors of youth in colleges. He also induced Joseph to expel them from the missions of Paraguay; to abridge the power of the bishops; and to prohibit the celebration of the "auto-da-fé" of the inquisition. The Jesuists not being able successfully to arrest the progress of reform determined to assassinate the king; but failing in this attempt, the whole order fell under the ban of the kingdom, and were officially declared a political organization under the mask of religion, and its members expelled from the kingdom as enemies of the public peace, and traitors to the government. Pope Clement XIII., enraged at this summary destruction of the most efficient department of his machinery, endeavored to intimidate the reformers by threats of excommunication, and commissioned a legate to adopt any means to arrest proceedings against the Jesuists. But his legate was promptly escorted out of the kingdom; and as the conduct of the holy father in protecting and defending an organization of traitors and assassins, implicated him in the guilt of an accessory, all connection with the See of Rome was declared dissolved until the imputation should be removed by the abolishment of the Jesuistical order. The vanity of Pope Clement could not permit him to suffer such a mortification, and the decree of dissolution was rigorously enforced; but his successor, at the hazard of disproving the papal infallibility, complying with the demands of Portugal, amicable relations were re-established.

On the death of Joseph I., in 1777, Maria Francesca Isabella, his eldest daughter, succeeded to the royal dignity. The superstitious temperament of this queen, and her natural infirmity, which terminated in confirmed mental alienation, disqualified her for the administration of the governmental powers on sound principles of public policy, and surrendered her to the selfish control of a corrupt priesthood and ambitious nobility. By the intrigues of these two classes, which seldom scruple to sacrifice the popular interest to their personal advantage, Pombal was deprived of his useful political influence, most of his regulations were abolished, and Portugal, from the dawn of a magnificent future, sunk into the obscurity and lethargy of her former condition.

In 1817 John VI., who had been regent during the imbecility of the queen, from 1795 to her death, ascended the throne. The spirit of French republicanism exerted a liberalizing influence over Europe generally, and had apparently a similar effect on the pope and his machinery.

Those who did not understand the profoundity of sacerdotal craft might have been stupefied with astonishment to see a pope, while professing to be infallible, discarding principles and policies which had been approved by the practice, and defended by the anathemas of his predecessors. He not only sanctioned the prohibition of Portugal forbidding Jesuists from entering the kingdom, and consented to the abolition of the inquisition, but even requested that all persecution against the Jews should cease, and that they should be admitted to greater rights and privileges. The popular current had set in too strongly in favor of change in the constitution and administration of the government for papal sagacity to oppose, and unobstructed by the sacerdotal machinery, it became daily augmented in volume and impetuosity. The liberal feeling of the nation, allowed spontaneously to flow, culminated in 1820 in establishing, without violence or bloodshed, a provisional government and a new **cortes**. **Tolerance on the lips of** a Catholic priest is treason to Rome; and, though this circumstance might have cautioned prudence against investing any of them with power, yet **as** they had warmly espoused the liberal cause, they were elected by the people as members to the cortes, **with the exception** of a few lawyers and governmental **officers. At the** assemblage of the cortes, under the presidency of the archbishop of Braga, the revolutionary measures were sanctioned, the inquisition forever interdicted, **and a constitution framed which** secured freedom of **person and property, the liberty of** the press, and legal equality. The king approved the provisions of this constitution, and swore to support it. But under this prosperous appearance of republican progress, **the demon of** religious intolerance **was secretly at work; availing itself of** every means to arrest the popular current. The portentous mutterings of an approaching storm were frequently heard; and it was not, therefore, a matter of surprise to the friends of freedom, that in 1832, a regency was established at Valladolid, under the bishop of Lisbon, with the avowed object of subverting the constitution, and inviting the people to rally under the standard of monarchy; nor that this regency was supported by the **queen,** Don Miguel, **the** clergy and the nobility. The machinations of the papal machinery had so successfully extinguished the popular enthusiasm which had won such important concessions to natural right, that no sooner was the standard of royalty raised, than an enormous reduction took place in the ranks of the liberal party. So many priests, noblemen, soldiers and people espoused the royal cause, that John VI. found no difficulty in declaring the constitution of 1822, which he had sworn to support, null and void, and to protect his perjury and his treason to the freedom of the people, by disarming the military and the national guards. The absolutists then proceeded to annul all the concessions that had been made, in accommodation to the popular feeling; they restored the church confiscated property, established a censorship over the press, imprisoned or banished the liberal members of the cortes, and organized a junta for the purpose of framing a monarchial constitution. But Don Migual, aspiring to become absolute king, could not submit to the restriction of a constitution; and, being commander-in-chief, and exercising the governmental powers, excited an insurrection against the Lisbon cortes, and arbitrarily proceeded to banish all liberals, constitutionalists, freemasons, and members of other secret societies. That he might successfully remove every obstacle that imperiled his ultimate designs, he forbade all appeals to the king. But the acts which his ambition dictated were too reprehensible not to acquire for his administration a dangerous and prejudicial notoriety. In spite of all precaution the rumor of his tyranny penetrated the royal palace, and Don Miguel was summoned into the presence of the king to explain the reasons for his arbitrary conduct. Candidly acknowledging or artfully assuming that he had been the innocent victim of craft and misrepresentation, he succeeded in obtaining the king's pardon.

In 1826 John VI. died, and Isabella becoming regent,

administered the government until Pedro IV. of Brazil, the brother of the deceased king, could make it convenient to visit Portugal, and assume the reigns of government. After having done so he established a constitution, providing two legislative chambers, and then abdicated in favor of his eldest daughter, Dona Maria da Gloria. Don Miguel, his brother, the chamberlains, and the magistrates swore to support the constitution. But the first, in violation of his oath of allegiance, and of his fraternal obligations, entered into a conspiracy for its overthrow. With this object in view he organized an apostolic party, and abusing the power and confidence with which he was honored, secretly filled the army, navy, and civil offices with his adherents. Having matured his plans he caused an insurrection to break out against the queen, in order to enable him to seize the royal authority under pretense of restoring public tranquillity. England, however, interfering, the revolution was checked, and the project of usurpation frustrated. But the treasonable plot was skilfully and comprehensively laid, and the zealous support which it derived from the papal machinery soon rendered it popular with the masses. As if enamored of slavery and despotism, the people began to crowd into the ranks of the apostolic party, to second its declaration in favor of Don Miguel as king, to unite in its shouts of "Long live the absolute king," "Down with the constitutions," and to denounce, abuse and assault those who refused to echo its suicidal acclamations. A few military garrisons which still withstood the popular frenzy, and adhered to the cause of constitutional government, raised the standard of revolt;

and being joined by other troops, an army was organized which marched against Lisbon. It was met by the apostolic army, which greatly outnumbered it; and being defeated, the liberal junta was dissolved and Don Miguel proclaimed absolute king. In 1834 Don Miguel was defeated by Don Pedro IV., and the constitution of 1826 was re-established by the cortes.

---o---

PAPAL POLITICAL INTRIGUES IN SPAIN.

We will conclude our history of Papal Political Intrigues, by a cursory glance at a few of its instances with regard to the government of Spain.

Catholicism was introduced into Spain in 586, under the reign of Reccared I.; and from that period the governmental affairs were controlled by the political intrigues of the clergy, until 711, when the kingdom became a province of the Caliph of Bagdad.

The Moorish government adopted a more liberal policy than was consistent with the spirit of Catholicism. It tolerated the free exercise of all religions. It permitted the subjugated to retain their laws and magistrates. Agriculture, commerce, arts and science flourished under its auspices. It established libraries and universities; and, from the hand of its civilization Europe has received the knowledge of arithmetical characters, of gunpowder, and of the art of manufacturing rags into paper. But the Infidels who conferred these advantages could not conciliate the proud spirit of the Spaniard to subjugation under foreign rule, nor the pope to the loss of revenues derivable from an opulent kingdom. A national struggle for indevisibility of empire, and primogenitureship in succession was consequently inaugurated; and a succession of conquests, from 1220 to 1491, ultimated in the reduction of the Moors under Castellian supremacy. With the achievement of nationality, and the discovery of South America, Spain began to rank with the first powers of Europe. But her decline was as rapid as her elevation. Besides the conflicting laws and customs which prevented national unity, and the political tyranny which oppressed the masses, a rigorous persecution was inaugurated against the Moors and Jews, compelling such as refused to be baptized to leave the kingdom.

In 1520 Charles V. became king of Spain, and subsequently, also Emperor of Germany. After suppressing an insurrection of his Spanish subjects, who demanded a liberal constitution, and annihilating the last vestige of civil liberty by separating the deliberative estates, he established over the kingdom a military, religious, and political despotism. So oppressive was his administration, and so reckless were his expenditures, that although Mexico, Peru, and Chili poured a continual stream of wealth into the public treasury, yet excessive taxes had to be imposed, and enormous loans negotiated to satisfy the demands of the rapacious monarch.

In 1555 Philip II. ascended the throne of Spain. The Catholic education of this prince fitted him better for a cloister than a throne. His rapacity empoverished the nation, and his religious intolerance perpetually convulsed it with sedition and war. His devoutest wish was to extirpate heretics, and his most pleasing sight was an auto-da-fé, in which he could behold his subjects expiring in the flames. Like Sigismund, the smell of burning heretics was never offensive to his nostrils. His inhuman and impolitic course having led his minister to intimate that he was depopulating his kingdom by his frequent massacres, he replied: "Better be without subjects than to reign over heretics." As cowardly as he was blood-thirsty, it was his custom when his army was engaged in battle, to retire to a safe retreat and pray for its success; and whenever a victory was achieved to assume the head of the command, as if the triumph was the result of his valor and military skill.

Although his Catholicism had transformed him into merely mechanical part of the papal machinery, without feeling or reason, yet when his truce with France was broken by the interference of Pope Paul IV., and his right to the kingdom of Naples was declared forfeited, he awoke from his lethargic slumbers, and commissioned the bloody Alva to proceed with an army to Rome and chastise the holy father for his insulting political intrigues. The pope alarmed, and, perhaps surprised at the belligerent attitude of a king once so remarkably obedient, thought it better to consult prudence than the divine prerogatives of his office, and to avert the impending chastisement by subscribing to articles of peace.

In 1109 Philip III. became invested with the royal dignity. By nature a tyrant, by temper a bigot, without any administrative capacity, and educated in superstition and intolerance, he seems to have been born for the the disgrace and destruction of the throne he inherited. In the most brilliant period of Spanish history her religious despotism was prophetic of her premature decay, and each succeeding reign verifying the prophecy, she now tottered on the verge of ruin. Favorites were allowed to waste the national revenues, England and Holland destroyed the Spanish commerce, frequent insurrections destroyed the public peace; eight hundred thousand Jews, and two million Moors were, during this and the preceding administration driven from the country; and to complete the national degradation Spain had to submit to the supremacy of England.

In 1665 Charles II. succeeded to the regal authority. At his death, which occurred in 1700, he made Philip of Anjou, grandson of his sister, consort of Louis XIV., the sole heir of his dominion, in order to prevent the division of the empire, which had been resolved upon by France, England and Holland. This will led to the war of the Spanish succession, notwithstanding which the Bourbon, Philip V., maintained himself on the Spanish throne.

In 1759 Charles III. succeeded to the throne of the Spanish monarchy. The decaying embers of liberalism which had began to scintillate amid the gloom of despotism, now shone forth with renewed brilliancy. Genius and intelligence, which alone are capable of grappling with the astute principles of government, and of developing the latent greatness of a people, were fortunately exhibited in the favorite publicists and statesmen of the monarch. Profound and elevated views of political economy began to characterize the administration; and the true principles of commerce, the national importance of agriculture, arts and manufacture, and the best means for their development, became more generally understood by the government and the people. With Count Florida Blanca, a man of extraordinary ability and activity, as ambassador at Rome, holding the pope in check; with Aranda, a man of penetrating genius, occupying the most influential position of the state; with Olavides enjoying the confidence of the monarch, and elaborating laws for public improvement; and with Campomanes, a scholar of varied and profound erudition, as fiscal gaent of the royal council of Castile, defending the enlightened policy of the government against the attacks of bishops; equalizing taxation; and reducing the number of mendicants, the nation could not but increase in splendor and prosperity, notwithstanding it had became involved in a formidable war which raged between France and England. By the co-operation of these patriotic statesmen, whose lofty spirit scowled on despotism and religious bigotry, a pragmatic sanction was obtained from the government which restricted the inquisition, banished the Jesuists from the Spanish dominions, and confiscated their property.

But Rome and her priests could not forgive these benefactors of the nation, although their liberal policy had improved every department of government, and had added, amid the disasters of war, wealth to the treasury, and a million men to the population. Florida Blanca was disgraced, imprisoned, and finally banished to his estates. Campomanes was removed from office, and disgraced. Aranda, who so greatly contributed to public security, good order, and the abolition of abuses, after passing through several trying vicissitudes, was banished to Arragon. And Olavides, in the midst of his beneficent and patriotic labors was arrested for heresy, and imprisoned in a monastic dungeon.

For the better protection, perhaps, of the monarchy from aggressions from without, and from insubordination from within, the pope, at the request of Charles III., declared the Spanish monarchy to be under the supervision of the Immaculate Conception. St. James, the former protecting genius of Spain, was formally deposed from office, and the Virgin Mary duly invested with his authority and jurisdiction. The truth of the Immaculate Conception was demonstrated beyond prudent dispute by the oaths of the emperor and the estates; and similar oaths were made the indispensable condition of all who should henceforth receive a university degree, or become a member of any corporation or association. As reverence for the clergy had become the substance of the Catholic religion, so now invocations to the Virgin Mary became the principal act of devotion.

In 1788 Charles IV. was invested with the imperial dignity. In 1808 the troops of Bonaparte having entered his dominions, he welcomed them as allies, and shortly aftewards resigned the crown in favor of his son, Ferdinand VII. A month had not elapsed before he secretly revoked his resignation, and finally ceded his right to the crown to Napoleon, who placed Joseph Bonaparte on the throne. Although the ministers of Ferdinand VII., and the greater part of the educated classes of Spaniards, acknowledged without hesitation the authority of Joseph, yet the monks and priests, whose principles and interests are identified with despotism, in conjunction with the absolutists, and supported by England, found sufficient available material in the change of dynasty, in the arrogance of the French, and in the national hostility to foreign domination, to excite a general insurrection against the French regime, and in favor of Ferdinand VII. as king. A junta was established at Seville which proclaimed war against France, and announced an alliance between England and Spain. A desperate struggle was now inaugurated, which, through six bloody campaigns, raged from 1808 to 1814; during which every important city was successively taken and lost, and every province was desolated and drenched in blood. Armies after armies, on both sides, were created and destroyed with melancholy rapidity. The papal machinery held the people in such absolute control that, though the French gained victory after victory, abolishing as they triumphed the feudal privileges, the inquisition, the monkish order, and endeavored by the most liberal concessions to conciliate the popular prejudices, yet they retained no place which they did not garrison. Their ranks were constantly thinned by the secret dagger, their communications cut off by guerillas, and their wounded murdered in cold blood. Insurgent bands everywhere carried on the bloodiest struggles, and women took a fiendish delight in torturing and assassinating the captives of war. At length the dreadful tragedy was closed, by the victory of the English at Toulouse.

    Peace being restored to the nation the cortes assembled, and shortly afterwards passed a resolution, declaring that before Ferdinand should be acknowledged as king, he should be required to swear to support the constitution which had been drawn up by the cortes of 1812, and which had been acknowledged by the allies of Spain. When interrogated as to his disposition of complying with the demands of the cortes, he replied in a tone of insolent indifference: "I have not thought about it." To fortify the absolute power he intended to usurp he professed to abhor despotism, and solemnly pledged his honor to grant the people a new constitution, founded on liberal principles, and which would afford ample protection to the rights of person and property, and to the freedom of the press. But the motives which induced him to make these promises did not urge him to fulfil them. While he nullified the old constitution, he did not restrict his authority by a new one; but in the exercise of absolute power arrested the officers who served under Joseph Bonaparte, and banished them with their wives and children; abolished freemasonry; restored the Jesuists; re-established the inquisition; put liberals to the rack; executed all who opposed the domineering pretensions of the priests; imprisoned those who ventured to remonstrate against his measures; incarcerated in monastic dungeons the members of the cortes; and domineered with absolute despotism over the lives and fortunes of his subjects. These severe proceedings, intended to intimidate insurgents, produced disloyalty, confusion and anarchy. The army became dissatisfied; the people insubordinate; the country infested with plundering and murdering guerillas; and, encouraged by this turbulent state of affairs, four battalions, in 1819, under Riago, declared for the constitution of 1812. The progress of this revolution was strenuously opposed by the allied forces of the monks, the priests, and the absolutists. The bishop of Cienfuegos defeated it at Cadiz. But the people inhaling the patriotic enthusiasm, arose in masses in its favor, and even the apostolics deserted their commanders. Ferdinand deprived of troops, and almost of adherents, found himself obliged to submit to the demands of the people. A provisional junta was established to conduct the public affairs, before which Ferdinand appeared and swore to support the constitution of 1812. The inquisition was abolished. The cortes assembled, and in a session of four months, endeavored by the means of moderate measures to conciliate the prejudices and interests of contending factions, and to restore harmony and vigor to the nation. The clergy and absolutists, whom no concession could satisfy, except that of unrestricted monarchy, organized a conspiracy for the overthrow of the constitution; and as the cortes had in their reformatory measures abolished some convents, and banished all non-juring priests, they appealed to the religious frenzy of the people, and succeeded in creating considerable opposition to the constitutions. In the interest of this counter revolution an apostolic junta was established on the frontiers of Portugal, for the avowed design of destroying the privileges of the crown and the clergy. Numerous bands of armed monks and peasants appeared in the different provinces; and their bold assassinations and barbarous acts produced such universal consternation, that the cortes declared the whole country in a state of siege. It was now evident that the priests and monks who had stimulated the peasants to insurrection had been instigated by the French government. But the cortes met the conspirators with skilful and vigorous measures, and having vanquished them in every engagement, succeeded finally in effecting the disbandment of their forces.

In 1822 another attempt was made to subvert the constitution. At Soi d'Urgel, on the confines of France, the absolutists established a regency under the Marquis Mataflounda. France was the instigator of this regency, and supported it with her influence and money. The army of the absolutists, composed of apostolic soldiers, and soldiers of the faith, were met by the united strength of the nation, and overwhelmed with defeat. The regency fled to France. But this evidence of the capability and determination of Spain to maintain a constitutional government, awakened into opposition every element of despotism, not only within her borders, but within all Europe. The pope refused to receive the Spanish ambassadors. The nuncio left Madrid; France, Austria, and Prussia demanded of the cortes that they should restore to Ferdinand full sovereign powers, and England advised acompliance with the demand. The Duke Angoulême, the commander of the French forces, established a junta which formed a provisional government on absolute principles, and declared the acts of the cortes null and void. France raised an army of the soldiers of the faith, who were received by the Spanish clergy with acclamations of joy, and termed by them "Good Christians." The peasantry, controlled by the priests, espoused the cause of the absolutists, but the army, the educated classes, and the people residing in cities generally adhered to the party of the constitutionalists.

The dictatorial interference of foreign powers in the internal affairs of a sovereign nation, and their attempts to defeat a governmental reform which they had sanctioned, and which, to achieve had cost the nation so much treasure, and so many valuable lives, fired the native pride and heroism of the Spanish character, and united the different factions of the constitutionalists in a solid body in favor of their country and its liberty. Though few in number, without allies, and without pecuniary resources, yet they were full of energy and heroic courage. The cortes repelled with patriotic indignation the insolent interposition of foreign powers, and prepared for the doubtful contest with consummate skill. As the church had been the chief cause of the national calamity, they appropriated its surplus plate to the necessity of the public treasury. The soldiers of the faith, and their guerilla bands, exclusively requiring the attention of the national guards and of the soldiers of the line, the cortes found themselves without an efficient army to oppose the march of the French troops, and the apostolic forces. This serious disadvantage enabled the absolutists to march on from victory to victory; and though some places made a good defence, and others a stubborn and desperate resistance, yet others submitted with scarcely a struggle. The gloom which now overshadowed the prospects of the constitutionalists, was ominously deepened by the defection of some of their generals. But the undaunted firmness of the remaining leaders, and the unequalled boldness and skill which characterized their manœuvres, desperately disputed inch by inch the progress of the monarchists, until the fall of Valencia terminated the eventful struggle, so honorable to the constitutionalists, so disgraceful to Europe, and so full of admonition to freemen. The bloody contests in which the liberals had been engaged greatly depleted their ranks, and now dungeons, exile, and the secret dagger nearly completed their annihilation. Under these depressing circumstances, the cortes invested Ferdinand with absolute power. The apostolics, the soldiers of the faith, the clergy and the uneducated classes, hailed him with acclamations of "Long live the absolute king;" "Long live religion;" "Death to the nation;" "Death to the negroes." Ferdinand then declared null and void all the acts of the constitutional government, and all the public approvals by which he had sanctioned them. An attempt was made to introduce the inquisition, but the liberals, supported by France, and even approved by the pope, successfully resisted the obnoxious measure. In 1832, the infirmities of Ferdinand having rendered him the dupe of designing favorites, he created Christina, the queen, regent for the infanta Isabella, his daughter. In 1837 the regent was obliged, by an insurrection, to proclaim the constitution of 1812. In 1843, Isabella having attained her majority, was declared queen. The constitution, revised and deprived of its democratic provisions, was substituted for that of 1837. After the adoption of this constitution the municipal privileges were abridged, the sale of the sequestered church property suspended, and extraordinary provisions devised for the support of the clergy.

CHAPTER XVI.

PAPAL INTRIGUES RESPECTING THE UNITED STATES.

Papal Intrigues—Catholic Persecution—Protestant Persecution—Catholics in the Revolutionary War—In the late Rebellion—Catholic Enmity to Civil and Religious Liberty—An Alliance formed for the Subversion of the American Republic—The Duke of Richmond's Letter—Catholic Immigration—Progress of Catholicism—Its Consequences—The Republic in Imminent Danger—Union Only Means of Salvation—Conclusion.

THAT the papal pretensions have been a fruitful source of the seditions and wars which, like successive tornadoes, have swept in fearful rapidity over Christendom, the records of history furnish the most unquestionable evidence; yet still no one will venture the assertion that popish machinations have been the sole cause of political discords. Treason and popular disaffection have revolutionized and annihilated government after government long before the throne of St. Peter was established; yet since that unfortunate period it cannot be denied, that whenever the causes of civil or foreign war became active, the sacerdotal monarchs have inflamed or soothed them according to the dictates of their interests. Through their intrigues the exterminating sword of Charlemagne compelled the Saxons to be baptized; and that of Otho I. compelled the Danes to accept the same rite. Through their intrigues Clovis was induced, by his Catholic wife, to consent to be baptized; and his troops who had followed him to the field of slaughter, were led to follow him also to the baptismal fount. By the same means Ethelbert, who wished to marry Bertha, daughter of Carobert, King of Paris, was persuaded to agree to matrimonial stipulations allowing her, upon becoming his wife, to bring her bishop with her, and permitting him to establish a Catholic church in the kingdom for her convenience. By the same artful means Ethelwolf was led to confer on the clergy the tithes of all the produce of the land; Alfred the Great, to expel from his kingdom all the Danes that refused to be baptized; Edward to accept the title of saint and confessor in lieu of an heir to his throne, and to consent to abstain from nuptial congress with his queen; Edward IV. to promulgate a law committing to the flames all persons convicted of the heresy of the Lollards; and Mary I., a person of good natural qualities and administrative abilities, to imprison Protestant bishops for high treason, to confine princess Elizabeth in the tower, to execute Lady Jane Gray and her husband Guilford Dudley, to provoke the insurrections of Cave and Wyat, to commit to the flames two hundred and twenty-seven of her innocent subjects, and to render herself a terror to her nation. By the same disgraceful and impertinent intrigues the reign of Queen Elizabeth was perpetually disturbed with efforts to overthrow her government. The popes excommunicated her; denied her legitimacy; endeavored to supplant her with Mary Queen of Scots; induced the French to support Scotland in a rebellion against her government; created a sedition in the north; incited Spain to promote a conspiracy against her, assisted by Florentine merchants, the Bishop of Ross, and the Scotchmen residing in England; and when all these efforts proved abortive, to organize a conspiracy to have her assassinated by Anthony Babington. By the same disastrous intermeddling the reign of Queen Ann was disturbed with efforts to restore the succession to James the Pretender, the pope's tool for the recovery of England; under that of George I. the Duke of Marleborough was led to proclaim the Pretender in Scotland; Cardinal Alberoni, minister of Spain, to form an alliance in his favor with Russia, Sweden, France and Spain; and Atterbury, Bishop of Rochester, to engage in a conspiracy for the same object. Similar papal machinations have interfered with the peace of France, Germany, Spain, Portugal, Belgium, Sweden, Russia, Poland, China, Japan, Egypt, Abyssinia, and of many other governments, all of which were fearfully productive of sedition, anarchy, war and revolutions.

Besides these intermeddlings with the national affairs of all governments, the Catholic church assails all non-Catholics with the most execrable persecution, openly when she dares, secretly when she must. In her fiendish malice she counsels the violation of every principle of justice, of every obligation of humanity, of all contracts, of all pecuniary engagements, of all oaths, and urges as a duty the persecution and extermination of all unbelievers, by means of corporeal punishment, by imprisonment, banishment, murder, fire, swords, racks, stakes and scaffolds. Hear the truth of these assertions from the sanctified lips of the holy mother herself:

"The Catholics believe that the Pope's authority is not only ministerial but supreme, so that he has the right to direct and compel, with the power of life and death."—*Ecc. Jacob. Mag., But. Reg. Oppos. c.* 138.

"Two swords were given to Peter, the one temporal, the other spiritual."—*Bernard de Consed. Lib.* 4: *c.* 3.

"She (the church) bears, by divine right, both swords, but she exercises the temporal sword by the hand of the prince, or the magistrate. The temporal magistrate holds it subject to her order, to be exercised in her service, and under her direction."—*Bronson's Rev., Jan.,* 1854.

"Both swords are in the power of the Pope, namely, the spiritual and the temporal sword; but the one is to be exercised by the church, the other for the church; the one by the hands of the priest, the other by the hands of the king and the soldiers, but as the sword of the priest."—*Pope Boniface, Corp. Jur. Con. ed. Bocher, tome* 11: *p.* 1139.

"Civil contracts, promises, or oaths of Catholics with heretics, because they are heretics, may be dissolved by the Pontiff."—*Pope Innocent X., Caron.* 14.

"Engagements made with heretics and schismatics of this kind, after such have been consummated, are inconsiderate, illegal, and in law itself is of no importance, (although made, per chance, by the lapse of those persons into schism, or before the beginning of their heresy), even if confirmed by an oath, or one's honor being pledged."—*Pope Urban VI., Bymer* 7: 352.

"Though sworn to pay he may refuse the claims of a debtor who falls into error or under excommunication. The debtor's oath implied the tacit condition that the creditor, to be entitled to payment, should remain in a state in which communication would be lawful."—*St. Bernard, Maynooth Report,* 260.

"There are various punishments with which ecclesiastical sanctions and imperial laws order heretics to be punished. Some are spiritual, and effect the soul alone; others are corporeal, and effect the body. . . Among the corporeal punishments, one which very much annoys heretics is the proscription and confiscation of their property."—*Alphonso de Castro, cap.* 5 : *p.* 98.

"Another punishment," says he, "is the deprival of every sort of preeminence, jurisdiction and government, which they previously had over all persons of all conditions; for he who is a heretic is, *ipso jure*, deprived of all things."—*Ib., cap.* 7 : *p.* 1055.

"The last punishment of the body for heretics," he informs us, "is death, with which we will prove, by God's assistance, heretics ought to be punished."—*Ib., cap.* 12 : *p.* 123.

But it will be said that Protestants have been guilty of persecution as well as Catholics. This assertion is unquestionably true. We confess, with regret, that Protestantism, although she admits the right of private judgment, has proved a foe to civil and religious liberty. But unlike Catholicism, she has made concessions; reluctantly, indeed, but still she has made them. Guizot confesses that her practice has necessarily been inconsistent with her profession of toleration. She, however, claims not, like Catholicism, to be the source and supreme controller of all political power; nor to be the sole disposer of crowns and kingdoms; nor has she elaborated a policy, adopted a systematic course of measures, and organized a clerical force for the acquisition of supreme and universal temporal and spiritual dominion. She has no central head, with spies penetrating all domestic and national secrets, and communicating to it the information they have acquired. She has no political machinery ramifying every part of Christendom, and acting in concert for the promotion of her interests. She has no convents, nor nunneries; nor monastic vows; no father confessors; no religious confessional; no religious orders, no military knights; and no spiritual guides. She imposes no oaths of allegiance on her priests, requiring them to adopt every available method of subjugating all government under her authority. She has no inquisition, no rack and torture for her opponents; no pretensions to absolve subjects from their oaths of allegiance; no interdicts to alarm superstitious minds by the suspension of religious worship in disaffected kingdoms. She has never interfered between rulers and their subjects, concocting treason, fomenting sedition, and producing anarchy. She has never organized armies for the extension of her dominion, and for the subjugation of kingdoms to her authority. She has never butchered whole cities for unbelief, nor in one day put one hundred thousand heretics to death. She has done none of these things, yet her hands are not unstained with innocent blood. Would they were. Henry VIII., of England, persecuted with equal severity those who believed in the pope's right to temporal power, and those who disbelieved the other dogmas of Catholicism. The Church of England, under Charles I., inflicted the most atrocious punishment on the Irish Catholics; under James I., on the Puritans; and under Elizabeth, it oppressed both Catholics and dissenters with tyrannical measures, and illiberal disabilities. The Puritan Cromwell persecuted both Catholics and Episcopalians. In Ireland he wasted the Catholics with fire and sword; in Scotland he put whole garrisons of dissenters to death; and as his schemes for obtaining the royal dignity suggested, persecuted Covenanters, Republicans, and Puritans. When Charles II. was elevated to the throne he deprived 2000 dissenting clergymen of their livings; and by his five-mile act prohibited them from approaching within five miles of their former parishes. But the rigor of Protestantism eventually relaxed its severity. Under William III. some of the disabilities which oppressed the dissenters were removed; and under that of George III. additional toleration was accorded. Still it must be admitted that the ablest agents in extorting these concessions to religious liberty were the Free Thinkers of that age. Yet the Quakers, always the most respectable body of citizens, and the professors of the most harmless of all creeds, were still punished with fines, confiscation, imprisonment and death. All who disbelieved in the holy trinity were also subject to similar persecutions. Not until 1813 did Protestant England cease to punish a belief in Unitarianism with imprisonment, and legal disabilities. John Calvin, at the head of the Consistory of Geneva, had John Guet beheaded on a charge of attempting to overthrow the doctrines of the Calvinistic church; and Micheal Servetus arrested and burnt alive for having attacked the doctrine of the holy trinity. Even in republic America, under the elevating influence of liberal institutions, the intolerant spirit of religious bigotry predominates more or less over the mind of the Christian republic. In Massachusetts Baptists and Quakers were once fined, imprisoned, and burnt alive. In Virginia all Quakers that disbelieved in the holy trinity, and all persons that refused to have their children baptized were scourged, confined, banished or put to death. In Pennsylvania, under the charter of William Penn, all Atheists were excluded from official position. In Maryland disbelief in the holy trinity was declared to be a capital offence; and not until recently was any person, who professed not to believe in Christianity, unless a Jew, eligible to any office of trust or profit in the State; nor even to this day is any person eligible who disbelieves in a God. The statute books of every Protestant country bear testimony to the same illiberality. Humboldt, Cuvier, Buffon, La Place, Gibbon, Voltaire, Hume, Jefferson, and other eminent scholars and patriots would, by the provisions of almost every State constitution in the Union, be debarred from filling the lowest office that they create. In fact the history of no religious sectary indicates it to be a bond of love, union, or concord. Every Protestant creed, sectary or conclave, is a perpetual source of mutual jealousy, animosity and persecution. The same intolerant spirit breathes its malignancy over the pages of the religious press. "If we are not Christians," says the *Church Union*, "let us make no hypocritical pretensions of founding governments on Christian principles. If we are, I believe that they should predominate over our whole life; let us have them incorporated in the basis of our government, and the national policy shaped by them. Let no one hold an office of trust or profit whose life is not conformably thereto." These holy ravings remind us of an attempt once made by the Puritans to incorporate the Bible into the British constitution. "The wrestlers with God," as they called themselves were, deliberating upon a motion to repeal the laws of England, and substitute in their place the laws of Moses and the prophets. But Cromwell averted the calamity by a peremptory dissolution of parliament, and a command to "the wrestlers" to go home; nor did he think it prudent to call them together again. The religious politics of the Methodist *Home Journal* are similar in tone with that of the *Church Union*. This infuriated orthodox theologian says: "They that deny the doctrines of Christianity, ignore the basis on which our government is founded. Can they be regarded as citizens? Ought any man who holds to this position be admitted to—or permitted to hold Christian citizenship under this government? We hold that to be consistent with ourselves Infidelity should not be tolerated in our country, much less encouraged by those who openly profess and teach its doctrines." These assertions are the evident irrepressible ebullitions of innate treason to the republic. They ingore the basis on which our government is founded, and, according to the logic of this fanatic the sect that holds them ought not to be regarded as citizens, nor permitted to hold Christian citizenship under this government. But the knife with which this madman would cut his own throat Infidelity would wrest from him. The sacred basis of our government is equal political and religious rights. Had Methodism been chosen as the basis of our government, would a republic have been thought of? Never! Did not John Wesley, its founder and spirit, oppose the American revolution? Did he not write against it, preach against it, and labor publicly and privately to arrest its progress? Was there a man in England that inflicted deeper injury on the American cause? While English Infidels aided the struggle for independence with their pens, money and valor,—while English statesmen blushed at the barbarous conduct of their government,—this bigoted priest, a fugitive of justice from the State of North Carolina, defended it without shame or compunction. Even at this day Potestant priests have dared to assert that Infidels have no rights which they are bound to respect; but such miscreants have no rights, (for they surrender them by their assertions,) which any person is bound to respect. Such self-accursed, self-outlawed bigots, in conjunction with unprincipled demagogues and political aspiring judges, are to-day laboring to incorporate in the national constitution the fanaticism of the *Church Union* and of the Methodist *Home Journal.* When their holy treason shall have become a success, liberty will forsake her desecrated abode; despotism will occupy her temple; and, we fondly hope that, in the course of coming events the fanatics will not discover that they have legalized their own extermination. Had Constantine the Great, though frenzied with ambition and crimsoned with guilt, beheld the boundless ocean of gore which was destined to flow from an incorporation of Christianity with the civil power, and to roll its heavy surge over all future time, he would have been more obdurate than a fiend had he not cowled his head in horror at the frightful vision, and dropped in mercy the pen already inked to inaugurate the tremendous catastrophe. Yet how sickening is the thought that the example of this ambitious tyrant, loaded with the curses of ages, is now attempted to be imitated by Protestant priests, political judges, and United States officials. But thanks to nature, the play of the natural principles of liberty in the minds of some priests, have been too strong to be repressed by dogmatic creeds. Gloriously inconsistent with their principles, they have inscribed their names in imperishable honor on the scroll of liberty. Thankful for the few names blazoned there, freedom must drop a tear over the smallness of the number.

It will be asked, perhaps, notwithstanding the facts which have been adduced showing the political nature and designs of the Catholic church, what has the American republic to apprehend from it? It will be asked, Did not Catholics fight for the establishment of a free government in the revolutionary war? Did they not fight to defend it in the war of 1812? Did they not fight to preserve its unity in the late rebellion? No well informed person will answer these questions in the negative; and no candid person will fail to acknowledge the distinguished valor and liberality which they displayed on these occasions. Catholics are men; and the love of liberty is a natural principle of the human constitution. Ignorance may blind it; prejudice mislead it; and superstition overawe it; but when the natural vigor of its disposition is aroused it will assert its rights in defiance of creeds, shackles and stakes. It is not the nature, but the education of Catholics, and the religious despotism with which they are enthralled, that has so often deprived freedom of their homage and allegiance. The frequent opposition of Catholic princes to the policy and measures of the popes, the numerous leagues which they have formed, and the vast armies which they have raised in their support, abundantly show how often their reverence for the pope has been displaced by defiance to his authority, and contempt for his pretensions. The liberal minded people of France have, from an early date, boldly opposed the pope's claim to temporal power. St. Louis IX., in 1269, declared in a pragmatic sanction, that the temporal power of France was independent of the jurisdiction of Rome. Charles VIII., of France, in a pragmatic sanction issued in 1433, asserted for France, in conformity with the canons of the Council of Basle, independence of Rome in all temporal matters. Louis XIV., in 1682 convened a national council of the clergy at Paris, which decided that the Pope of Rome had no power to interfere, directly or indirectly, in the temporal concerns of princes and sovereigns; that the usages of the French church are inviolable; that the authority of the general councils is superior to that of the pope; and that the pope is not infallible in matters of faith. The popes, by the means of bulls, have attempted to nullify these acts, but nevertheless they form the distinctive principles of the Gallican Church, and also of other Catholic churches in different kingdoms of Europe. The Fenian order is another happy instance of the predominance which patriotism may gain, in the minds of Catholics, over their reverence for the church and its despotism.

If Catholics have at various times chastised the pope, deprived him of temporal authority, assaulted his person, imprisoned and deposed him, it is not surprising that they fought in the defence of the independence and freedom of America. No one that has an adequate conception of the papal policy, will be much astonished that the Catholics were prominent leaders in the revolutionary war. It was a cause in which the pope himself, in perfect consistency with his pretensions, might have personally engaged. The pope claims England as his fief, and denounces her kings as usurpers. The success of a revolt intended to deprive England of her colonies was as gratifying to his revenge as it was flattering to his ulterior designs on the colonies themselves. In a republic he could plant his machinery, build up at will his monastic penitentiaries, erect his strong castle-like and secret-celled churches, leisurely select and occupy eligible and strategic points for citadels, and collect from every kingdom his most faithful and reliable subjects. Bishop Hughes asserted that Catholicism was friendly to republics, for they allowed its free development. But the development of Catholicism involves the subversion of republics, and the establishment in their place of political and religious despotism.

The insincerity of any proposed attachment to the American republic by popes or priests, is attested by the very occurrence of the Southern rebellion. Had the pope and priests been opposed to it a Catholic rebel would scarcely have been known; and had not the Catholics North and South been in favor of the rebellion, it could not have taken place. That singular and unnecessary intestine collision, in which the South gained nothing but disgrace, the North nothing but depopulation and empoverishment, and at the mystery of which leading secessionists were so much puzzled that they declared it to be the effects of a general lunacy, was nevertheless in perfect harmony with the profound and masterly policy of the Roman See, which comprehends in its toils the events of ages, and from the first projection of a plot to its final consummation, shapes every intervening circumstance to the fulfilment of its grand design. The Catholics North supported the cause of the Union, and the Catholics South the cause of the rebellion with votes, money and men; the rebellion, therefore, was not contrary to the teachings of the church. The depopulation of the native element of the North, the influx of foreign Catholics, the creation of an oppressive national debt, the demoralization consequent on civil war, the engenderment of civil antipathies, and the supplanting of colored servants by white Catholic servants, were all known prospective results of the rebellion; were all in harmony with the papal designs; and to realize which the Catholics of the North, and the Catholics of the South were stimulated by their priests to meet each in deadly conflict.

But dismemberment could not possibly have been intended by the secret projectors of the rebellion. It was an impracticable idea. The geography of the country interposed to its success an insurmountable obstacle. It was also inconsistent with the papal designs. But monarchy was not an impracticable idea. It encountered no difficulty in the country's geography. It was in harmony with the policy of the Roman See. The Catholic blood which was poured out in such torrents in the civil conflicts was not intended to effect dismemberment, but to create the elements conducive to the establishment of a monarchial government. Shortly after the close of the rebellion this soil, hallowed by the blood, and consecrated by the sepulture of millions of freemen, Catholic as well as non-Catholic, was attempted to be desecrated by the establishment of presses for openly advocating that execrable treason; and it has been asserted by the leaders of the late rebellion, that the civil war is not at an end; but that it will again break out, and then the battle field will not be the South, but every State, city and village in the Union. Perhaps they mean to intimate that it will be a repetition of the massacre on St. Bartholomew's eve.

To those who fondly dream that the republic of America has nothing to fear from the pretensions of the Pope of Rome, and his loyal subjects, we submit the following extracts:

"Heresy (Protestantism) and Infidelity have not, and never had, and never can have any right, being, as they undoubtedly are, contrary to the law of God."—*Bronson's Rev.*, Jan., 1852.

"Heresy (Protestantism) and unbelief are crimes, and in Christian countries, as in Italy and Spain for instance, where the Catholic religion is the essential law of the land, they are punished as other crimes."—*Bishop Kendrick.*

"Protestantism of every form has not, and never can have any right, where Catholicism is triumphant; and therefore we lose all the breath we expend in declaiming against bigotry and intolerance, and in favor of religious liberty, or the right of any one to be of any religion, or of no religion, as best pleases him."—*Catholic Rev.*, Jan., 1852.

"Religious liberty is merely endured until the opposite can be carried into effect without peril to the Catholic world."—*Bishop O'Connor, of Pittsburg.*

"If the Catholics ever gain, which they surely will, an immense numerical majority, religious freedom in this country will be at an end."—*Archbishop of St. Louis.*

"Catholicity will one day rule America, and religious freedom will be at an end."—*Bishop of St. Louis.*

"The Catholic church numbers one-third of the American population; and if its membership shall increase for the next thirty years as it has for the thirty years past, in 1900 Rome will have a majority, and be bound to take the country and keep it."—*Hecker.*

"Should the said church go on increasing for the next twenty years, the papists will be in a majority of the people of the United States."—*William Hogan.*

"St. Thomas Aquinas, in his second book, chapter 3, page 58, says: 'Heretics (non-Catholics) may justly be killed.' But you will answer, there is no danger of this. They can never acquire the power in this country to sanction that doctrine. How sadly mistaken are you! How lamentably unacquainted with the secret springs or machinery of popery."—*William Hogan.*

Quoting from an author Hogan writes:

"America is the promised land of the Jesuists. To obtain the ascendency they have no need of Swiss guards, or the assistance of the holy alliance, but a majority of votes, which can easily be obtained by the importation of Catholic voters from Ireland, Austria, and Bavaria. . . . I am not a politician, but knowing the active spirit of Jesuitism, and the indifference of the generality of Protestants, I have no doubt that in ten years the Jesuists will have a mighty influence over the ballot box, and in twenty will direct it according to pleasure. Now they fawn, in ten years they will menace, in twenty command."—*Synopsis, p.* 106.

In the above quoted authorities we have a unanimous declaration of Catholic bishops, priests and periodicals, that the Catholic church is radically opposed to religious liberty; that she regards Protestants and Infidels as criminals; that whenever she obtains the political power she punishes them as such; and that the success of her policy and measures in this country has been sufficient to justify her expectation, that in 1900 she will be enabled to accomplish all her bloody and treasonable designs. That these hopes are not altogether chimerical, we have also the reluctant and alarming concessions of her opponents. Those who abuse liberty should be deprived of its benefits; and those abuse it most who take advantage of its generous indulgence to plot for its destruction. The rights of toleration subsist only by mutual consent; their obligations are reciprocal; and whenever the silent compact is violated by one party, the other is exonerated from its obligations. No man possesses a right which is not possessed by another; nor has he any authority for claiming for himself that which he does not concede to others. When, therefore, the Catholic priests proclaim that Protestantism in any form has no right where Catholicism is triumphant, they surrender their rights where Protestantism in any form is triumphant. When they assert heresy and unbelief are crimes, and where the Catholic religion is the essential law of the land, are punished as crimes, they authorize heretics and unbelievers to consider Catholicism a crime, and where heresy and unbelief are the essential law of the land, to punish Catholics as criminals. When they say that Catholicity will one day rule America, and then religious liberty will be at an end, they appeal to the instincts of self-preservation, and justify freemen in adopting any measure that is necessary to render their avowed treason and destructive designs abortive. They assail the fundamental principles of the Constitution, and forfeit all right to its protection. Neither Protestants nor Infidels may be disposed to avail themselves of the privileges of these concessions, while forbearance is a virtue; but they may be provoked to consider the further tolerance of the Jesuists in this country as inconsistent with the peace and stability of the republic.

As the treasonable designs of the Catholic priests are undeniable, it is important to understand by what means they expect to accomplish their infamous purposes. The subjoined letter of the Duke of Richmond, formerly Governor-General of Canada, will explain their policy, their system of measures, and the co-operation which they are to receive from the sovereigns of Europe. "*It* (the American republic) *will be destroyed,*" says he, "*it ought not, and will not be permitted to exist.* The curse of the French revolution, and subsequent wars and commotions of Europe, are to be attributed to its example, and so long as it exists no prince will be safe on his throne, and the sovereigns of Europe are aware of it, and *they are determined on its destruction, and they have come to an understanding on the subject, and have decided on the means to accomplish it;* and they will eventually succeed, by subversion rather than by conquest. All the low and surplus population of the different nations of Europe will be carried into that country. It is, and will be, the receptacle of the bad and disaffected population of Europe, when they are not wanted for soldiers or to supply navies; and the governments of Europe will favor such a cause. This will create a surplus majority of low population, who are so very easily excited, and they will bring with them their principles, and in nine cases out of ten adhere to their ancient and former governments, laws, manners, customs and religion, and will transmit them to their posterity, and in many cases propagate them among the natives. These men will become citizens, and by the constitution and laws be invested with the right of suffrage. Hence discord, dissension, anarchy and civil war will ensue, and some popular individual will assume the government, restore order, and the sovereigns of Europe, the immigrants, and many of the natives will sustain him. *The church of Rome has a design on this country, and it will in time be the established religion, and it will aid in the destruction of the republic.* I have conversed with many sovereigns and princes of Europe, and they have unanimously expressed their opinion relative to the government of the United States, and their determination to subvert it." According to this admonitory letter an alliance has been formed by the European powers and the Pope of Rome, for the subversion of the American republic, the substitution of a manarchy in its place, and the establishment of Catholicism as the national religion. Had the Duke of Richmond been silent, still no well informed person could doubt that all the European sovereigns, whether Protestant or Catholic, would act upon the avowed principle of the Holy Alliance in their conduct with regard to North America. Would England consent, it may be asked, to ally herself with the papal despot? Why

not? She has done so before; in the recent troubles of
the Roman See she sent her war vessels to protect the
pope; and she assented to the principles of the Holy
Alliance, which was for the extinguishment of all freedom in Europe. The good sense of the English people
would never have recognized a policy which inevitably
involved their own destruction; but they are a cypher
in the great account of the short-sighted government.
That England heartily co-operates with the papal
priests in their infamous work, may be learned from the
subjoined extract of the *Dublin Evening Mail*, elicited
by the news from America that certain teachers had
been dismissed from a school of the West on account of
their foreign birth, &c.: " The foreign birth and Roman
Catholic proclivities of the teachers thus dismissed,"
says he, " are sufficient evidence that they have been
imported into the United States by the Church of Rome,
with a view to pervert the secular education of the
country to the purposes of proselytism. They are, in
fact, emissaries of the *College de Propaganda Fide*, and
have been trained and qualified, no doubt, by its education, to carry out abroad the principles it has been so
successful in disseminating here in Dublin. *The pope
has not a more efficient free-handed institution at his back
than the imperial parliament of the united kingdom,*
which spares no expense to furnish his holiness with
zealous and well informed agents for the spreading of
his dominion over the face of the globe. Does he require priests to publish and extend it wherever the
English language is spoken, the halls and dormitories
of Maynooth are enlarged, and their larder abundantly
replenished to keep a constant supply of young ecclesi-

astics for his service. Do these in turn send home a requisition for more teachers to assist them in their work, *the Chancellor of the Exchequer adds some ten thousand pounds for his yearly estimate for national education in Ireland*, and continued re-enforcements of propagandists are thus maintained, in readiness to move in obedience to the call, whenever Rome may need their service."

According to the Duke of Richmond's letter, one of the means by which the tyrant of Rome and his colleagues have adopted for accomplishing the downfall of the government of the United States, is that of foreign immigration. Let us examine the operation of this device. The editor of the *Louisville Journal*, in discussing the question of foreign immigration, makes the following statement: "In 1850 our native white population was about 17,300,000. In the same year our foreign population was about 2,300,000. In 1852 the immigration was about 398,170. At that rate it would take only about six years to double the foreign population here in 1850. This is about five times our population's increase, which is in a ratio of three or four per cent. per annum, while the increase of foreigners is from fourteen to sixteen per cent. on the census of 1830, 1840, and 1850.

"In 1852 our presidential vote was about 3,300,000. In 1848 it was about 2,880,000. In 1852 our foreign arrivals, as shown, were about 400,000, and 240,000 of these were males, thus showing that in one year, the arrivals of foreign males into this country, was nearly as great as the increase of our whole voting population during four years."

The foreign arrivals by sea alone were —

In	1850	315,333
"	1851	403,828
"	1852	398,470
"	1853	400,777
From Canada and Mexico during the same period about		700,408
		2,118,408

It appears from the census of 1850 that the total aggregate of foreign population of the United States in 1849 was 2,210,829. If the tide of immigration has added but two millions to the number of the foreign population every four years since 1849, it must have amounted, in 1869, to 7,210,829.

All the immigrants are not, however, Catholics. Some are Protestants, some Infidels, and some Radical Republicans. The Turners, the Free Germans, and the members of the Revolutionary League are all firm friends of free governments. The proportion of Catholics among the immigrants, at a fair computation, is presumed to be about three-fourths of the entire number. They must, therefore, add to the Catholic numerical strength about 3,750,000 at every decade

Besides the numerical augmentation of the Catholic church through the medium of foreign immigration, there are other appliances acting powerfully in its favor. "It is not long," says William Hogan, "since I saw a letter from the Catholic bishop Kendrick, of the diocese of Massachusetts, in which he informs the authorities of Rome that he is making converts of some of the first families in the diocese."—*Synopsis, p.* 169. "I have often conversed," says he, "with American Protestants on this subject, and regret finding many of them—especially those of the Unitarian creed—are strong advocates of popery, and in favor of its introduction among the people." John L. Chapman, a Methodist clergyman, in a work written before the Southern outbreak, says in substance, according to my recollection, that a Methodist preacher cannot now address his congregation upon the subject of Catholicism with the same freedom he could formerly; that those who imagine a Methodist preacher can now utter in the pulpit, or at a tract or bible meeting, the sentiments of John Wesley respecting popery, are entirely mistaken; and that those who suppose that an editor of a Methodist periodical can now assail the errors of Catholicism without the loss of subscribers, are laboring under a great deluions. While the pulpits, revivals, and evangelical enterprises are making no converts of any account among Catholics, the confirmation services of the Catholic bishops show the great number of adult non-Catholics which they are adding to their church. The number of children kidnapped, and the extraordinary number confirmed by Catholic bishops, might suggest a suspicion that the church has not abandoned its historic mode of adding to its members. Every non-Catholic child educated in a Catholic school becomes a Catholic, or strongly biassed in favor of that church. We hear of Protestant priests, and sometimes of Protestant bishops, and of whole bodies of theological students becoming Roman Catholics.

It is an undeniable fact that the annual increase of

the Catholic population far outstrips that of **the non-Catholic population ;** and that at some future period its numerical strength will **be** capable of deciding in favor **of the church every election** that takes place. When that unfortunate hour arrives every policeman, councilman, mayor, judge, governor, delegate, congressman, senator, president, civil official, **army or naval** officer will be a Catholic. Then the non-Catholics will be powerless, and **at the mercy of those who believe they have no rights. Then, by the secret operation of the papal machinery, one faction will** be inflamed against another, and one section of the land against another. Then rapine, violence, assassination, sedition, massacre—everything that can render **life and property insecure—** will distract every state, **city and village in the Union.** Then, amid the anarchy and confusion thus produced, **some Catholic tyrant will arise, and—the civil disorders subsiding at the bidding of the** pope—will be **proclaimed dictator.** Supported by the Catholic and **Protestant kings of Europe, he will** abolish the republic, **and establish in its place a** Catholic monarchial government. Then, **according** to **Bronson,** heresy and Infidelity will be declared to **have no** rights. Then, according to Archbishop Kendrick, Protestantism will be declared to be a crime, and punished as such. **Then,** according to the archbishop of St. Louis, **religious liberty** will no longer be endured. Then, according to Hecker, the Catholic church will **be** bound to take the country, **and keep it.** Then inquisitions will be introduced, **and stakes erected.** Then the darkness of the middle ages will settle over the land. Then the schoolhouses, the colleges, the asylums, and the churches built with Protestant funds will be applied to Catholic purposes. Then the fortunes which non-Catholics have amassed will be confiscated. Then the territorial acquisitions of the Government, all its resources, all the advantages it has acquired by arms and treaties, its navy and its army, will become the property of the papal monarchy, and applied to its defence and extension. Then it will be the business of Americans, not to create magistrates, but to obey despots; not to share in the sovereignty of the government, but to toil in slavery to support an execrable despotism. Then liberty of speech and freedom of the press will be no more. Then the ecclesiastical dungeons, which the supineness of Americans have allowed Catholicism to erect among them, will be the homes and graves of freemen. Then will arise a government constructed of schemes for public plunder; where an aristocracy are privileged robbers; where moral worth and dignity are the helpless victims of power and injustice; where laws are made for subjects, not for rulers; and where the people are inherited by royal heirs, like so much land and cattle. Then will the monarchial demon, the God of slaves and aristocrats, seated on the people's throne, with his feet on the people's neck, quaff blood like water; and eye with scornful indifference the squalid millions whom he has doomed by an enormous taxation to huddle in hovels, without light or air, with cloathing scarcely enough to hide their nakedness, with food scarcely enough to sustain life, or fire scarcely enough to keep them from freezing.

When the pope shall have succeeded in his attempts to establish such a monarchy over the American people, he will next proceed to enlarge its dominions by the annexation of Canada, Mexico, all South America, and all the Pacific and Atlantic islands. With such a dominion, such resources, such an army and navy, he will be master of the land and the ocean. He will then proceed to plunder and discrown the very kings that had assisted him in erecting his colossal power. He will then enforce, by the thunders of American monitors and war steamers, his claim to the crowns of England and Russia; his claim to be the disposer of all crowns; his claim to be the only monarch that ought to wear the token of royalty; in fine, his claim to the supreme temporal and spiritual monarchy of the world. Then England will awake, but it will be in the vengeful folds of a serpent crushing out her life. Then the European despots will awake, but it will be amid the crumbling of their thrones. Then the papal allies will awake, but it will be to find their limbs fettered, and the foot of the sacerdotal monarch placed in malignant triumph upon their necks. Then the world will awake, but it will be to find that it has suffered the extinction of the last star of liberty, and involved itself in a night of despotism without the hope of a morn.

But the spirit of freedom is immortal; its conflict with despotism will be eternal. Bolts, dungeons, shackles cannot confine it; racks, flames and gibbets cannot extinguish it. To annihilate it, the most formidable efforts of bigotry, the most ingenious arts of statesmen, the combined power of church and state, have been applied in vain. Though the blood of freedom's sons have streamed in torrents, and the smoke of their stakes have darkened the face of heaven, yet their spirit has still walked abroad over the world. So it has been in the past; so it will be in the future. If the Catholic demon should massacre all the freemen in one age, they will rise up more powerful in the next; and successively as time rolls on, shake with their energy the accursed throne. Hence civil war will never cease, fields will eternally reek with gore, burning cathedrals and convents will illuminate the night, till the world, instructed by its past errors, will unite in a natural union for the extinguishment of Catholicism.

We have now alluded to the dangers which begin to blacken our political firmament. Can the storm be averted? We believe it can. A union of the Protestants, Jews, Spiritualists, Free Religionists, Infidels, Atheists, Turners, Free Germans, and of all non-Catholics, without regard to creed, race or color, on a basis of universal civil and religious liberty, with a judicious policy, and a corresponding system of measures, will prove adequate to the emergency. Such an organization, if sufficiently liberally constituted, might command the support of Gallic and Fenian Catholics. The life, liberty and welfare of all non-Catholics, if not, indeed, of the Fenians and Gallicans themselves, are in equal danger, and why should they not organize for mutual safety? Does prejudice forbid it? Millions of lives must be sacrificed if a union be not effected. Who would, then, hesitate to sacrifice a prejudice that it may be effected? A tyrant may demand concessions without rendering an equivalent, but freemen can not. Can Americans sleep in peace, while the clang of the hammers that are forging their chains are sounding in their ears, and the pillars which support their government are tottering over their **heads?** It seems impossible. Their obligations to their country, to posterity, to the world, demand union. **Union or slavery ; union or confiscation ; union or** the rack, the stake, the gibbet. One **or** the **other is inevitable.** Which do you now chose? **A few more years hence you will** have no choice.

Every citizen **knows** that under the present form of government **his** merits have rewards, **and his industry has encouragements** enjoyed by no **people** in any country, or under any other form of government. The **poorest and the richest are here** accorded equal **chances,** equal **privileges; and an equal** voice in **selecting** legislators, **judges and rulers. They are equally untrammelled by legal impediments in seeking the highest positions in the government. Each citizen is an integral part of the sovereignty of the nation ; he participates in its management, and shares its greatness and glory.** It is a consolation enjoyed only by an American, that if fame nor fortune should gratify his ambition, he can still bequeath to his children a richer inheritance than that of either fame or fortune, the inheritance **of a free government.** Judging of the future by **the past, it is his privilege to** believe that the republic will **continue to grow in power and greatness** with each succeeding age, until **the light of her glory shall fill the earth;** until **despots shall tremble before the majesty of the people ; until the clank of slavery, and the groan of the** oppressed shall **no more** be heard; **and until the united world shall rise to** the majesty and greatness **of equal privileges,** equal rights and equal laws.

Such are the blessings guaranteed, and the expectations warranted by the continuance of the republic; but monarchy, like a deadly blast, annihilates them all. With the liberty, it lays the greatness and glory of the nation in the grave. Intolerance will then re-establish its racks and torture. Industry will then be oppressed, and enterprise annihilated. This land, which has so long resounded with the song of liberty, will then reverberate with the clanking irons of servitude. This nation, which is now the wonder and glory of the earth; which is so powerful and prosperous; this nation will be no more. Her life and splendor will have departed with her freedom. History may record her eventful story; her sons may clank in chains around her tomb; future freemen may curse the degenerate sons who wanted the valor or unanimity to transmit to their posterity the government which they inherited from their ancestors; but these will not call her to life and glory again. Like a wave she will have rolled away; like a dream, she will have departed; like a thunder peal, she will have muttered into eternal silence. Like these she had but one existence, and that will then have ended.

www.ingramcontent.com/pod-product-compliance
Lightning Source LLC
Chambersburg PA
CBHW030408230426
43664CB00007BB/797